THE GREAT NORTHERN IN THE EAST MIDLANDS

The Rise and Fall of Colwick Yards
Nottingham London Road - Gedling - Basford

ALFRED HENSHAW

THE RAILWAY CORRESPONDENCE AND TRAVEL SOCIETY
1999

© **RCTS 1999**

ISBN 090 1115 843

121 Green End Road
Sawtry
Huntingdon
PE17 5XA

Cover Photo: The scene across Colwick Yards in October 1949 facing east from footbridge 6A at LNWR MPD. The pilot engine LNER Class J50 in the foreground is shunting the departure end of No. 1 Down Yard. In the distance, exhaust from another pilot at Carlton Field can be seen shunting the south end departure sidings. *John R. Bonser.*

Title Page Photo: This fine portrait of a GNR E2 2-4-0 and posing staff at Nottingham unfortunately has no information with it. The engine which appears to have been well cleaned prior to leaving the engine shed, is painted green with brass beading around the splashers. This engine of the 206 series was built at Doncaster in 1891 and had Timmis helical springs under the driving axle boxes instead of laminated springs with which earlier ones were fitted. Patrick Stirling designed this locomotive with 6 ft 7 in coupled wheels for use on slow passenger, fast parcels and special goods trains. No 864 was withdrawn from service in June 1923. Note the tubular type of point rodding connected with pins through sleeves used by the GNR, and the second brick warehouse in the background. The first warehouse is in the distance behind the tender, with the gas holder appearing above it.

H H Mather

Printed by Birlim Litho Limited
230 Cinderhill Road, Bulwell, Nottingham, NG6 8SB.

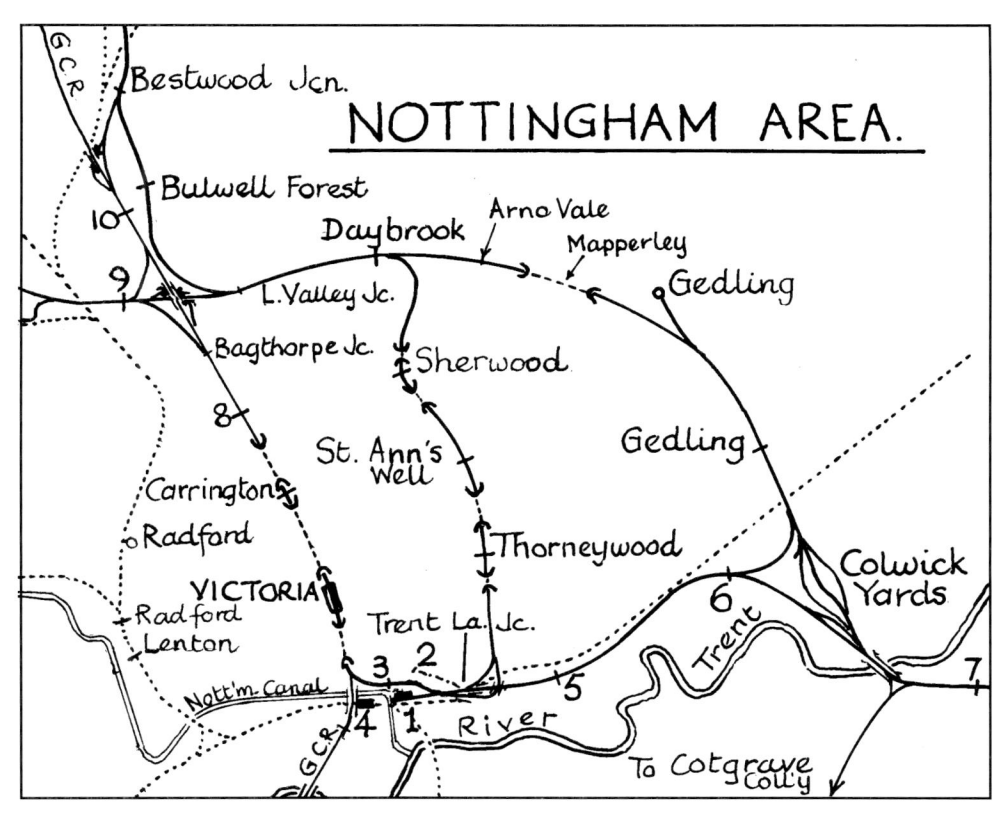

1. London Road Low Level.
2. Manvers Street (Goods).
3. London Road High Level.
4. Midland Station.
5. Race Course Station.
6. Netherfield & Colwick.
7. Radcliffe-on-Trent.
8. New Basford.
9. Basford & Bulwell.
10. Bulwell Common.

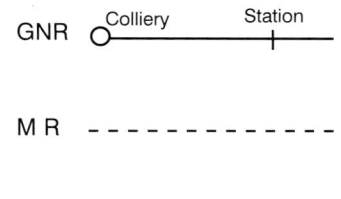

KEY TO DIAGRAM ABBREVIATIONS AND SYMBOLS

BH - Booking Hall.
BO - Booking Office.
CB - Clearance Locking Bar.
CLC - Cheshire Lines Committee.
FB - Foot Bridge.
FP - Foot Path.
GCR - Great Central Railway.
GNR - Great Northern Railway.
LC - Level Crossing.
LDECR - Lancashire, Derbyshire & East Coast Railway.
LR - Lamp Room.
MP - Mile Post.
MR - Midland Railway.
PLH - Platelayer's Hut.
SB - Signal Box.
SM - Station Master.
SP - Signal Post.
TC - Track Circuit.
TT - Turntable.
WB - Weighbridge.
WR - Waiting Room.
MPD - Motive Power Department
LMR - London Midland Region (BR)

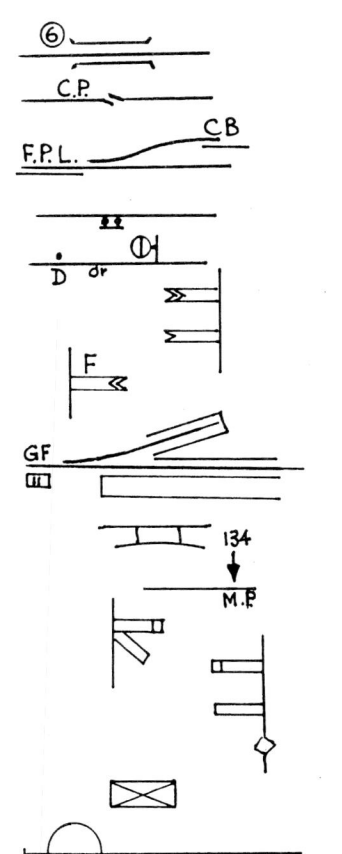

Bridge & Numberplate.
Catch Points.
Clearance locking bar.
Facing Point Lock.
Detonator Placers.
Disc or Ground Signal.
Distant Signal worked from Signalbox illustrated.
Distant Signal NOT worked from Signalbox illustrated.
Distant Signal Fixed at Caution.
Dock (loading).
Platform.
Ground Frame.
Loading Gauge.
Mile Post.
Signal Slotted with next signalbox.
Stop Signal worked from signalbox illustrated.
Stop Signal NOT worked from signalbox illustrated.
Track Circuit Indicator.
Signalbox
Turntable and Water Column.

iii

1st time table of the Basford Line

GREAT NORTHERN RAILWAY.

NOTICE FOR FEBRUARY, 1876.

The Great Northern Train Service for January will, with the following exceptions, be continued **throughout February**, and until further notice :—

WEEK DAYS.

OPENING

OF THE FIRST SECTION OF THE

NEW NOTTINGHAMSHIRE LINE

FOR

PASSENGER TRAFFIC.

Trains will run as under :—

DOWN.

	A.M.	A.M.	A.M.	P.M.	P.M.	P.M.	P.M.
Nottingham ... Dep.	7 30	9 50	11 20	12 40	3 50	5 8	6 20
Gedling and Carlton ... ,,	7 40	10 0	11 30	12 50	4 0	5 18	6 30
Bestwood and Arnold ... ,,	7 47	10 7	11 37	12 57	4 7	5 25	6 37
New Basford (for Dob Pk. & Bulwell) Arr.	7 52	10 12	11 42	1 2	4 12	5 30	6 42

UP.

	A.M.	A.M.	A.M.	P.M.	P.M.	P.M.	P.M.
New Basford (for Dob Pk. & Bulwell) Dep.	8 10	10 35	11 55	1 35	4 25	5 35	7 0
Bestwood and Arnold ... ,,	8 15	10 40	12 0 P.M.	1 40	4 30	5 40	7 5
Gedling and Carlton ... ,,	8 23	10 48	12 8	1 48	4 38	5 48	7 13
Nottingham ... Arr.	8 35	11 0	12 20	2 0	4 50	6 0	7 25

Skegness and Firsby Branch.

The 6.45 a.m. Train from Skegness will run as under :—

		A.M.
Skegness ... Dep.		6 38
Wainfleet ... ,,		6 53
Firsby ... Arr.		7 5

To stop at Cowbank, Croftbank, and Thorpe Culvert if required.

CITY AND SUBURBAN SERVICE.

The 4.5 p.m. Train, Moorgate Street to Enfield, will start at 4.3 p.m., and be 2 minutes earlier to King's Cross (G.N.)

The 4.32 p.m. Train, Broad Street to Enfield, and 5.25 p.m. Train, Enfield to Broad Street, will be discontinued.

New Trains will leave Broad Street at 5.32 p.m. for Enfield and intermediate Stations, and Enfield at 6.25 p.m. for Broad Street and intermediate Stations.

The 6.45 p.m. Train, King's Cross to East End, will be run to Highgate only.

SUNDAYS.
West Riding District.

The 6.50 p.m. Train, Shipley to Bradford, will be 10 minutes earlier throughout.
The 8.0 p.m. Train, Kirkgate to Bradford, will be 10 minutes later throughout.
The 8.25 p.m. Train, Ardsley to Bradford, will be 10 minutes later throughout.
The 8.50 p.m. Train, Shipley to Bradford, will be 15 minutes later throughout.

King's Cross Station,
27th January, 1876.

HENRY OAKLEY,
General Manager.

Please attach this Notice to the January Time Books and Bills.

CONTENTS - COLWICK - NOTTINGHAM

1. Historical Introduction - by John Marshall — *Page 2*
2. Colwick Yards and Motive Power Depot. — *Page 5*
3. Netherfield and Colwick - Nottingham London Road — *Page 39*
4. Gedling - Leen Valley Junction - Basford and Bulwell — *Page 57*
5. Nottingham Suburban Railway — *Page 84*
6. Appendices — *Page 97*

    1. List of Tunnels:
       Stationmaster Area Control Responsibilities — *Page 98*
    2. Booked Shunting Engine Duties — *Page 99*
    3. Specimen Allocation of Traffic at Colwick — *Page 101*
    4. Marshalling of Traffic for Junctions and Stations in Manchester and Western Districts — *Page 102*
    5. Weekday Passing Times at Arno Vale Signalbox October 1899 — *Page 104*

GRADIENT PROFILES

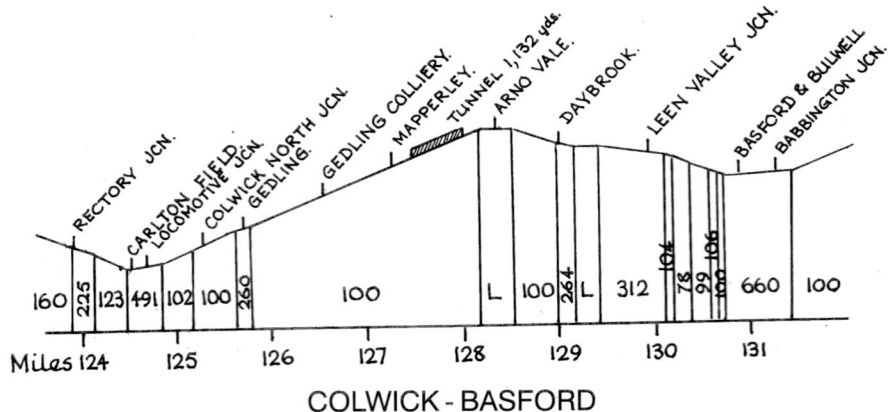

COLWICK - BASFORD

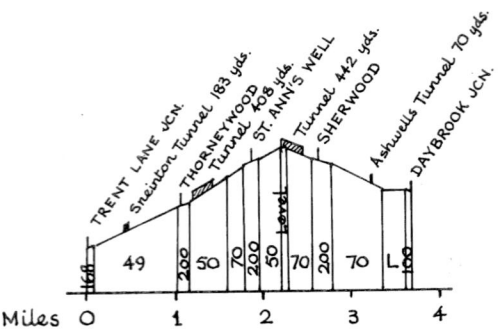

NOTTINGHAM SUBURBAN LINE

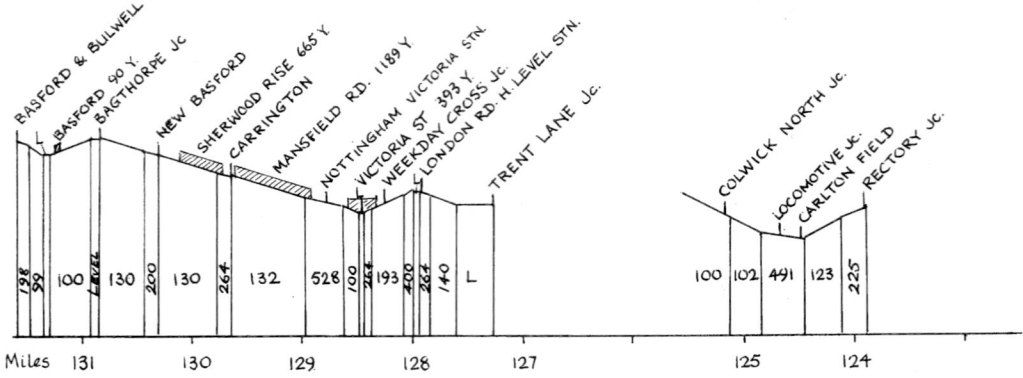

BASFORD - NOTTINGHAM VICTORIA - HIGH LEVEL

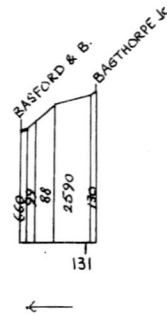

← DOWN LINE

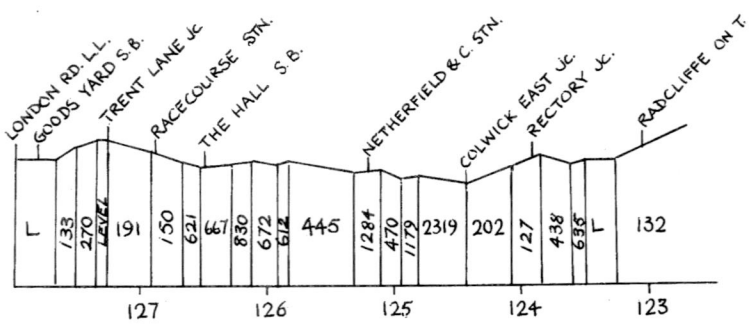

NOTTINGHAM LONDON ROAD - RADCLIFFE ON TRENT

AUTHOR'S NOTE

The scale plans of layouts for Colwick Yards and the lines west and north thereof are taken from GNR drawings dated 1903 and 1904 by kind permission of BR Public Relations Officer and the Engineer's Department. In the few cases where these were unavailable use has been made of OS 1:1250 scale maps, First or Second Editions.

The Signalbox diagrams are not to scale. They show details of lever frame connections to points, signals, etc, and other relevant information, and are taken from the author's (including H H Mather's) collections and date from 1935 to 1970. They should make a useful comparison with the scale maps, revealing closure of early collieries/works together with the opening of such new sites as Opencast coal sidings in the Second World War.

Distances shown on the scale plans are from the GNR Appendix to the Working Time Table of June 1912 and agree with the re-measurement of the lines from King's Cross Passenger Station undertaken during 1895-6. Mile posts on early OS maps do not necessarily coincide with official mileages.

Gradient profiles have been taken from LNER charts of the 1930s, and particularly in colliery regions, where subsidence has occurred differ from original GNR drawings made at the opening of the lines. Earlier figures are shown in brackets.

Apart from early Post Cards, and Bridge photographs from BR archives, many illustrations are of the post-war era. Every effort has been made to include early pictures, and the date together with the photographer is always mentioned where known.

The lines covered have been walked and photographed recently to indicate what remains to be seen of a once busy railway.

ACKNOWLEDGMENTS

Having been left the task of writing the text for the second section of the GNR in the Nottingham District due to the sad demise of Harold H Mather in 1985, I must thank his son, David H Mather, for his co-operation and assistance in providing his father's notes, and many documents which he has inherited relating to the area. My thanks also extend to the following:-

British Rail Engineers and Publicity staff at Nottingham; J Cupit and staff of the Nottinghamshire County Records Office; Staff of Derbyshire Records and Museums Offices; C H Eggleston, J W D Miller, the late F Pike, P Stevenson, W Taylor, M J Hitchens, M Back, S Checkley and G H R Gwatkin. For the generous use of photographs all of which are acknowledged in the text where known, my thanks include J P Wilson, John Marshall, John R Bonser, the late R W Sheppard, C A Hill, the late A G Cramp, H J Priestley, and B Walker.

Much assistance has come from reminiscences with friends too numerous to list in the Railway Correspondence and Travel Society, the Railway and Canal Historical Society and ex-colleagues from LNER days. They will know to whom I refer and forgive me for omitting their names, I trust.

NOTES ABOUT THE AUTHORS

Work on this history of the former London and North Eastern Railway in the East Midlands first started after two former colleagues, Alfred Henshaw and Harold Mather, began reminiscing about their careers and the fact that there was no complete record of the lines they had once worked on.

Harold had been involved with the local railways all his life. His grandfather was engaged in the construction of the GNR Derbyshire Extension and when this was completed was stationed at Breadsall as foreman ganger until his retirement in 1915. Harold's father started work with the GNR as a locomotive cleaner in 1898 at Nottingham London Road Locomotive Depot, then as Fireman at Derby before transferring to Colwick in 1915 and retired from the Nottingham District Control Office in 1947. Harold joined the LNER in 1924, spending all his railway career in Derbyshire, Leicestershire, Northamptonshire and Nottinghamshire. After working through the clerical grades and as relief clerk working at many stations in the East Midlands he became Station Master in 1944. For twenty years his stations featured in the Best Kept Station and Gardens Competitions, winning many First Prizes. He became Area Manager in 1965 and finally retired with the closure of Colwick and the Derbyshire Extension Lines in 1970. Harold Mather also had a wide interest in the preservation of our heritage and was the author of the History of Kimberley and the History of the Clock and Watch Makers of Nottinghamshire. Sadly Harold became seriously ill in 1985 and died before the work on the four volumes could be completed, leaving Alf to finish the work.

Alfred joined the LNER in 1934 and served as goods and booking clerk at several stations in the Nottingham area until 1938 when he transferred to the Nottingham District Control Office. Apart from his army service he spent the rest of his railway career working on the three control sections which were responsible for the operation of services over the lines covered by this history. Alf left the railway service at Nationalisation in 1948 to train as a school teacher. However, his keen interest in the railway industry continued and over many years he has lectured on the local railway history.

After many months of hard work completing his diagrams, maps and photographs, Alf has rewritten the early manuscript using Harold's original detailed notes and documents which have been generously made available together with much helpful advice by his son, David H Mather.

John Marshall is a well established railway historian, author of several books and articles for the railway press. Upon learning of the efforts of Alf Henshaw to complete the books on the GNR in the Nottingham area, after the death of Harold Mather, John offered to use his wealth of material and knowledge of the area to write an introductory historical chapter for each volume.

Fig. 2

1. HISTORICAL INTRODUCTION - BY JOHN MARSHALL

A Bill was presented for the 1872 Session of Parliament for an extension from two junctions with the Nottingham-Grantham line at Colwick, round the north of Nottingham to Awsworth, beyond Kimberley. From here one branch would go up the Erewash Valley to Pinxton, and the other through Ilkeston and Derby to join the North Staffordshire Railway near Egginton.

The Bill passed through Parliament and received Royal Assent on 25th June 1872 *(GNR (Derbyshire and Staffordshire) Act of 1872 c139, 25 June)*. Section 19 imposed a penalty of £50 per day if the railway was not opened in five years from the passing of the Act. Power was given to raise £1m by new shares, to borrow £333,000 and to create and issue debenture stock. No time was lost, for on 16th August 1872 the order was given for the Railway from Nottingham to Pinxton to be proceeded with as rapidly as possible.

The work was carried out under Richard Johnson as the resident engineer William Henry Stubbs (1847-90) who was later to become Chief Civil Engineer of the MSLR. Contract No 1, Colwick to the east end of Ilkeston viaduct was let to George Benton and Abraham Woodiwiss for £298,744 on 4th March 1873. Heavy engineering was required in cuttings, tunnels and embankments.

From Colwick East Junction, about 500 yds west of the Trent bridge, and Colwick West Junction, the lines joined at Colwick North Junction. Inside the triangle so formed the GNR built a locomotive depot and extensive sorting sidings, causing the development of what became a new railway town. The tender of J Parnell & Son, £7664, for Colwick loco shed was accepted on 19 February 1875 *(A long article on the railway and its works appeared in the Nottingham Daily Guardian, Thursday 12 August 1875, p 4, cols 5 and 6)*. A further contract for an extension of the shed, for £11,310, was awarded to E Wood on 6 May 1881.

Beyond Colwick North Junction the MR Lincoln line was crossed by bridge 10 of three iron plate-girder spans as required by Section 16 of the Act. Shortly after the village of Gedling at 4 1/2 miles, where an attractive station was provided, the line entered Mapperley cutting through heavy clay, with a maximum depth of 70 ft for a considerable distance, involving nearly 300,000 cu.yd. of excavation. A stream was carried over the cutting in a brick aqueduct which also carried a farm road. The cutting led to Mapperley tunnel, straight, 1132 yd long, passing under the 'Plains' at a maximum depth of 210 ft. Six shafts were sunk for construction and, on completion of the tunnel, which consumed 5 million bricks, three of the shafts at 10 chain intervals were retained for ventilation. Beyond another vast cutting at the west end of the tunnel the summit was reached at Arno Vale. A single-span through plate-girder bridge with brick arches over the pavements carried the line over the Nottingham-Mansfield road into Daybrook station, 7 1/2 miles and to Basford, 9 1/4 miles.

At Leen Valley Junction extensive sidings were laid out and a long loop was added on the Up side between there and Daybrook where, with permissive block working, coal trains and iron-ore empties would await their turn to blast their way up to Arno Vale summit. William Rigley's Wagon Works were established at Leen Valley Junction and at Bulwell Forest where they turned out the brightly painted wooden-framed and bodied four-wheeled coal wagons for colliery companies which were such a familiar feature of the British railway scene until the second world war. In 1940 another loop was built on the down side at Leen Valley Junction which involved considerable excavation.

Passengers travelling from Nottingham to stations beyond Daybrook had first to make the circuitous journey of 7 1/2 miles round Nottingham before they arrived at Daybrook where they were only 3 miles from Nottingham station in a straight line. To shorten this journey a group of Nottingham businessmen formed the Nottingham Suburban Railway Company to promote a line through the eastern suburbs from Trent Lane, about a mile out of Nottingham station, to Daybrook.

Edward Parry (1844-1920), who from 1879 was County Surveyor of Nottinghamshire, was appointed engineer. He laid out a steeply-graded route with deep cuttings, high embankments and four tunnels which cost about £70,000 a mile to build. Construction was authorised by the Act of 1886 which incorporated the company with a capital of £250,000 in shares of £10 and power to borrow £83,000 when all shares were issued *(Nottingham Surburban Railway Act 1886 c94, 25 June)*. The railway was to be 3 3/4 miles long with a short branch of 9 chains to the works of the Nottingham Patent Brick Company at Thorneywood. On 8 December 1886 the tender of J P Edwards for £111,501 was accepted for construction. At the time he was engaged on the MR line from Ripley to Heanor in Derbyshire. There were several changes in the planned junction at

Fig. 3

Trent Lane. As built, the Down line climbed at 1 in 49 to the bridge over the MR. The Up line descended on easier gradients over the Grantham line by two bow-string lattice-girder through spans, crossed Trent Lane by a brick arch and the MR again by a through lattice-girder span before joining the main line. The bridge carrying both tracks over the MR was a lattice deck-girder span in two parts: the Down line crossed on a gradient of 1 in 49 while the Up line crossed on the level. The railway crossed Sneinton Dale by a three-arch brick viaduct and passed through Sneinton tunnel, 183 yd, to reach Thorneywood station, 1 3/4 miles. Here there were extensive sidings and a goods shed. A branch from behind the station passed through a tunnel 109 yd long under Thorneywood Lane just large enough to pass open wagons which were hauled up to the brickworks by a small winding engine at the top. Next was Thorneywood tunnel, 408 yd, and a short distance beyond that a skew lattice-girder deck span over The Wells Road. At Saint Ann's Well station, 2 1/2 miles, were more sidings and another goods shed. The line reached a summit of 296 ft just south of Sherwood tunnel having climbed 201 ft in 2 1/4 miles from Trent Lane Junction, mostly at 1 in 50. The line dropped through the tunnel, 442 yd long, at 1 in 70 to Sherwood station, 3 1/4 miles. From a siding on the right a steep cable-worked incline led up to the Mapperley works of the Nottingham Patent Brick Company. This branch was not included in the Act. There was no goods shed at Sherwood. The line dropped again at 1 in 70 through Ashwells tunnel, 70 yd, and rejoined the GNR just east of Mansfield Road bridge at Daybrook. By this route Daybrook station was 4 1/4 miles from Nottingham, a reduction of about 3 1/4 miles.

The railway was opened on 2 December 1889. In January 1890 the passenger service consisted of ten trains from Nottingham and nine back including four to and from Newstead. Pinxton and Derby trains continued to run *via* Netherfield where they connected with trains to and from Grantham. Nottingham passengers could travel *via* the Suburban line and change at Daybrook.

Although the Nottingham Suburban Railway remained in private ownership until the grouping on 1 January 1923, it was operated from the start by the GNR, with standard GNR signalling. The heavy gradients, and its avoidance of Colwick yard, made it suitable only for light passenger trains and local goods trains. The stations were in rural districts and by the time housing developments had reached the railway electric trams were taking passengers directly to and from Nottingham at low fares. So the local passenger traffic had no chance to develop and on 1 July 1916 the intermediate stations were closed as a wartime economy measure. Another factor leading to its decline was the opening of the Great Central Railway through Nottingham and the connections with the GNR.

The additional coal traffic coming in from the Leen Valley made it necessary to provide greater capacity at Colwick yard so, on 13 April 1888, the tender of Parker & Co, £15,012, was accepted for an extension of the yard and also widening between Saxondale and Radcliffe on the Grantham line for the iron ore traffic. The new sidings replaced part of the line from Colwick North Junction to Colwick East Junction and necessitated construction of a new through line to the Grantham line at Rectory Junction close to the Trent bridge. This and the new sidings came into use on 23 November 1891. On 5 November 1896 Dennett & Ingle were awarded the contract, for £15,481, for an additional engine shed and wagon shop at Colwick. These were completed in 1897.

Fig. 2
A similar viewpoint to Fig. 140 p58 is chosen here, but behind the signal gantry is a new signal box. The train signalled on the Up line is routed for Netherfield & Colwick station, and most probably Nottingham. Standing at the Down platform a sparklingly clean H A Ivatt-designed LNER Class D3 heads a four-coach train of six-wheeled coaches from Nottingham to Basford & Bulwell. This locomotive was built at Doncaster Works in May 1898, and was not withdrawn from service until December 1950. Such engines regularly worked the GNR passenger trains in the Nottingham area and throughout LNER days. *c.1912 the late F H Gillford*

Fig. 3
Another official photograph of the station footbridge with the oval number plate clearly visible on the right hand pillar, but which embraces much more detail. Beside the name board on the Down side platform (left) is the gradient post indicating an easing of the climb from Trent Lane Junction of 1 in 49 to 1 in 200, to assist drivers to get away. At the foot of the steps are posts holding the notice board to passengers to cross the line by the bridge. Beyond this the buildings and an enamelled plate advertising one of Nottingham's staple industries - Player's Navy Cut tobacco. Beneath the awning on the left, is part of the Goods shed and its awning, whilst the steps and doorway to the signal box appear on the Up platform. The long footbridge in the distance spans the cutting from Thorneywood Rise (left) to Thorneywood Lane, now Porchester Road on the right. There are two GN lettered wagons behind the Up platform above which is the gable end of the Station House. *c.1904 G Cawthorne collection*

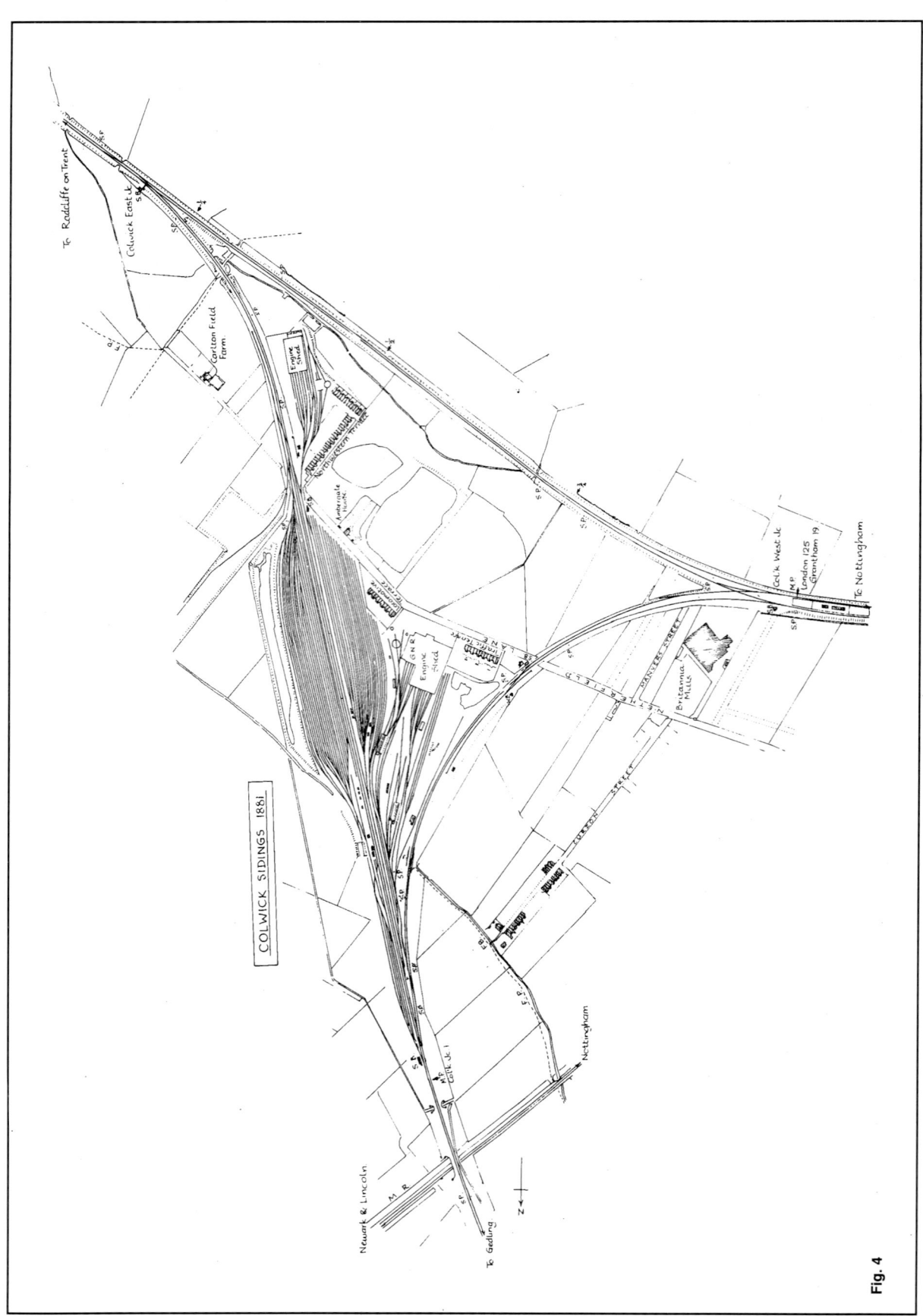

Fig. 4

2. COLWICK YARDS AND MOTIVE POWER DEPOT

Fig. 5
This view looking south from bridge 10 over the MR Nottingham-Newark line shows the fine lattice bracket of Up Home signals at Colwick North Jc. The signal box shows above the right hand parapet. Ex LMS Class 8F 48526 has arrived on the Down Main with a freight trip from Nottingham London Road, and is about to set back on to one of the six Old Bank reception sidings.

August 1966 A Henshaw

The Ambergate Company did not operate a goods service into Nottingham Midland station upon the opening of the line, but built sidings and a warehouse at Colwick for such traffic in the Spring of 1850. From here it was carted to and from Nottingham by horse and dray. By 1857, after the opening of London Road Station, these early sidings were lifted, and the embankment on which they had been built was removed, except for one stone pier which had carried the lines over the flood plain of the river. This remaining pier was incorporated into the transhipment dock on the Jitty (No 31 road) in the Down sidings of No 1 Yard near Locomotive Junction.

In June 1872, with the Derbyshire Extensions Act having been passed by Parliament, the GNR lost no time in purchasing 150 acres of land at Colwick for the construction of Up and Down side sorting sidings, a locomotive shed and workshops, and some dwelling houses. By 23rd August 1875, the double line connection between Colwick West Junction and Colwick North Junction was opened, forming a triangle of lines with Colwick East Junction where the Extensions westwards began. By the following Spring, sidings for 650 loaded on the Up side and 500 empty wagons on the Down side were completed, as were the houses of Traffic Terrace and Locomotive Terrace. The first engine shed of four roads, later called the 'Old Shed' was also finished with small outbuildings which later became the Joiners' Shop etc. *(H H Mather).*

Colwick Passenger Station was opened on the old Ambergate line from Grantham 250 yards east of the original Carlton Junction in May 1878, together with a brick built Goods Shed and Office, and a small Goods Yard 29.5 chains (649 yards) away where the west to north lines crossed Netherfield Lane. Collection/delivery services for the surrounding area including Gedling was by railway-owned drays drawn by horses of the Truman family. After 1st April 1929 these services were continued by three-wheeled motorised units called Karrier Kobs from Nottingham London Road Depot. Alongside the Goods Yard towards the North Junction Workshops and sidings were built for the District Engineer. At the Level Crossing of Netherfield Lane, a Signal Box of that name was built to control the gates and entrance to the Goods Yard.

Fig. 6
Mr Charles H Eggleston was one of the few dedicated railwaymen who owned and used a camera to advantage whilst about his duties. He was Assistant Yardmaster at Colwick shortly before its demise, after which he transferred to Lincoln. Here is a detail of the tranship stage and shed beside the Jitty, with the bracket and appendages, but minus the arc, of the loading gauge (Fig 38 P21). On the left are the Shunters' cabin and Signal Box at Locomotive Junction.

April 1970 C H Eggleston

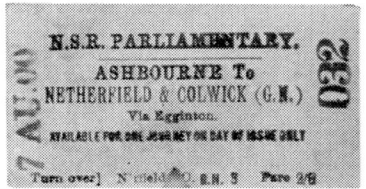

5

Fig. 7
An early view (pre-1909) of Netherfield station as seen from the road approaching bridge 41 which shows Colwick West Junction signalbox on the right beyond the buildings, together with its Up Home signals, one with a sky arm for early visibility over the bridge. The platform displays a variety of advertisements and posters together with 'penny-in-the-slot' machines. Note the unusual support for the long awnings over this island platform which served as a junction station for trains from the Derbyshire Extension lines west of Gedling into Nottingham London Road, and the Grantham/Newark trains heading east from there. The faintly visible chimney beside the signals is at Britannia Mills.
H H Mather collection

Fig. 8
The same train as in Fig 23, p13 travelling down the Branch towards Carlton Field. Left of the train are the Engine Line and six Arrival roads to No 1 Down Empties Yard, known as 'Spike Bank'. Further left are the Avoiding Lines which swept round to join the Main Lines at Colwick East Junction. The Down Goods has been removed from behind the second lamp post in the direction the train is travelling.
January 1966 A Henshaw

On September 1st 1879, the GN and LNWR Joint Line was opened between Saxondale Junction and Melton Mowbray. As the LNWR had been granted running powers over GN lines to collieries along the Derbyshire Extension, a temporary engine shed, and siding accommodation was built for them at Colwick in that year, near the south end of the yard, later becoming No 2 Down Yard.

The increasing traffic from lines to the west; its working east and south to London, together with the opening of the Leen Valley line in 1881 serving new collieries as far as Newstead and Annesley led to an additional engine shed to hold 50 locomotives (the Large Shed), and workshops being built in 1882. Two years later, six new reception sidings were built for coal traffic at Colwick North, which became known as the New Bank, the earlier ones to the west being called the 'Old Bank'. Additional Land Powers were taken for improvements, alterations and enlargements by Acts of 1877, 1885, 1890 and 1903, but these do not specify for what purpose *(H H Mather)*.

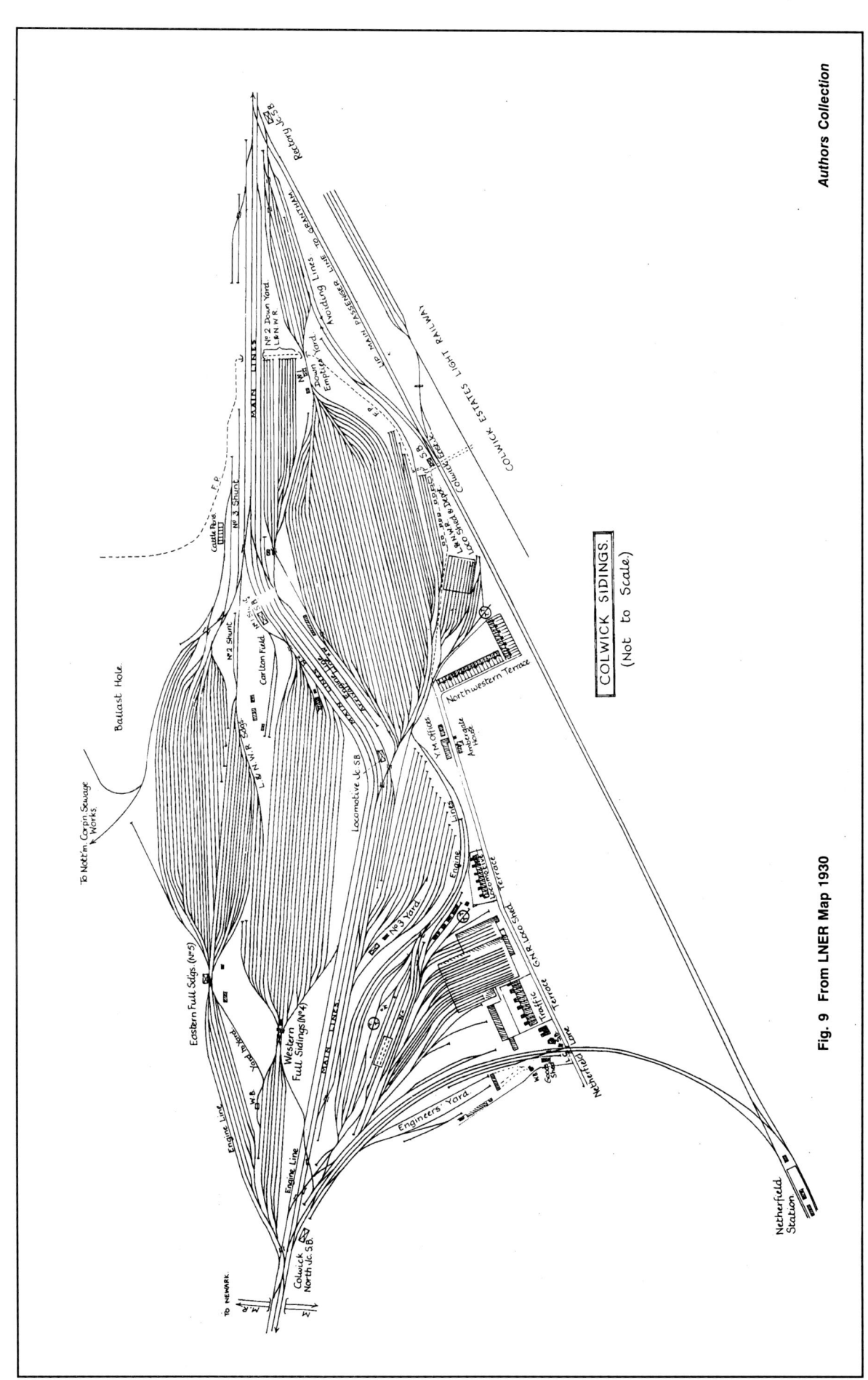

Fig. 9 From LNER Map 1930

Authors Collection

Fig. 10
The view from Carlton Field signal box looking south towards Rectory Junction, showing a reduced, or rationalised layout from that illustrated in Fig. 9, p7. The brake van on the left is at the end of No 1 shunt, adjacent to the exit from No 2 section. Further left is the exit from Nos 3 and 4 sections behind which are the cattle pens. The line right of the point rodding is the Up Goods beside the Up Main. The Down Main is not continuous here any longer, and the Down Goods line which lay beneath the signal gantry has also been removed. The steel-sided mineral wagons containing iron ore from the Leicestershire mines around the Vale of Belvoir are in No 2 Down Yard, and above them is the Shunters South cabin. The difference in levels is again obvious from this angle: No 2 Yard being level; the running lines to Rectory Junction climbing at 1 in 123 to cross the River Trent, and the downward slope of No 1 Yard sidings to allow gravity shunting.
April 1970 C H Eggleston

A private residence called 'Ambergate House' on the opposite side of Victoria Road to the Traffic Offices was provided for the Yardmaster. At the rear of this residence was Graves' Pond noted for its fishing. This was created by excavating material for construction of the embankment from Colwick East Junction to Netherfield Station.

In 1885, The Railway Institute was opened close to the Level Crossing on Netherfield Lane, and a Lodging House for train crews was built to the rear of Traffic Terrace. During the same year, a new and separate Parish called Netherfield was created because of the concentration of railwaymen around the expanding yards and Engine sheds. Its name was taken from the nether (lower) fields of the Parish of Carlton Netherfield. The furthest point for the Beating of the Bounds at Rogationtide in the Ecclesiastical Parish of Colwick was beside the River Trent. The new Signal Box soon to be built at the south eastern end of the extended marshalling yards was named Rectory Junction. Powers were granted to replace the Level Crossing at Netherfield, west of the station, with a bridge to take the road from Colwick to Carlton, and give access to the station at the same time.

In 1890 additional land powers were granted, and during the following few years, the marshalling yards were extended to their final extent (Fig. 2, p7). The original double line from Colwick North to East Junctions was slewed northeastwards to Carlton Field (named after the farm) (Fig 4, p4), and back again to meet the Grantham lines just west of the River Trent at Rectory Junction, where six reception sidings for the new Down sorting sidings (No 1 Yard) were built. Up and Down goods lines were provided between Carlton Field and Rectory Junction, together with a block of eleven sidings (No 2 Down Yard) replacing the temporary Engine shed for use by the LNWR traffic. This yard was controlled by Carlton Field signal box and also known as Ladysmith. The double line junction at Colwick East was reversed in direction, and connected to Rectory Junction, giving two additional running lines known as the Avoiding Lines. These were connected to the outlet of No 1 Down yard at Locomotive Junction which also controlled access to the new nearby LNWR Engine Shed and also to Engine Lines to the GN sheds at Colwick North. Another small yard of sixteen sidings, site of the first Down sidings, became No 3 Yard and dealt with Goods and Perishable traffic.

By 1900 on the Up side, the original reception roads were extended and increased to six for Goods Traffic, six more of similar length built alongside to the east for mineral trains, and an additional 29 roads forming no 5 Yard were laid, making Colwick the largest marshalling yards on the GNR, with a total capacity of 6,000 wagons. Two points boxes now controlled the marshalling by gravitation into the two large sets of sidings; No 4 Goods Yard and No 5 Minerals. The LNWR, having built their sidings and an Engine Shed on the Down side had sidings on the Up allocated to them in 1892 which included three goods and eleven mineral roads, all being controlled by Carlton Field. These were at South End Departure No 2 Section (Fig. 62 p30). Their Engine Shed had eight roads, workshops, offices, a turntable and coal stage. Also, at the end of Netherfield Lane (later Victoria Rd) the LNWR built 39 houses for their employees, named North Western Terrace. Access to the Engine Shed from NW Terrace was across a single line at the end of Netherfield Lane by level crossing until 1890, when a lattice girder footbridge, No 6A was built. This was demolished in 1962. The staff complement of this depot consisted of

1 Depot Supervisor, 4 general clerks, 2 stores clerks
1 Mechanical Foreman, 1 Leading Fitter, 6 fitters, 6 mates
2 Boilersmiths 2 mates 2 boiler washers
3 general storesmen, 4 coal stage men, 3 general labourers
101 Drivers, Firemen and Cleaners, 12 Guards, 2 callers-up.

No 2 Down Yard was manned by one inspector, three foreman shunters and six shunters.

Fig. 11
Senior Fitter Sid Checkley standing outside the Stores building at Colwick Loco. Behind him is the low wall of the deep well with its pipes and valves leading to the Pump House above which was the storage tank. In the foreground is the connecting rod of locomotive No 60102 which began as A1 Pacific No 4471 in 1922 and named Sir Frederick Banbury after the Chairman of the GNR at that time. *S Checkley*

Fig. 12
The view inside the Erecting Shop showing J6 in the foreground and 36-ton Royce gantry crane right, above an 'Austerity' 2-8-0. The wagons would have brought boiler tubes in for unloading.

1955 C A Hill

The vast expansion of traffic for Colwick led to delays for the goods and empties trains awaiting acceptance from Radcliffe-on-Trent, and two Goods or Slow lines were laid between Saxondale Junction and Radcliffe, operated under Permissive Block Regulations and opened in August 1890. Up to eight trains could be held nose to tail on the Down line, and Cabins for relief of train crews were built at Netherfield and Radcliffe stations, the former being a signing on/off point manned round the clock by timekeepers. A similar Up Goods Line was laid between Leen Valley Junction and Daybrook which could hold five trains. In 1897 a third Engine Shed of four roads was built. Wagon shops as well as additional sidings were completed in 1897.

The Nottingham Colwick Estates Light Railway Company laid lines on a new Industrial Estate between the River Trent and the Nottingham-Grantham line in 1916, and in January 1918 the Company was granted powers to connect to the GNR at Colwick East Junction. The GNR were to place the traffic into Exchange sidings to the south of their running lines. By August 1919 the Light Railway was completed, and an Electric Power House built to serve the Estate. Electric power and lighting was supplied to Colwick Yards, Loco, and buildings from this Power House. Prior to this a small supply of electricity for machinery at Colwick Loco had come from a generator driven by a gas engine. On 18th April 1922 agreement was reached with the Light Railway Company to work the line, but leaving maintenance in the latter's hands. The GNR had control of the rates. The GNR engines then worked the traffic over the Colwick Estates Light Railway from the exchange sidings, under 'One Engine in Steam' regulations. After the closure of Colwick East Junction signalbox in June 1972 the railway connection was maintained using it as a Ground Frame released from Rectory Junction until 1st April 1985. The Estate, now served by road is flourishing with many new units and has been extended to the north side of the lines to Grantham since the closure and clearance of the marshalling yards.

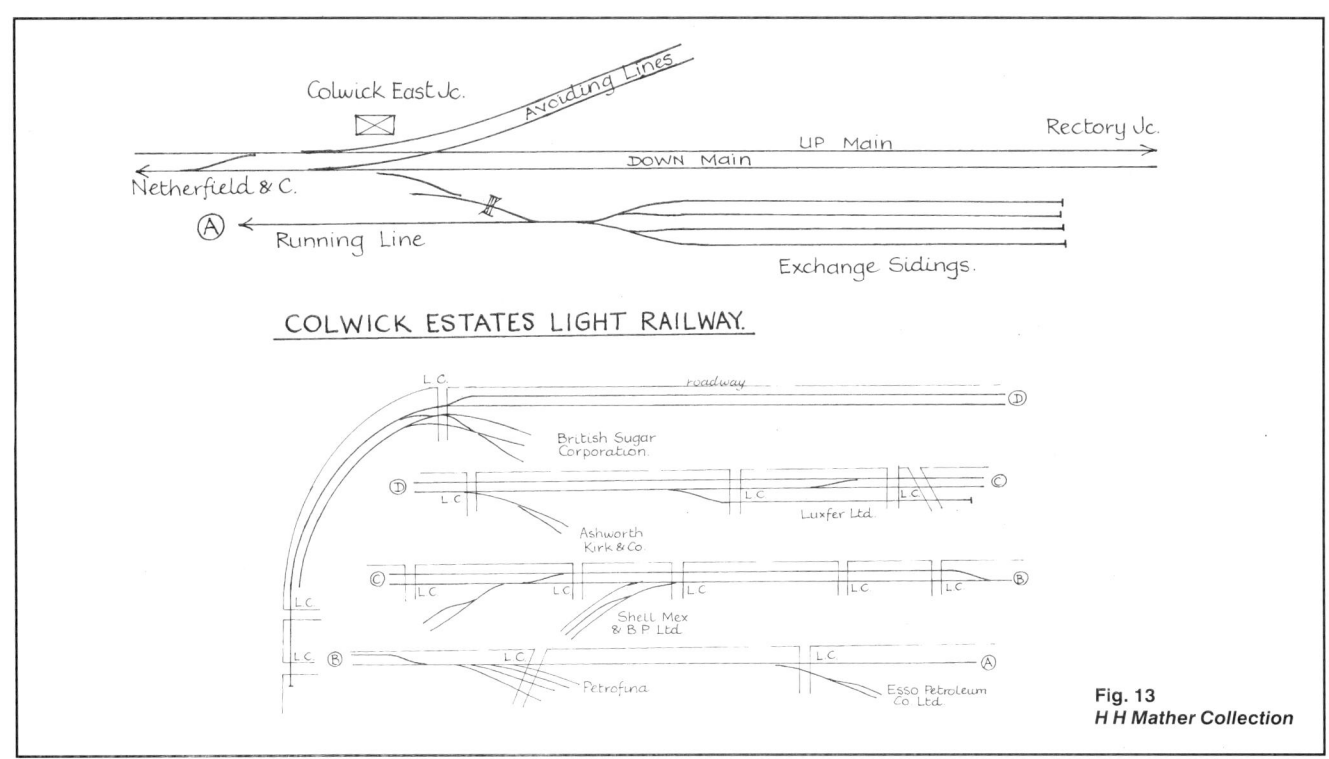

Fig. 13
H H Mather Collection

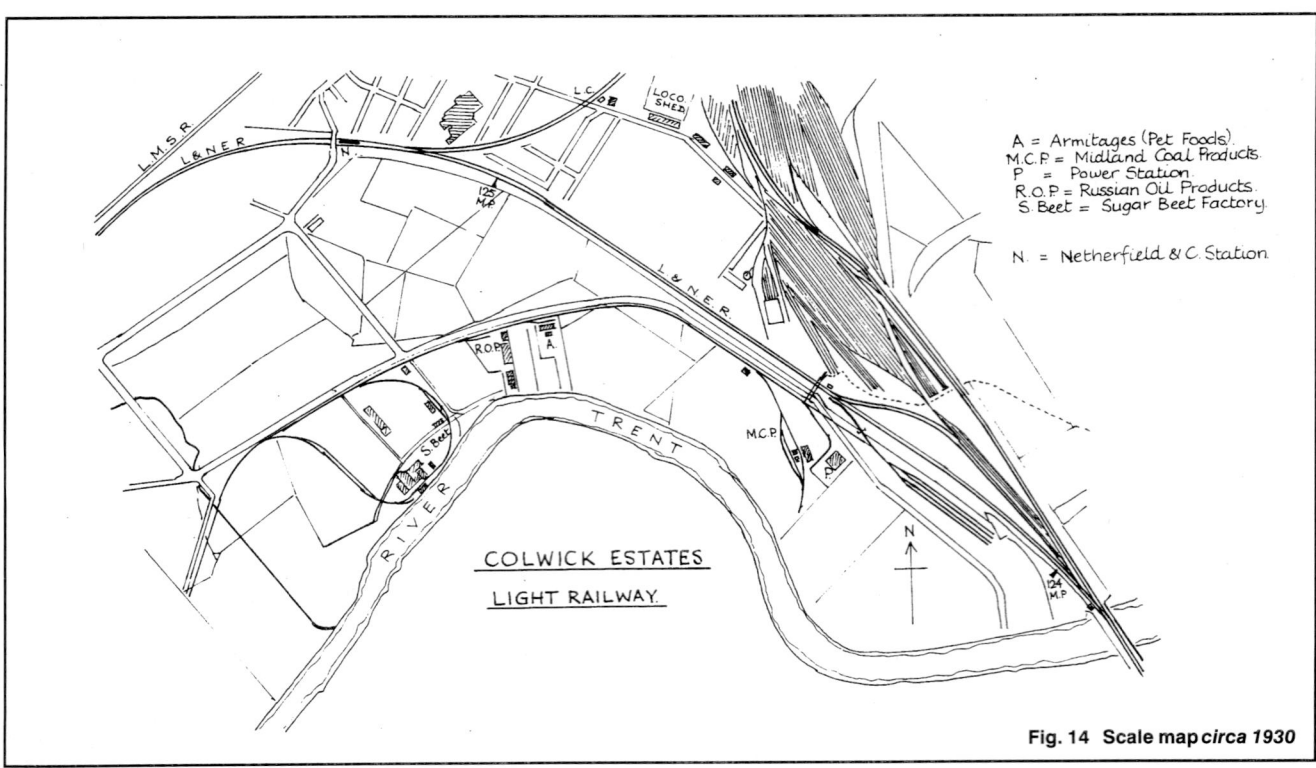

Fig. 14 Scale map *circa 1930*

In 1924, now under LNER management, the Shearlegs to lift 35 tons was transferred from GCR Grimsby Loco Depot to Colwick Depot replacing the former timber structure, which was under cover. Staff at this time in the Motive Power Department were:-

Locomotive Superintendent, Chief Clerk, 15 general clerks, 3 time clerks, 2 roster clerks, 3 stores clerks
730 drivers and firemen, 3 running shed foremen, 3 foremen's assistants, 3 ashpit foremen, 4 foreman fitters, 1 chargehand fitter, and about 40 loco fitters
1 boiler washer foreman, 6 boiler tube cleaners, 9 steam raisers, 8 fire droppers, 4 coalmen, 1 tank diver and mate to clean engine tenders
1 electrician and mate, 2 lampmen, 1 joiner and assistant, 2 fitters and 2 mates to attend turntables and watercolumns at both the Depot and outstations, 3 stationary machine attendants, 1 turner
3 foremen engine cleaners, 30 engine cleaners, 1 toolman and 1 labourer to supply rakes, shovels, detonators, spanners and to shaft pick hammers, and 3 gas fitters. Other attendant staff were tinsmiths, coppersmiths and 1 painter and mate, along with 70 to 80 men in the wagon shops and saw mill engaged on painting, repairs and supply of timber. The wagon cripple dock consisted of two roads in the fitting shop, and most of the work on wagons was at piece rate.

In September 1928 the LNWR Motive Power Depot closed and their engines were stabled at GN sheds, drivers and firemen signing on and off at Colwick Locomotive Depot and guards at the Yard Traffic Offices. The LMS crews were rostered by LNE Foremen but came under LMS Nottingham MPD authority, who also provided relief for their own crews on overtime. This was under the pooling arrangements between the LMSR and the LNER.

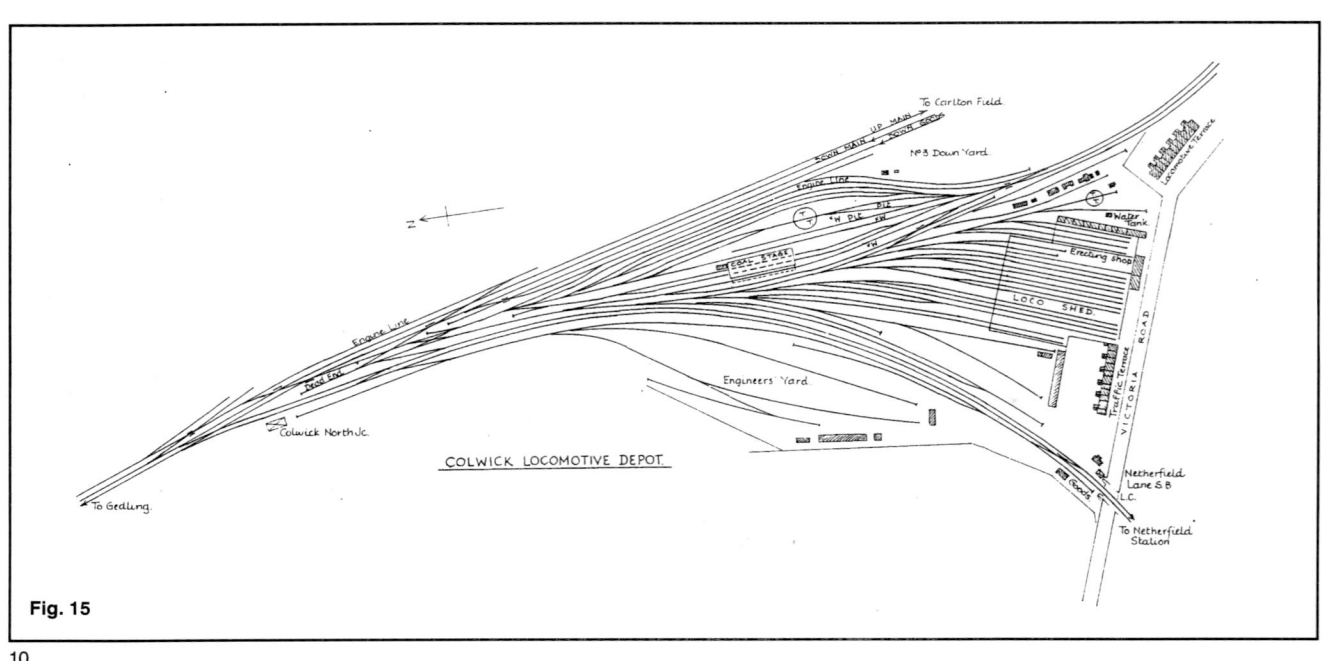

Fig. 15

Colwick Motive Power Depot was modernised in 1936 with the erection of an overhead coaling plant, known as the 'Cenotaph', a vacuum-operated turntable, a 36-ton Sheldon & Cowan breakdown crane, and a 35-ton traverser crane. A stud of approximately 200 engines was maintained. After the second World War, the LNE Classes A3 Pacifics and V2 Green Arrows of Leicester GC Depot were maintained at Colwick. The erecting shops had five lathes of various sizes, one locomotive wheel lathe, one wagon wheel lathe, two drilling machines, one bolt screwing machine, one hydraulic pump for the wheel drop, four forges with a big fan of 8 feet diameter. In the blacksmith's shop were one shaping machine, one slotting machine, one upright engine to drive shafting working all machines, and three stationary boilers. The gas plant with two retorts and gas engine supplied power for lifting gear. All axle boxes were boiled in a large tank, the grease skimmed off and reclaimed. Firelighters were made 6 inches long by one inch square, the ends dipped in tar and shavings and packed in threes. Three large tanks stored ordinary cylinder oil, mineral oil for bearings and superheater oil. Distribution of oil, firelighters and sponge cloths was in the hands of three oilstoremen.

At the old coal stage 30 tons were shovelled in each eight-hour shift for the rate of 4 1/4 d (1.75p) a ton. the double rate of emptying the ashpit and loading into wagons was 6d (2 1/2p) a ton. Smoke box ashes were sent to fire the two retorts driving the gas engines.

A well sunk into the sandstone aquifer provided water pumped into an overhead tank, which in turn supplied the water requirements of the Locomotive Depot, Marshalling Yard, cottages, Railway Institute, Lodging house and the two jib water cranes at Netherfield passenger station. A gas fitters' shop was provided in the tower carrying the water tank. Three time recording clocks were provided at the entrance to the Locomotive Depot. From the Time Office a lever operated the steam 'bull' blown at 6.0 am, 10.0 am and 10.0 pm, and this could be heard over a radius of five miles.

Fig. 16
A view of BR Standard Class 4MT 2-6-0 beneath the coaling plant at Colwick. This was erected in 1936 and was known as 'The Cenotaph'. To the right is the vacuum-operated turntable. *1967 R Askew*

Fig. 17
A steam-operated grab clearing the ash pits. The curved corrugated asbestos roof in the background was in the Engineers' Yard beyond the branch to Netherfield Station. *1963 C A Hill*

11

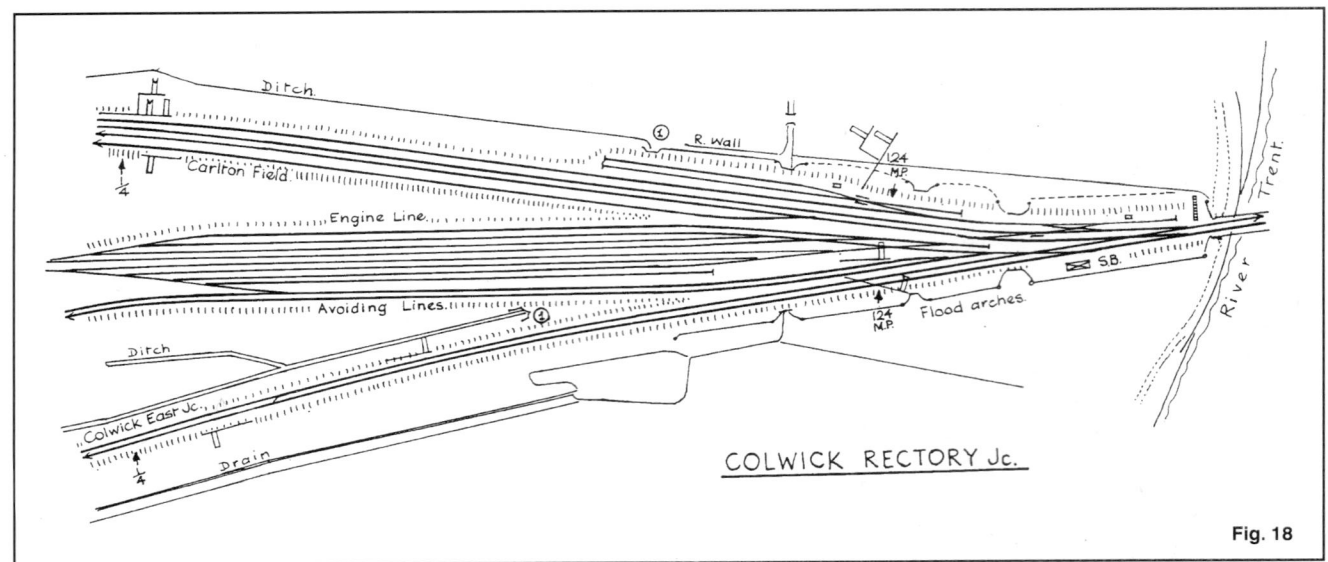

Fig. 18

RECTORY JUNCTION 123 m 71 1/4 ch

This large signal box was situated on the embankment west of the bridge over the River Trent, and controlled all movements into and out of Colwick at the south end, from the Nottingham-Grantham lines. Trains leaving for destinations *via* Radcliffe-on-Trent could approach along the Up Slow or Goods line or the Up branch from Carlton Field. Down trains as late as 1932 passed beneath a gantry of five posts of somersault signals as they crossed the River Trent. From left to right they signalled routes to (a) Colwick East Junction *via* the Main line; (b) Colwick East Junction *via* Avoiding Line; (c) One of the six reception roads for No 1 Down Yard, known as Spike Bank; (d) Branch Goods Line to Carlton Field; (e) Branch to Carlton Field. This gantry was replaced by a bracket signal with three posts of upper quadrant arms at the western end of the bridge by 1936, (Fig. 22 p13) and in BR days by a colour light signal with horn indicators (Fig. 24 p14).

The six reception roads could each hold approximately 60 wagons, but a few trains of 80 Private Owners' coal wagons were scheduled from Peterborough to Colwick during the 1930s often hauled by Gresley Class 02 2-8-0 locos nicknamed Tangos. Two empty reception roads were needed to handle such trains, which would draw down one clear road, and continue along the engine line from Shunter's South Cabin until the brake van was clear at the east end. The leading 25 or so wagons were then uncoupled, drawn forward clear of points, and the engine released for Loco *via* Locomotive Junction. The Pilot then fetched the wagons on the Engine Line, shunting them first back into another reception road. The signalmen had the assistance of Train Register Lads as at Colwick North Junction to report all train movements except Stopping Passengers to Control. An order was issued from King's Cross on the 22nd December 1910 that no two large eight wheel coupled or 'Atlantic' type engines or two eight wheel coupled tank engines, or one of the above with ordinary engine to run over the bridge crossing the River Trent, or over any bridges or viaducts west of Colwick in the same direction at the same time. After closure of Colwick Yards in April 1970, the Up and Down Branch lines to Carlton Field were stopped 520 yards from the junction to form an Oil Terminal, and the reception roads were used for extra sidings. The Up and Down Avoiding Lines were classified as sidings, blocked by a buffer stop at Colwick East. The connection from the Down line to No 1 Reception line, formerly released electrically by Colwick East Junction, was secured in the normal position. On August 1st 1976 the facing points to the Oil Terminal were taken out, movements afterwards using the crossover No 8 at the Cotgrave Branch connection.

The Cotgrave branch is out of use, but under consideration for a proposed Light Rapid Transport service to the village from Nottingham, like the Gedling branch (Fig. 144 p59)

Fig. 19
A fine view of the large span and arches of the Radcliffe viaduct from the west side which shows a Market Harborough -Nottingham London Road passenger train hauled by ex-Midland railway 2-4-0 passing the gantry of somersault signals which were Rectory Junction's Down Homes.
July 1932 E C Haywood

Fig. 20
A Grantham-Nottingham passenger train hauled by an Ivatt Class J6 six-coupled loco is passing the bracket of Down Home signals which replaced the gantry on the viaduct. On the right is the coal bunker at the foot of the steps to Rectory Junction signal box. The photographer was standing at the lamp post beside the brake van in Fig. 8. p6.
1955 F Quenby

On 12th February 1996, following instructions from Health & Safety Executive officials, Rectory Junction signalbox was temporarily closed for emergency re-wiring which needed complete disconnections. All connections were secured for through running. Signal arms and lamps were removed from Nos 55 and 74. Discs and lamps were removed from Nos 59, 61, 69 and 78. Colour light signals Nos 54, 56, 57 Up and 64, 65, 79 Down had lamps removed and heads covered.

Under the supervision of an Operating Inspector working into Total Oil Company's Private Siding was to be controlled by a shunter with a 2-way radio handset to the driver who would receive a similar handset after bringing his train to a stand. The Points Operator would give permission to enter and leave the Oil Terminal after which the driver's handset would be returned to the shunter, when these movements were over and the empties had departed. Points would then again be secured for through running. Normal working was resumed on 17th April 1996.

Fig. 21
The Engine Line (left) and six Arrival roads to No 1 Down Empties Yard seen from the Shunters South Points Box.
Rectory Junction signal box is in the distance, with the Avoiding Lines to the right, beyond which are the Main Lines to Colwick East and Netherfield & Colwick Station. The low parapets on either side are of Bridge No 3 housing a footpath beneath the rails.   *July 1969 A Henshaw*

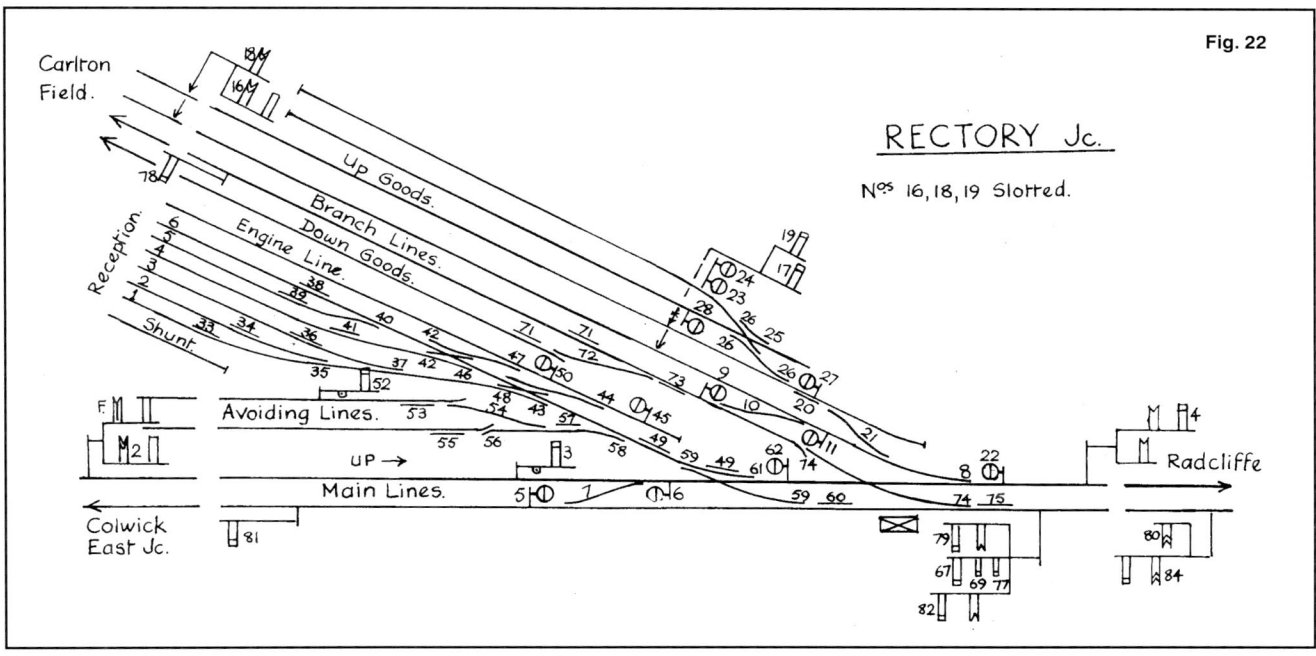

Fig. 23
A view from Rectory Junction signal box looking towards Radcliffe-on-Trent which shows an ex LMS Class 8F 2-8-0 heading a train of iron ore from Belvoir. Notice the colour light routing signal (right) which replaces an earlier gantry of semaphore signals (Fig. 19). In the misty background is the viaduct carrying the branch to Cotgrave Colliery.
January 1966 A Henshaw

COTGRAVE COLLIERY BRANCH

Work began on this new colliery in April 1954, the sinking of shafts taking place between 1956 and 1960. Coal production began in 1964. As with the postwar opening of Calverton, predictions were for a high output to serve the new electric power stations along the Trent Valley. Indeed one such station was planned at Holme Pierrepont near Radcliffe-on-Trent, but was not built, being superseded by the large Ratcliffe-on-Soar station, which began production in December 1967.

After crossing the River Trent east of Rectory Junction and still on the brick arched viaduct over the flood plain, the branch to Cotgrave curved away from the main lines to Radcliffe and Grantham in a southerly direction on a concrete viaduct.

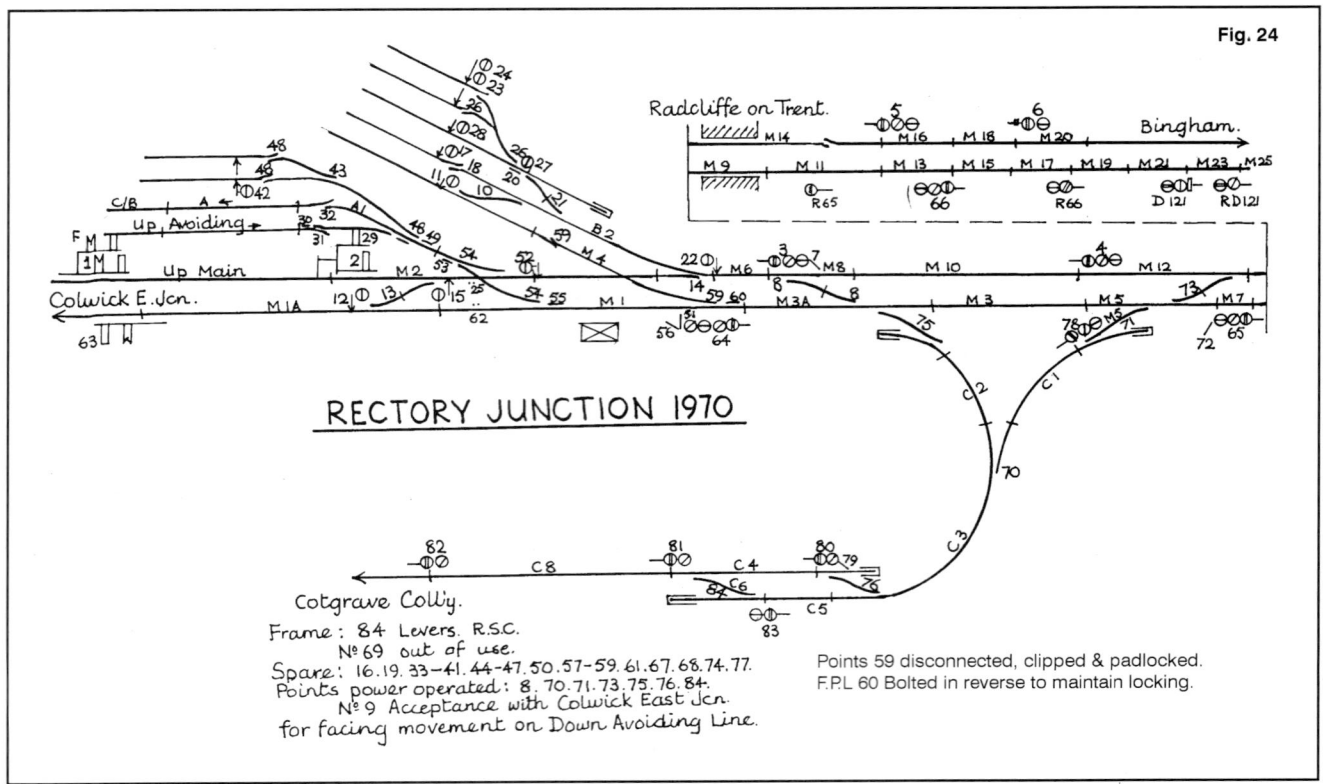

Fig. 24 RECTORY JUNCTION 1970

Frame: 84 Levers. R.S.C.
No 69 out of use.
Spare: 16.19. 33-41. 44-47. 50. 57-59. 61. 67. 68. 74. 77.
Points power operated: 8. 70. 71. 73. 75. 76. 84.
No 9 Acceptance with Colwick East Jcn.
for facing movement on Down Avoiding Line.

Points 59 disconnected, clipped & padlocked.
F.P.L 60 Bolted in reverse to maintain locking.

An embankment carried it above the countryside until the A52 Nottingham-Grantham road was bridged, and further still until another bridge crossed a minor road to Cropwell Bishop. Shortly after this the line ran alongside the Grantham Canal to the colliery.

A south to east curve was built on an embankment to join the Grantham line west of Radcliffe-on-Trent station, for there were hopes of high output from the new colliery. But the quality of the coal was not suitable and although a few trains went east to Whitemoor or Peterborough, the working did not last, and this curve was removed on 23rd May 1976. Trip working with empties from Colwick, returning with coal operated until closure of the Yard in April 1970, after which the LMR worked the traffic from Toton on the MR Erewash Valley Line.

Fig. 25
The bridges spanning the River Trent being crossed by an Up diesel-hauled coal train. The signal bracket in Fig. 20 is replaced by a colour light routing signal. Detail of maker's plate on the main span across the river is shown inset the main picture. *October 1967 late R W Sheppard*

Fig. 26
In commemoration of the 150th anniversary of the opening of the Midland Counties Railway between Nottingham and Derby, British Rail organised several special events and railtours which were very well patronised. One such railtour on 6th May was the 'Jolly Collier' which ran from Nottingham station to Calverton colliery, returning *via* Netherfield to Cotgrave colliery and thence back to Nottingham. The trips were made with a class 20 diesel locomotive at either end of a ten-coach train. This view illustrates the sharp curve of the concrete viaduct as the train approaches Rectory Junction on the return from Cotgrave. *May 1989 A Henshaw*

Fig. 27
The approach to Rectory Junction and Colwick Yards from the east was over a viaduct with a bridge spanning the River Trent. In January 1964 a branch line was opened to Cotgrave Colliery with east and west connections on the viaduct. D 8162 is seen taking a train of empties to Cotgrave over the new ferro-concrete viaduct. *October 1967 late R W Sheppard*

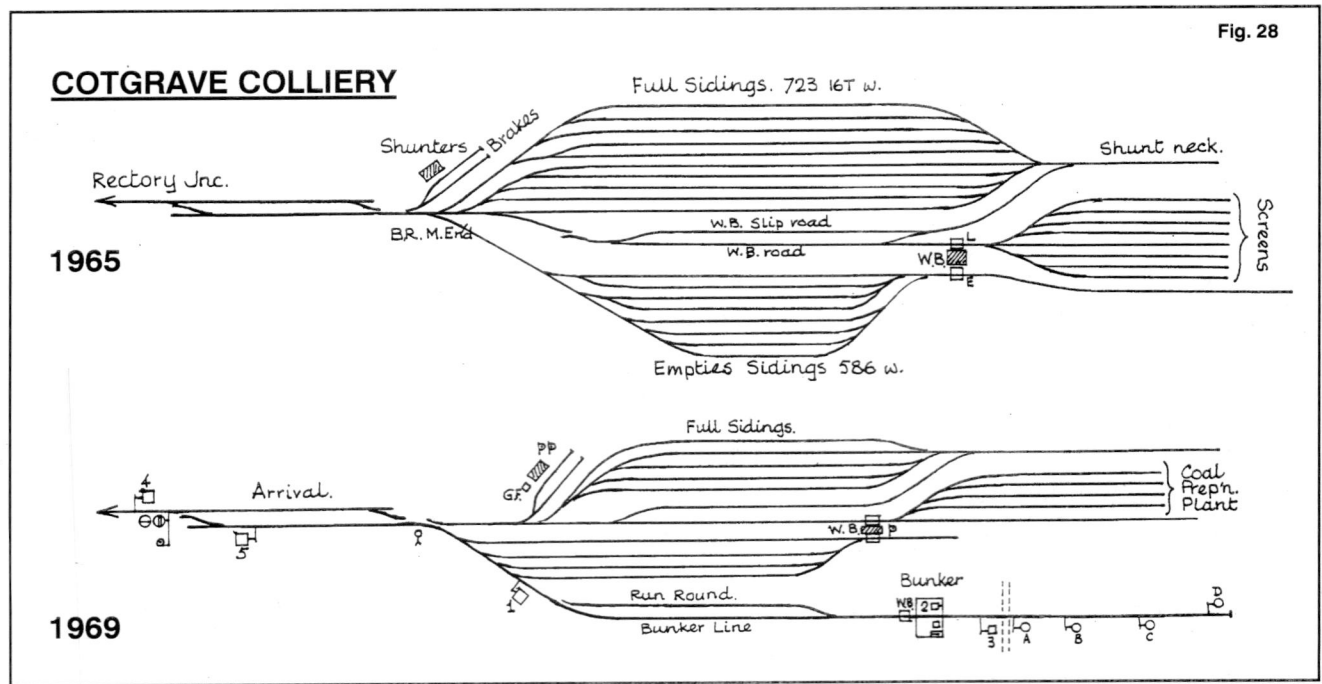

1965 All wagons were weighed inwards empty and outwards loaded. NCB locomotives transferred empties to the screens, and loaded wagons from the weighbridge road to the full sidings *via* the shunt neck.

1969 Square Notice Boards read as follows:
1. (Double sided) These points must be left set for the Bunker Line
2. Locomotives must not pass this point until authorised to do so by Bunker operator after loading.
3. Whistle
4. STOP. commencement of Yard Working. Proceed with caution.
5. Departing trains must not pass this point unless signal is clear.

The plunger between the sidings and departure line operates three klaxon horns situated beside the Arrival Line at distances of 200, 300 and 400 yards from the plunger.

Telephones are situated as follows:
RJ 82. Beside Departure signal to Rectory Junction.
Beside Shunter's Cabin : to Rectory Junction and to Weighbridge.
At Bunker Control Panel: to Rectory Junction.

An elevated position light ground (disc) signal 25 yards on the Rectory Junction side of the bunker reads through the bunker to the buffer stop.

The four signals A B C D facing the bunker apply to movements during loading, and are controlled by the Bunker Operator.

Fig. 29
Cotgrave Colliery rapid loading bunker as seen from the departing special, with stockpiles of coal occupying the ground where the empties sidings were. The buildings in the centre are the coal preparation plant fed by several covered conveyor belts, the steeply rising one right filling the huge bunker.
May 1989 A Henshaw

Fig. 30
Cotgrave colliery as seen from the train approaching the rapid loading bunker, beneath which it passed before returning along the branch. The pit shafts are on the left. The vacant ground left of the running lines was occupied with sidings for empty and loaded wagons when the branch was opened, but many were removed after the new bunker was installed (Fig. 28).

The colliery was finally closed on April 30th 1993, and the site subsequently cleared.

May 1989 A Henshaw

Fig. 31
Very little remains of the empties sidings on the left of the run round road as the passenger train proceeds slowly along the bunker line. Left of the two pit shafts is a conveyor belt conveying spoil to a lengthening bank.

May 1989 A Henshaw

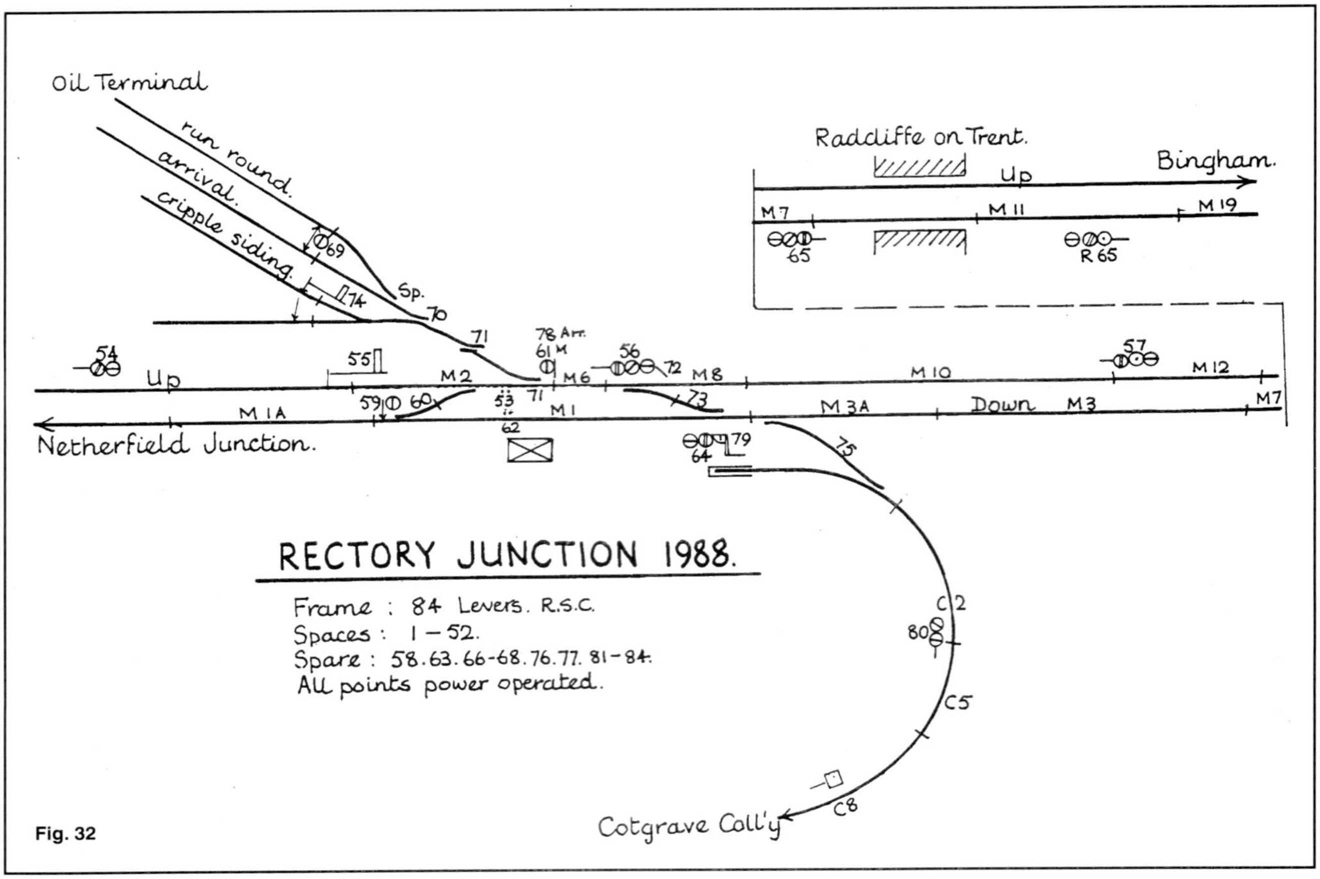

Fig. 32

RECTORY JUNCTION 1988.

Frame : 84 Levers. R.S.C.
Spaces : 1 – 52.
Spare : 58. 63. 66-68. 76. 77. 81-84.
All points power operated.

Fig. 33
A LNER Class J5 Ivatt six-coupled is seen here passing Rectory Junction hauling a Down mixed goods train, Class D, or pick-up from the headlight on the tender, into one of the six reception sidings for No 1 Down Yard. The lines on the extreme right are the Main Lines to Colwick East Junction and Netherfield & Colwick Station.

1955 F Quenby

Fig. 34
Rectory Junction Signal Box still intact, but with far less work done than there was twenty-five years ago. The two lines lead to an oil terminal a little way further along to where fuel is brought for discharge and storing, in tankers like the one standing on the bank. This is possibly a cripple awaiting repair on a reception road, most of which have been recovered. The lines to the terminal were previously the Up and Down Branch to Carlton Field and Colwick North.
March 1991 A Henshaw

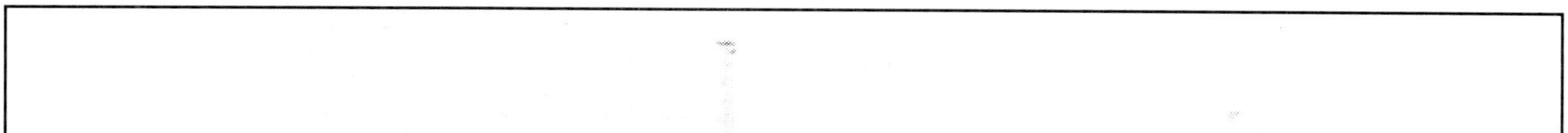

Fig. 35
The oil terminal at the end of the branch. No other sidings are left apart from the Avoiding Lines in the distance to the left. Above and beyond the embankment on the right is a huge pond for slurry which was piped from Gedling Colliery before its closure.
March 1991 A Henshaw

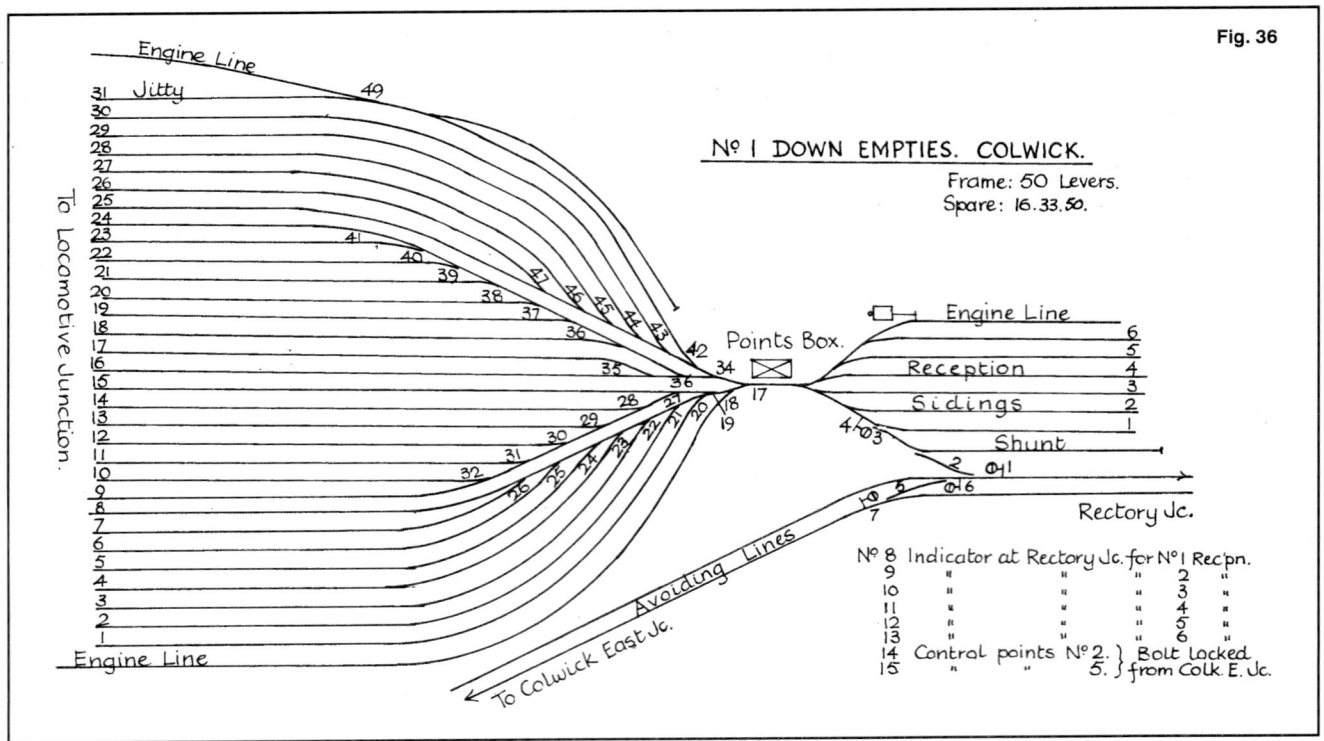

Fig. 36

Fig. 37
This shows the Pointsman's view of No 1 Yard in from the Shunters' South Points Box (Fig. 36 above). The ladders of connections to the thirty-one sidings can be clearly seen. The engine release line from trains arriving from the east is on the right of the fan of sidings. Behind the wagons on the left side are the houses of North Western Terrace, next to which are the taller buildings of the GN Loco sheds. Beside these are the white barge boards on the gable of Locomotive Junction signal box which controlled the departure of trains from the Yard. A little further right between two prominent lamp posts is the bracket of the loading gauge at the Tranship stage alongside No 31 road known as the Jitty (Fig. 6 p5). Between that and the furthest right lamp post is the tower of the coaling stage and Carlton Field Signal Box. Note the bench seat with armchair at the end in the foreground. The shunters who uncoupled the shunts of trains on the reception roads, then chased them down the slope to apply hand-brakes as they rolled towards other wagons had to be very nimble and alert, especially in icy or foggy weather and during darkness. They deserved a rest between marshalling trains!
July 1969 A Henshaw

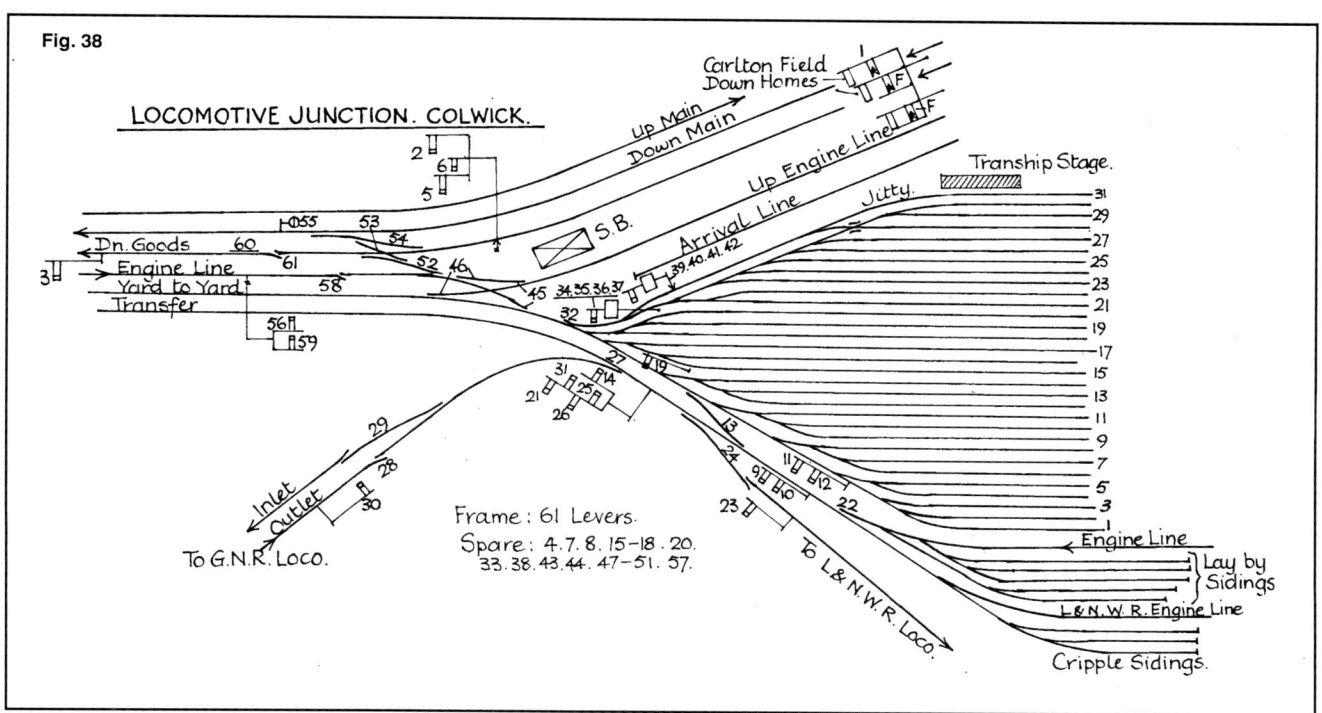

Fig. 38

Fig. 39
This view is taken from the 'platform' in front of the windows of Locomotive Junction signal box, and shows the departure end of No 1 Yard. Note the two departure signals with route indicator boxes which have replaced separate groups of arms. On the right beyond the fencing and gate stands the second LNWR Engine shed, closed since 1928, and in use commercially. The end of the houses of North Western Terrace appear to the right of the lamp post.
April 1970 C H Eggleston

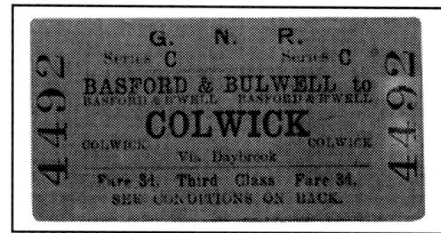

Fig. 40
This view of Locomotive Junction Signalbox is taken from the Traffic Offices looking northeast. Note the bricked up windows and blast protection wall beneath the stairs - introduced as a war time measure in 1939. This was a higher than usual lever frame to enable better visibility over the departure end sidings of No. 1 yard and the engine lines which it controlled. The Class 4 Mixed Traffic Locomotive left of the signalbox is shunting No 4 yard (Fig. 60 p29).
August 1966 C H Eggleston

Fig. 41
A clear view of the LNWR Locomotive shed and depot taken from the footbridge near North Western Terrace, which shows plenty of motive power and activity. The engines on the left of the group are 8-coupled goods of the G1 or G2 (super D) class which worked coal and goods trains from Colwick to Willesden *via* the GN and LNWR Joint Line, in addition to working trains to and from the collieries west and north of Colwick in pre-grouping days. Further to the right are several smaller 6-coupled engines, and the water tank. Note the coal stocks behind the telegraph pole, to the left of which is the fenced footpath to Colwick East Junction and the fields beside the River Trent. The line on the extreme left leads to the GNR cripple sidings.
Stephenson Loco Society

LOCOMOTIVE JUNCTION 124 m 59 1/4 ch

Opened on November 23rd 1891, this important box signalled the Down Main and Goods Lines from Carlton Field to Colwick North; the outgoing trains from No 1 Down Yard; the Lay-by sidings and Cripple Dock sidings after removal from their initial place in the Locomotive Depot. It took its name from the convergence of engine lines from various parts of the Yard including the LNWR for despatch to both Loco Sheds, and dealt with engines from both sheds for Down trains, as well as Up trains from Carlton Field. Probably as many engines were dealt with here as at Colwick North Junction. On occasions, a Light Engine for the GN Shed would be used to assist the departure of a heavy train along the Down Goods Line to climb the gradient up to Colwick North Junction instead of using the Inlet road to the shed. The signalbox was closed on 12th April 1970.

Fig. 42
Facing the opposite way from Fig. 40, the footbridge affords a good view of the sidings in No 1 Down Yard. The line to the right of the sidings separated by two lamp posts is the engine line from Shunters South Cabin. Further still to the right are the Layby sidings and Cripple sidings with wagons on them. On the extreme left above the wagons and vans can be seen the gantry of Carlton Field's Down Home signals.
September 1959 John R Bonser

Fig. 43
This is the view from Locomotive Junction signal box towards Carlton Field, seen left of the tall bracket signal, beside the Up Main Line. The Down Main Line has been lifted as have some of the sidings from No 4 Yard on the left. The line left of the Shunters Cabin was the Down Goods, and the two on the right were the Up Engine Line and Arrival road for No 2 Yard. No 1 Yard sidings spread across to the right with the Transit shed half obscured by the white post.
April 1970 C H Eggleston

Fig. 44
Locomotive Junction signal box at the departure end of No 1 Yard facing Colwick North Junction, with 13 crossover (Fig. 38 p21) left of centre, and the line to the old LNWR Loco shed extreme left beside the fence. The buildings beyond the fence are the Yardmaster's and Telegraph Offices, and that behind the signal (right) is the Shunters' cabin and mess room.   *July 1969 A Henshaw*

Fig. 45
A view of the Shunters South Cabin from which wagons were directed into the necessary road by hand signals from the shunter. The train was pushed slowly towards the Points box by the pilot engine, and individual or groups of wagons for one destination uncoupled. On passing the Points Box they rolled rapidly downhill away from the next shunt whilst the pointsman set the route for the succeeding wagons.
1955 F Quenby

Fig. 46
Standing against the parapet of Bridge 3 with the footpath beneath, we see the south side of Shunters' Cabin South, with the sidings it controlled on the left. To the right are the sidings of No 2 Down Yard which all ended in buffer stops, and here hold trains of iron ore in steel mineral wagons destined for Stanton Ironworks at Ilkeston. The gradient of the downward slope into the sidings left shows clearly against the level of No 2 Yard. Faintly visible above the mineral wagons is Carlton Field Signal Box and the gantry of Down Home signals.   *April 1970 C H Eggleston*

Fig. 47
A view of the Loco' (MPD) buildings from across Netherfield Lane showing offices (left) above which is the roof of the erecting shop and the coaling plant. Near the centre is the water tank, with the stores building before it. Next right is the Joiners' and paint shop, with brick arch man's shed adjoining. Far right was the Electricians' shop.
H H Mather

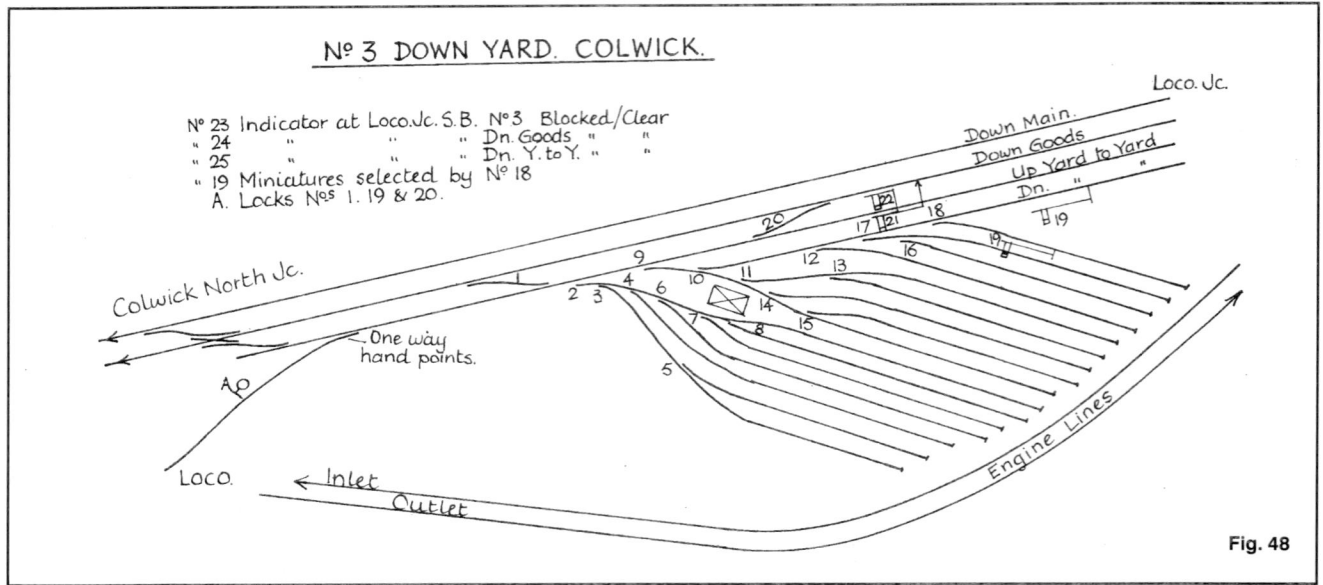

Fig. 48

No 3 DOWN YARD (Colwick Shunters' North)

Like No 2 Down, this yard, the site of the original Down side sidings of 1875 (Fig. 4 p4) was a flat group of 16 dead end sidings. It was used for the marshalling of Goods and perishable traffic going west and north until 1940, when the pooling of privately-owned mineral wagons for collieries removed the need to marshal them. No 1 Down Yard then marshalled goods and empties, its gradient into the sidings being eased somewhat for the heavier traffic, and all coal empties (Private Owners Wagons) were sent to No 3 Yard and dispatched from there to the collieries.

The points box, Colwick Shunters' North, signalled trains arriving and departing *via* the Down Goods line, and Yard to Yard transfers only. After the transfer of goods traffic during the war, the Up Yard to Yard road was used as an engine line to Locomotive Junction. Because of declining coal traffic the Yard was closed in the early 1960s, and the sidings and signal box removed after the summer of 1965.

Fig. 49
Adjoining buildings further left of Fig. 47 with the engine shed roof and ventilators showing above the main roadside offices. The buildings with gable ends facing the road (right of engine shed, with coaling plant behind) were used by running fitters and boilersmiths. The new Engine shed with four roads is on the extreme left.
H H Mather

Fig. 50
Further along Netherfield Lane from the MPD buildings stands the Yardmaster's Office, from the upper storey of which he could survey much, if not all, of the workings of the five yards. Alongside were the telegraph and other traffic offices. A little further along to the right was the LNWR Loco shed and NW Terrace.
H H Mather

Fig. 51
GNR 0-8-0 Class K1, (later LNER Q1) at Colwick c1918-1920 being oiled by its driver before leaving to work its train from the yard. Fireman Bemrose is at the cab. These engines were designed by H. A. Ivatt for hauling heavy mineral trains, the first one No. 401 being built in 1901, and was soon followed by 40 more. No. 409 was built in Doncaster in 1902 and because of the long boiler these locomotives were called 'Long Toms' after a naval gun with a long barrel. After working traffic from the collieries into Colwick, and coal trains into Peterborough and Ferme Park this engine was withdrawn from service in August 1931.
B B Johnson

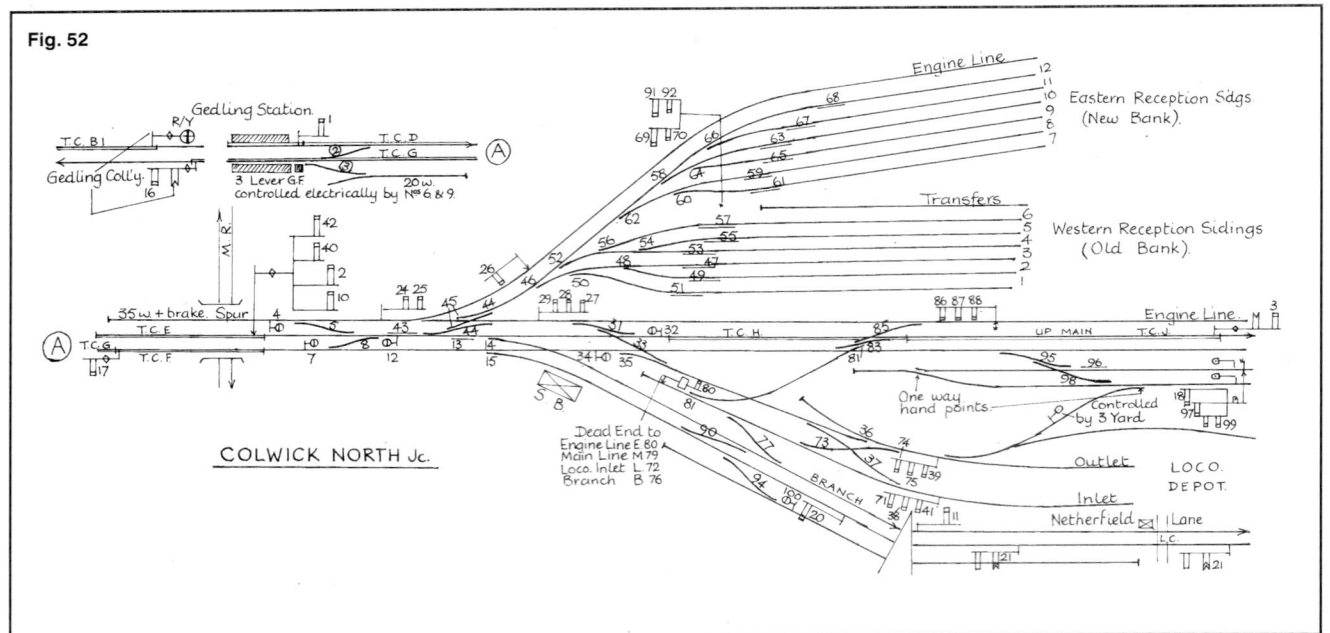

Fig. 52

COLWICK NORTH JUNCTION 125 m 17 ch

This very busy box was manned continuously. It controlled all westbound traffic from the Yards *via* Daybrook, and incoming trains from the Derbyshire Extensions, and Leen Valley with its Extension to the LDEC at Shirebrook North. A double line branch to the right led to Netherfield Lane, and the main Grantham-Nottingham lines at Netherfield Station. Between the angle here was the Locomotive Depot. From the Up Main Line two sets of six reception roads accommodated incoming Goods trains on the western side, and mineral trains on the eastern side together with Engine lines for released engines to return to Loco. The two main lines continued through the yards past Locomotive Junction to Carlton Field. Down trains leaving the No 3 Yard came along the Down Goods Line, and those from Nos 1 and 2 Yards from Locomotive Junction *via* either the Down Main or Goods Lines. Drivers used a system of whistles to indicate their presence and destination to the signalman, who was assisted with a Train Register Lad, whose duties were to keep the Train Register of bookings, and advise other signalmen of the number and destination of trains on the Single Needle telegraph instruments. All incoming trains were reported *via* this telegraph too. In addition all train movements except Local Passengers were reported to Control Office at Nottingham Victoria. After the closure of Mapperley Tunnel in 1960, trains from the west were routed *via* Nottingham Victoria and Netherfield to reverse on to the Up reception roads, and with the reduced traffic, much of which was now handled by the old Midland Railway, two western reception roads were closed, and No 1 became a departure road in the Down direction (Fig. 73 p34). On August 3rd 1966 the branch to Netherfield was singled, and on 11th August 1968 the box was closed and subsequently demolished, the single line from Netherfield Junction to Gedling Colliery being classed a siding.

Fig. 53
Here, the single line from Gedling Colliery is seen from beneath the loop road bridge as it curves towards Victoria Road (formerly Netherfield Lane). The building in the distance between the two dark posts was the Railway Institute, and the newer buildings left of the track are on the site of the Loco depot.
May 1993 A Henshaw

Fig. 54
This view taken from near the site of Colwick North Junction shows the curve of the Down line from Netherfield Lane, once used as the single line to Gedling Colliery. The colliery has been closed and the site cleared, but the track is left for the possibility of a branch from the proposed Light Rapid Transport system of the City of Nottingham to Gedling. The bridge carries the new loop road round Netherfield over the track. Buildings of an industrial estate where the 4 and 5 yard sidings were can be seen through the wire fence on the left.
May 1993 A Henshaw

Fig. 55
Taken shortly after Fig. 5 p5 this photograph shows from left to right miniature signals 24 and 25 beside the shunt siding. Above the disc signal 12, between the main lines, is the lead to the Up Reception sidings with ex LMS Class 8F 2-8-0 48526 and train beyond the bracket signal. The branch to Netherfield Lane swings away right past the signal box, and the coaling plant in the MPD is on the extreme right. Another Class 8F stands near the signalbox on the Down Main Line.
August 1966   A Henshaw

Fig. 56
Carlton Field Signal Box standing alongside the Up and Down Main Lines through the Yards, with the crossover 30 between them (Fig. 64 p31). The lever frame of 75 was Railway Signal Co with four-inch centres and 3ft 6in of space at either end. It was opened on July 5th 1889, and controlled the Up side working at South End Departure as well as the No 2 Yard on the Down side. The Signal Box took its name from a farm which was swallowed up in the great expansion of sidings in the 1890s (Fig. 4 p4). It controlled the departure of all Up trains from numbers 4 (Goods) and 5 (Mineral) traffic with the inclusion of the central block of sidings allocated to the LNWR known as number 2 section (Fig. 62 p30). With three shunting necks serving different sections there was plenty of activity here, and cattle pens were provided for feeding and watering beasts in transit if necessary. On the eastern side was a branch to Stoke Bardolph Sewage Works. Before the advent of mains sewage in Nottingham, earth closets were cleared at night into carts, drawn by horses to London Road Station, and there the 'night soil' was transferred to wagons and taken to the sewage works *via* Colwick. Locomotive coal stacks were also located on this side of the yards. In addition to all the traffic movements, the crews of trains working through the Yard such as Derby/Pinxton East Coast expresses would be relieved at Carlton Field.
April 1970 C H Eggleston

Fig. 57
The scene from the rear of Carlton Field signal box towards the Full sidings Yards 4 and 5, shows No 1 shunt in the bottom left corner and a rake of brake vans stretching into the distance. Next are the deserted sidings of No 2 Section and their departure road minus the head shunt! Right of the lamp post are four stock roads west of No 5 Yard Eastern Full Sidings holding a train of coal - perhaps destined for Welham Sidings? All of No 5 Yard sidings have been lifted but a good idea of the vast spread of lines across these Up side yards can be gauged from this view.
April 1970 C H Eggleston

Fig. 58
These are the sidings, almost deserted, of No 4 Yard, or Western Full Sidings as seen from Locomotive Junction signal box. They were used much less after the closure of Mapperley Tunnel, because traffic from the west had to travel via Nottingham Victoria and Netherfield & Colwick to Colwick North Junction, and then reverse into the reception sidings after a few wagon brakes had been pinned down. Goods traffic from west of Derby travelled via the Midland Railway, but some coal traffic for the south was transferred at London Road, Nottingham, brought to Colwick to go via the GN and LNWR Joint Line through Melton Mowbray to Welham. The train of coaches stands in No 9 road. Left of the sidings is the Up Main Line from Colwick North Junction beside which is the once Down Slow or Goods which becomes the Down Main beyond the miniature signal. No 3 Yard has been lifted by now, left of the bracket signal, and crippled wagons for repair were brought from near the LNWR Loco shed to the GN Locomotive shops to be dealt with. The 'Cenotaph' coaling plant shows up prominently in the distance.
April 1970 H H Mather

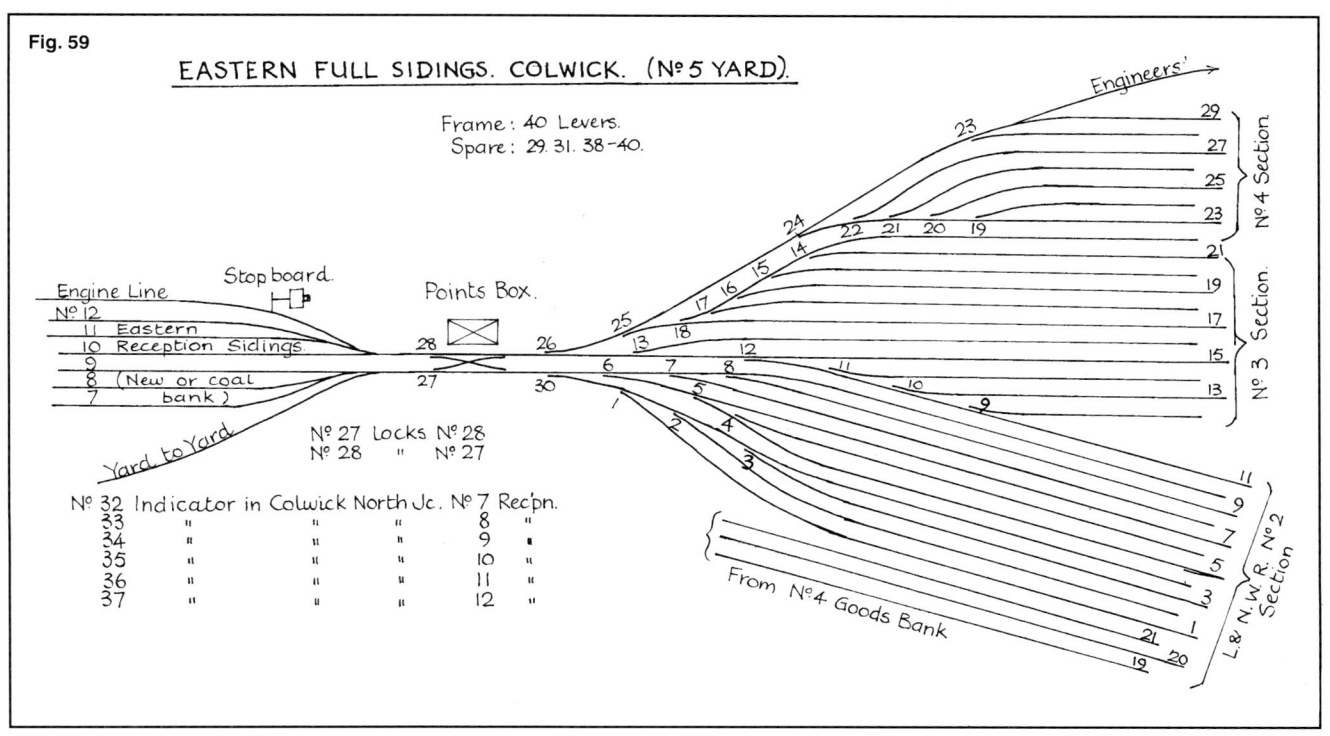

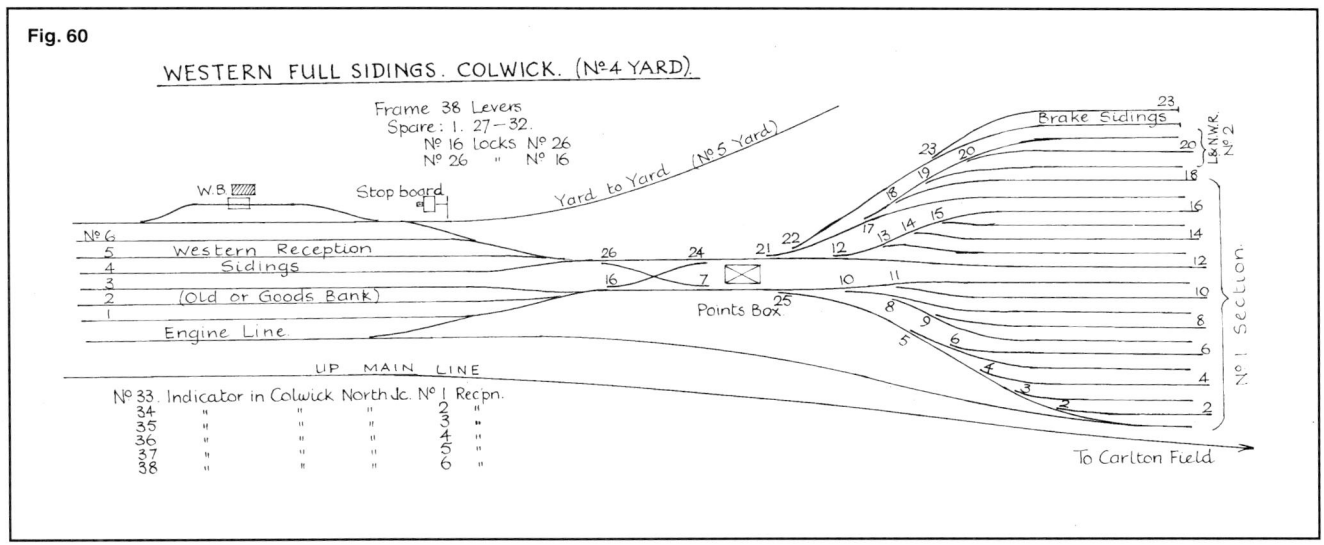

CARLTON FIELD 124 m 41 1/2 ch (see p27)

This box, on the two lines from Colwick North through the yards to Rectory Junction opened July 12th 1887 and signalled both running lines and the Down Goods line, as well as movements in and out of No 2 Down Yard, at first the LNWR Company's. Its main function was to control engines and trains from the south end departure of the Up sorting sidings of No 4 (Goods) Yard and No 5 (Mineral) Yard. Such trains could leave by the Up Main or Up Goods line to Rectory Junction.

Crews of through workings such as East Coast Excursions from Pinxton or Derby were relieved at Carlton Field, as was the 6.25 pm Burton-York braked Goods. Urgent traffic could be attached at the same time here. Block loads of coal etc for one destination would be sent up the Main line to Carlton Field to be shunted into the sidings at the south end, instead of using a reception road needed for trains to be marshalled. Three shunting necks were provided for the four sections of sidings, No 2 section, for LNWR traffic had its own pilot (shunting engine), and its southbound traffic went via Saxondale Junction and the Joint Line. Separate pilots worked No 4 (Goods) and 5 (Mineral) Yards. Cattle pens were provided beside No 3 shunt for feeding/watering beast in transit when necessary, and a single line connection led to Stoke Bardolph sewage works, much used in the days before water closets, when night soil from Nottingham was brought to London Road Goods, for transport by rail to the treatment plant.

After nationalisation in 1948, No 2 Down Yard was used for ironstone traffic from the Leicestershire field, which went mainly to Stanton Ironworks, and did not need marshalling. This signalbox was closed on 12th April 1970.

Fig. 61
Carlton Field Signal Box in the centre is seen from between the Up Main and Up Slow or Goods Lines. The signal gantry which straddled the Down Goods now has but one upper quadrant arm to control the Down Main alongside. To the right of the signal box are the Eastern Full Sidings, and departure lines leading to both Up Main and Up Goods in the foreground. Just visible between the gantry legs is the gable end of Locomotive Junction signal box (see also p27).
July 1969 A Henshaw

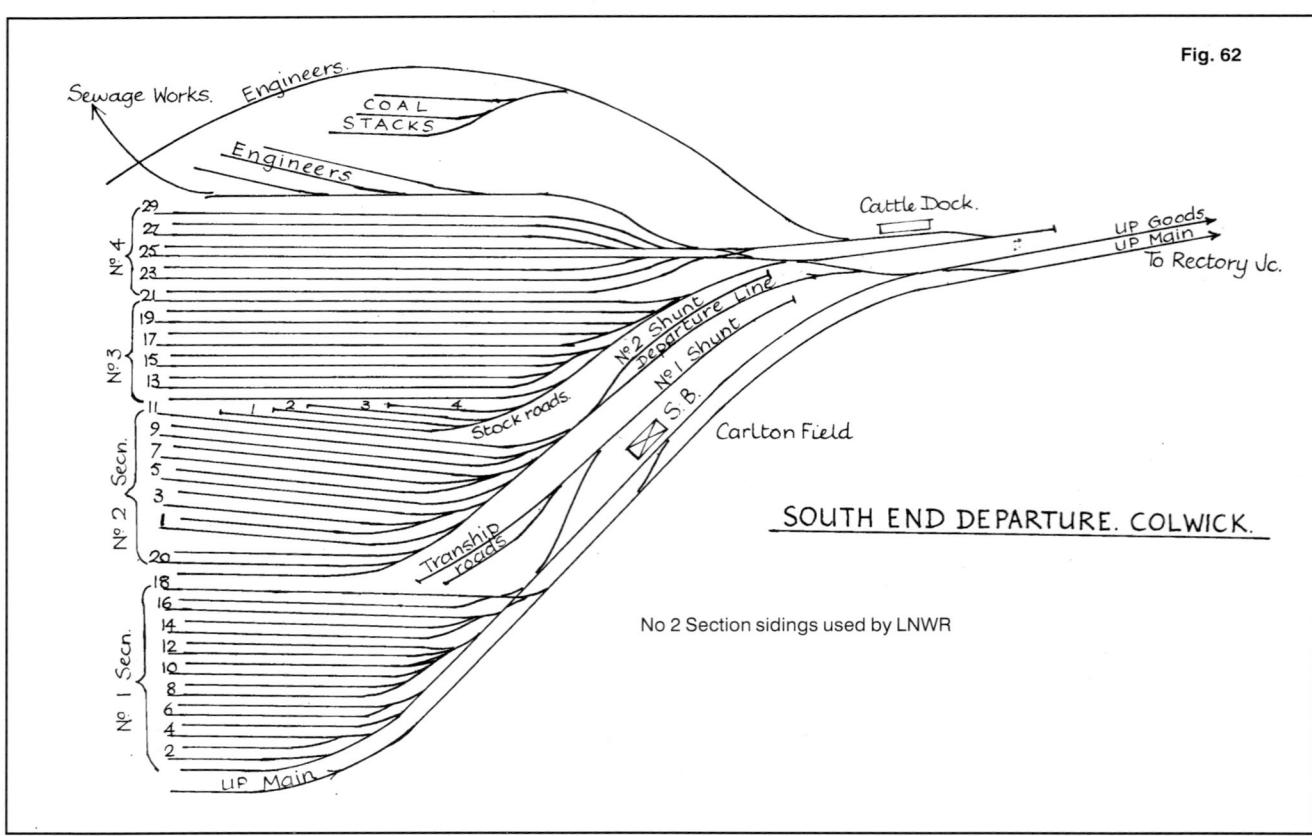

Fig. 62

SOUTH END DEPARTURE. COLWICK.

No 2 Section sidings used by LNWR

Fig. 63
LNER Class B1 4-6-0 61000 *Spingbok* is approaching Locomotive Junction with a train of iron ore from the Denton branch at Belvoir Junction in 1961. The sidings in the foreground are the departure end of No 1 yard. Above the boiler of the locomotive the up home signals 33 and 36 of Carlton Field can be seen with the cabins at South End Departure on the left. After the war a number of refugees from eastern European countries fled from the Baltic States and Poland to Britain and the west. Two such woman employed as 'packers' maintaining track work in the yard stand resting on the shovels whilst the train passes, but the 'foreman' adopts a much more relaxed position!
C A Hill

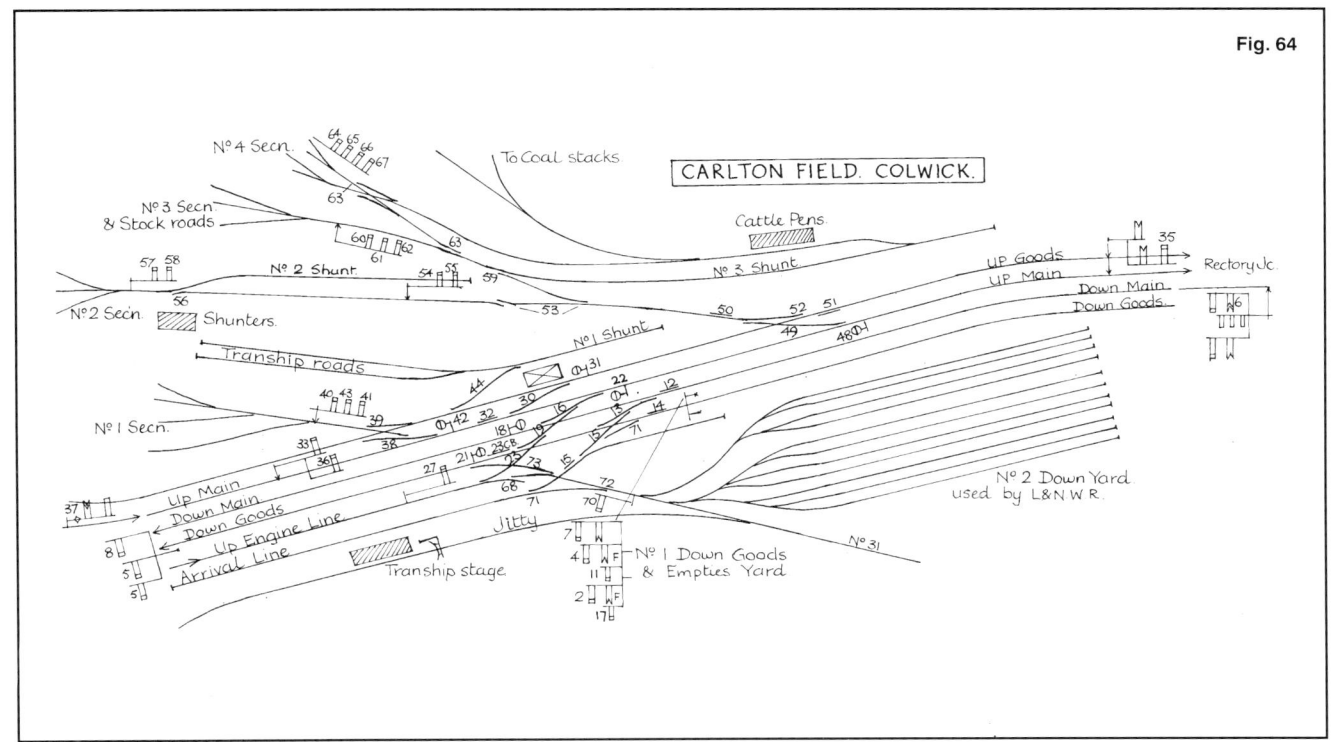

Fig. 64

Fig. 65

COLWICK EAST Jc.

Layout in 1888

Colwick Sdgs.
Up branch.
Down branch.
Down Slow.
S.B.
Rectory Jc.
Colwick West Jc.

Fig. 66

COLWICK EAST Jc.

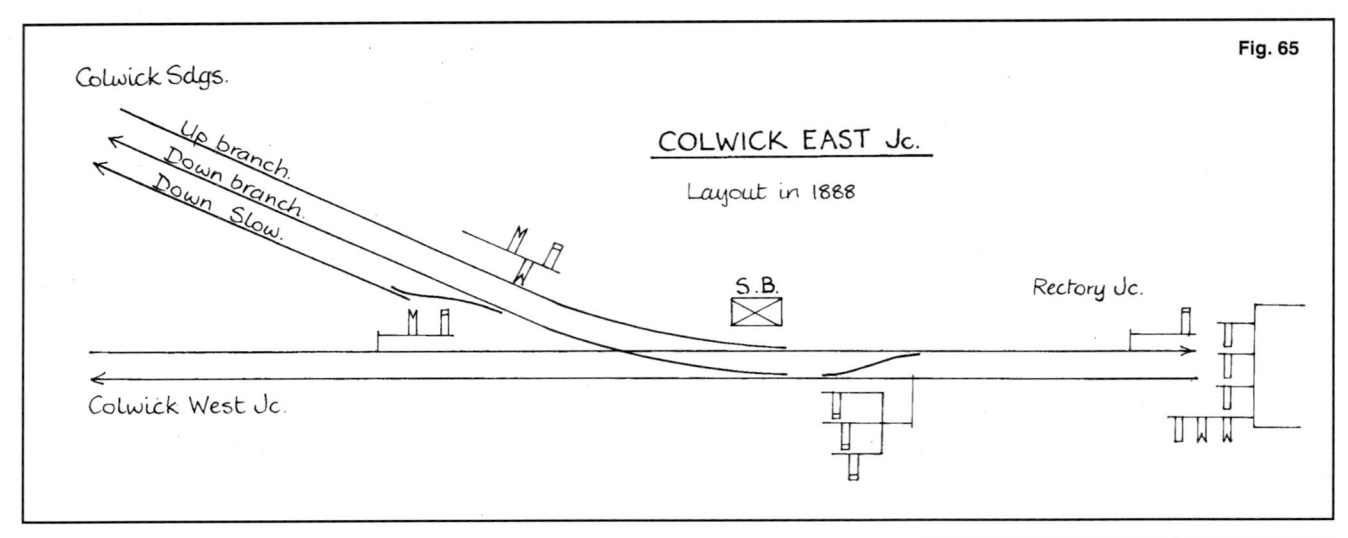

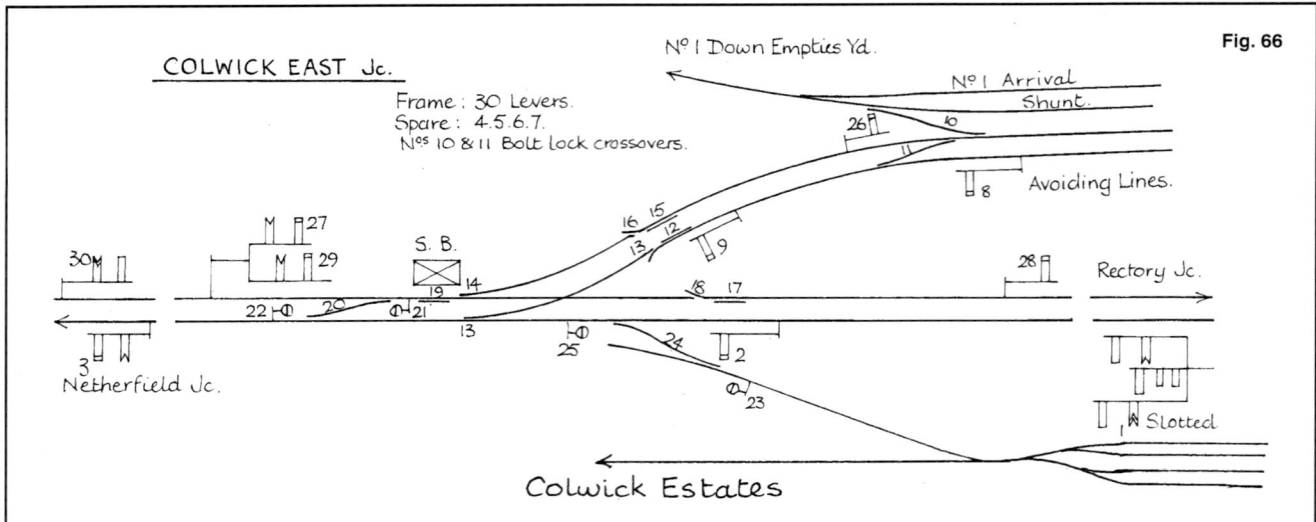

Frame: 30 Levers.
Spare: 4.5.6.7.
Nos 10 & 11 Bolt lock crossovers.

No 1 Down Empties Yd.
No 1 Arrival Shunt.
Avoiding Lines.
Rectory Jc.
Netherfield Jc.
Colwick Estates
Slotted

COLWICK EAST JUNCTION 124 m 32 1/2 ch

Originally this was the junction for the Derbyshire Extensions from the Grantham-Nottingham line, which opened in 1875 and formed a triangle with Colwick West and North Junctions, and inside which was built the first locomotive shed and sorting sidings (Fig. 4 p4). In 1891, the junction was reversed in direction to form the two Avoiding Lines to the newly-built Rectory Junction, with a connecting line from one to the Reception Roads at Shunters' South Cabin. The Colwick Estates Light Railway with four exchange sidings was constructed in 1919, and connected to the Down Main Line at Colwick East Junction. The double junction to the Avoiding Lines was replaced by a single facing point on the Up in BR days. The Avoiding Lines were used regularly by the return working of the 1.15 pm Colwick to Eaton ironstone empties. This train would return with loaded ironstone hoppers for Staveley Works, and be run on to Colwick East where the crew was relieved, and the train examined on the Avoiding Line before continuing *via* Netherfield, Nottingham Victoria and the GC route through Chesterfield Central. The signal box was closed on June 25th 1972, and used as a ground frame released from Rectory Junction to provide access to Colwick Estates. The severed connection to the Avoiding Lines was blocked with a buffer stop. Trains were allowed to propel over the Down Main line to Rectory Junction until after the last day of working there, on April 1st 1985.

Fig. 67
This is a view from the new loop road bridge which crosses the Main Lines between Netherfield & Colwick Station and where Colwick East Junction was sited. Colwick Estates to the right has much new development together with some on the left where the ground has been cleared. *March 1991 A Henshaw*

Fig. 68

COLWICK ESTATES LIGHT RAILWAY.

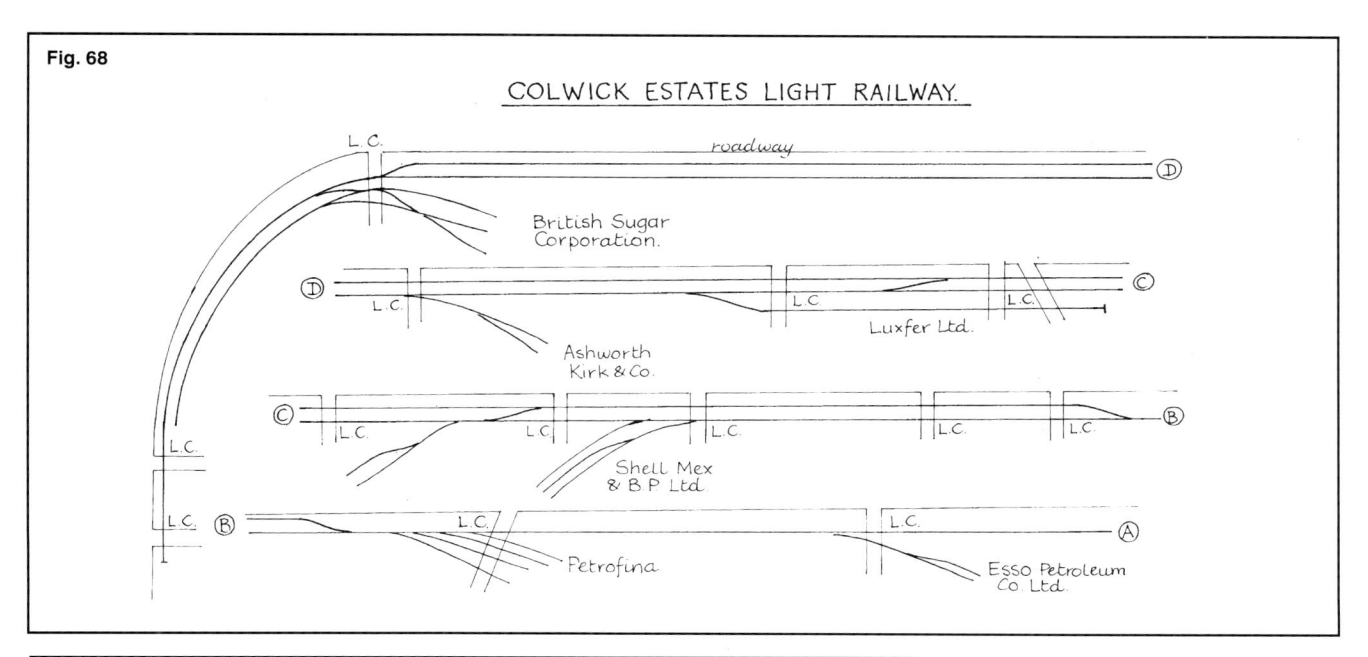

Fig. 69
Although the sidings have all gone and some new development is taking place, most of the southern half of the Yard is an empty desolate space with hardly a land mark to indicate where things once were. However between Rectory Junction and Colwick East are the Avoiding Lines still in place. This view towards Colwick East (itself demolished on 26 June 1972) shows the growth of scrub around the lines. The train of oil tanks is on the Down Main Line before being reversed into the exchange sidings. Beyond the Main Lines much new development is occurring on Colwick Estates, which is now all served by road access. *August 1966 A Henshaw*

Fig. 70
Colwick East Junction facing east and Rectory Junction, showing the single facing connection from the Up Main to the Avoiding Lines which curve to the left behind the signal box. The facing point lock bar detector mechanism is between the point blades. The connection to Colwick Estates Exchange Sidings from the Down Main Line is seen right. Earlier there was a double line junction to the Avoiding Lines. *July 1969 A Henshaw*

Fig. 71
ASBSC No 1 Industrial Locomotive at the British Sugar Beet factory sidings on the Colwick Estates Light Railway. There were a number of industries on this estate including Armitages Pet Food, Shell Mex and BP, Esso, Petrofina, Luxfer plant and an electricity generating station, all served by rail. The connection to the GNR was made in 1919 to the Down Main Line at Colwick East Junction, and four exchange sidings were provided here. *March 1954 John R Bonser*

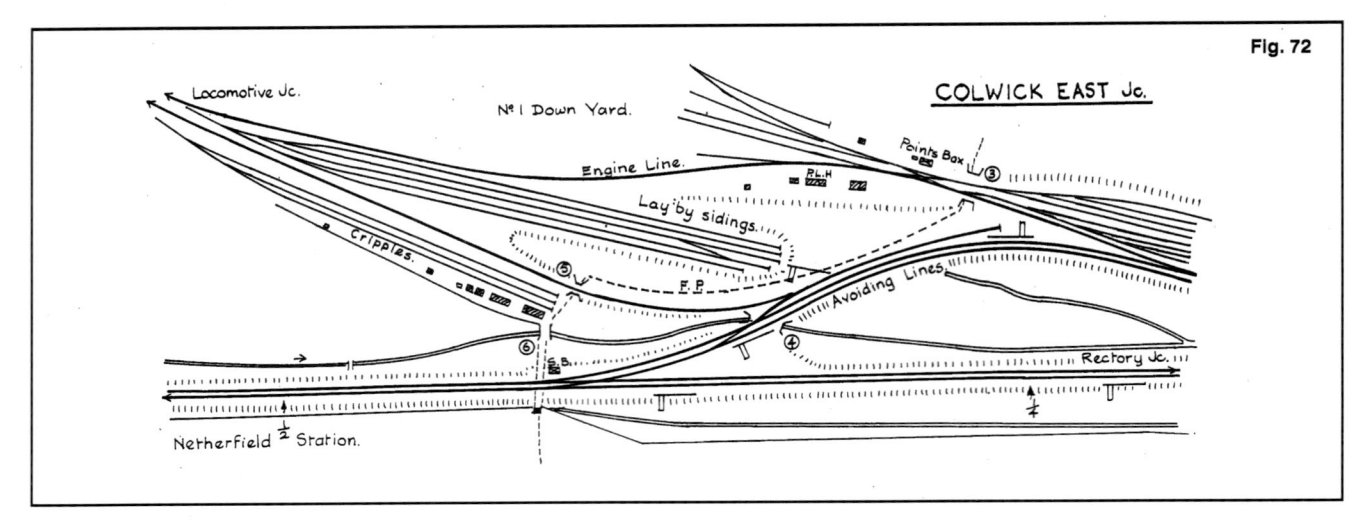

Fig. 72

(Diagram: Colwick East Jc., showing Locomotive Jc., No 1 Down Yard, Engine Line, Lay-by sidings, Cripples, Avoiding Lines, Points Box, Rectory Jc., Netherfield Station)

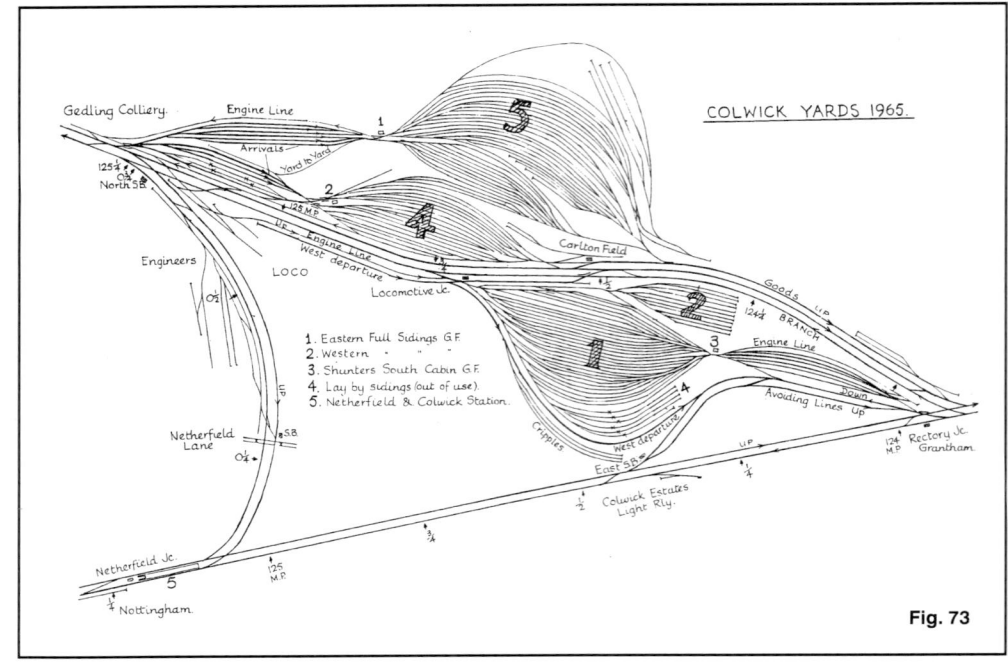

Fig. 73 — COLWICK YARDS 1965

(Diagram showing Gedling Colliery, Engine Line, Arrivals, Yard to Yard, Up Engine Line, West departure, Loco, Locomotive Jc., Carlton Field, Goods Up, Branch, Engine Line, Avoiding Lines Up, Cripples, West departure, East SB, Colwick Estates Light Rly., Rectory Jc. Grantham, Netherfield Lane, Netherfield Jc., Nottingham)

1. Eastern Full Sidings G.F.
2. Western "
3. Shunters South Cabin G.F.
4. Lay by sidings (out of use)
5. Netherfield & Colwick Station.

The staff complement of the Marshalling Yards after nationalisation in 1948 consisted of one Yardmaster, three assistant Yardmasters, one Chief Clerk, 7 clerks, 6 traffic inspectors (there were no foremen), 18 class 1 shunters, 3 class 2 train despatchers, 52 class 3 shunters including chasers, 3 class 4 shunters for screwing up fitted goods, 9 number-takers, 3 telegraph lads, 4 callers up, 3 lampmen for tail lamps, 1 signal lampman with lad assistant, and 260 guards.

Following the formation of the railway regions under nationalisation on 1st January 1948 there came a decline of activities at Colwick. Much of the Nottinghamshire and Derbyshire coalfield fell into the London Midland Region of BR, which extended to the east end of Mapperley Tunnel situated on the GN line, known as the 'Back Line', between Colwick and Daybrook. The operatiions of the area to the east including Colwick Yards continued to be worked by the Eastern Region BR, until well into the 1950s. During this period several collieries were closed in the area and where there was dual servicing from the GN and Midland lines, the GN side was invariably closed.

The LM Region closed Mapperley Tunnel on 4th April 1960, saying that it was unsafe. An independant enquiry established that it was not beyond repair, but to no avail. This cut off the main route into Colwick. Traffic was then routed *via* Nottingham Victoria and Netherfield. No 3 Yard was closed and lifted piecemeal after this. On 3rd January 1966, Colwick was returned to the LM Region, which finally spelt the end. The line was singled from Gedling Colliery to Netherfield Junction on August 3rd 1966, and traffic was rerouted away from Colwick allowing a rapid run down of the yards and motive power depot.

The end finally came on 13th April 1970 when Colwick Yards and Locomotive Depot closed and were subsequently demolished, the coaling stage (Cenotaph) being toppled on 29th December 1971. The Midland reigned supreme once more, the GNR having been 'a thorn in their side' for 118 years.

In the month of July 1925 Colwick Yard marshalled 147,913 wagons (more than New England, Doncaster or Wath), but these figures dropped to 89,815 in 1957 and 55,979 in 1961.

Fig. 74
Facing Netherfield & Colwick Station between the Up Main and Avoiding Lines, this view shows the Up Home signal bracket (Nos 27 and 29 Fig. 66 p32) with the Down Starter (No 3) in the far distance. The buildings and chimney right of the signal box are the old LNWR Loco Depot. *July 1969 A Henshaw*

Fig. 75

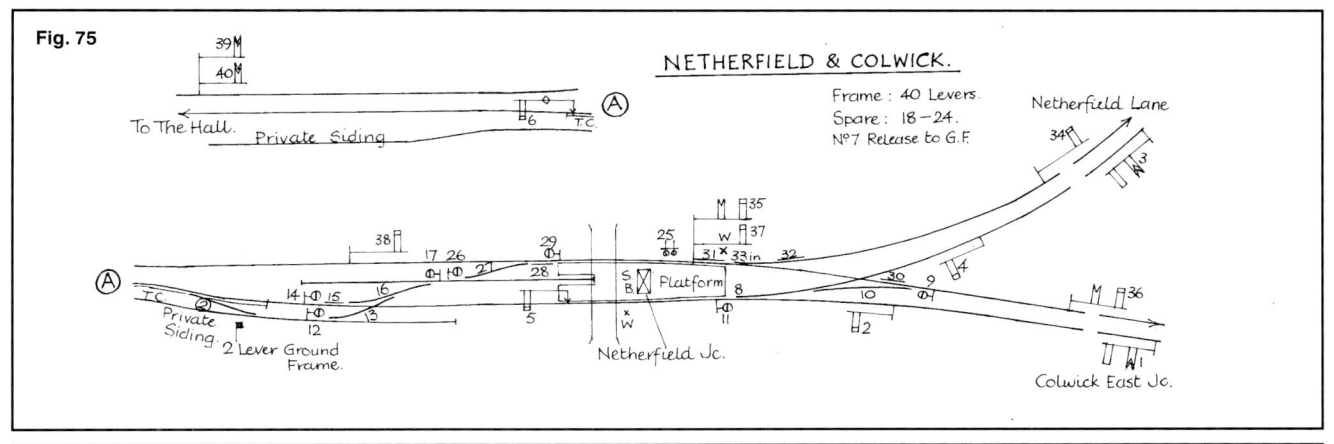

NETHERFIELD & COLWICK.
Frame: 40 Levers.
Spare: 18–24.
No.7 Release to G.F.

Fig. 76

NETHERFIELD STATION

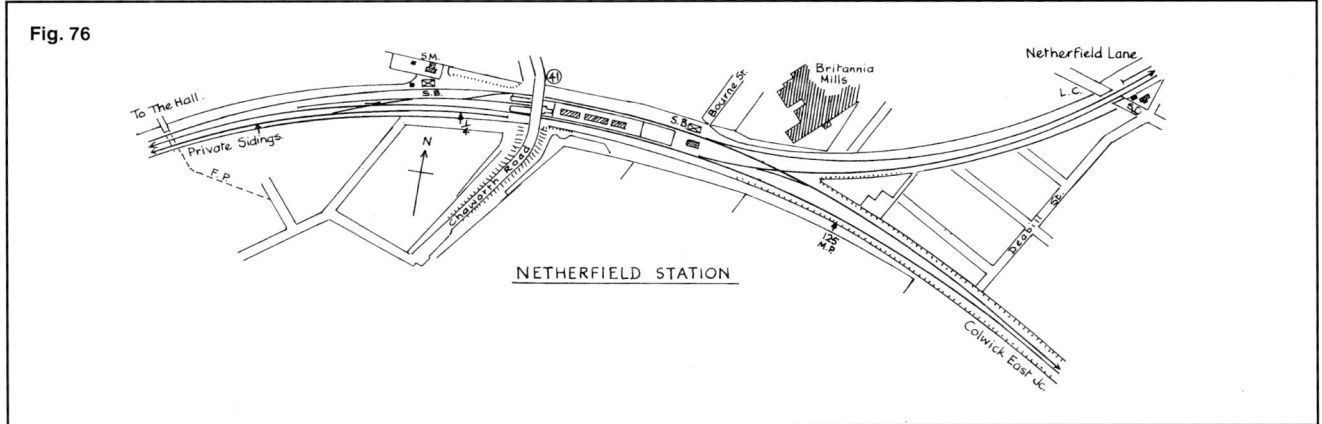

Fig. 77
This view from about the same spot as the postcard (Fig. 7 p6) reveals a different scene at the east end of the platform. The West Junction signal box has been removed, and the tall Home signals replaced with eye level upper quadrant arms, still on separate posts, close to which is the circular water tank and column. A similar tank was placed at the east end for Down trains to use.
September 1959
John R Bonser

Fig. 78
A recent picture to compare with what was there once! After the closure of Nottingham Victoria and the reinstatement of the connection to the Midland lines at Netherfield all passenger trains used the Midland Station at Nottingham. Intermediate stations were reduced to unmanned halts in the country, but at Netherfield & Colwick the old buildings were demolished and replaced with new. The semaphore signals are upgraded to colour lights, the branch to Gedling Colliery now singled and track-circuited is signalled by the 'horn' above the three aspects. The Britannia Mills factory is replaced with new housing.
March 1991 A Henshaw

NETHERFIELD JUNCTION 125 m 8 ch

The first signal box here was opened in 1850 to connect the Ambergate Line from Grantham to the Midland Railway's Nottingham-Newark-Lincoln lines at Carlton Junction. With the opening of London Road Station in Nottingham in 1857 this junction was redundant and was severed in 1866. But in 1875 the first of Colwick Yards and Loco Depot was opened, and a curve from Colwick North Junction to the Grantham-Nottingham line at Colwick West Junction was built (Fig. 4 p4). The passenger station was built west of this junction in 1878 on an island platform. The West Junction signal box was closed on 19th April 1909, having been replaced by Netherfield Junction, incorporated in the Station buildings across the middle of the platform, which replaced the original Colwick Station Signalbox when the Level Crossing to the west was closed, and the road from Colwick to Carlton diverted over bridge 41 from which access to the station was gained. Besides controlling the West Junction, the signalman could release the Ground Frame to allow access to the Private Sidings on the Down side, west of the bridge. In 1960, a new signal box was built immediately west of the bridge to control the re-connection of the GN to the Midland lines, laid in 1964 and this allowed the closure of Nottingham Victoria station in 1967. Netherfield Junction and Rectory Junction are the only two signal boxes now left at Colwick. The line from the West Junction to Gedling Colliery was singled with the closure of the Yards and is still *in situ* covered in weeds, for possible future use by Nottingham's proposed Light Rapid Transport system (electric trams).

Fig. 79

NETHERFIELD STATION & JUNCTION 1980.

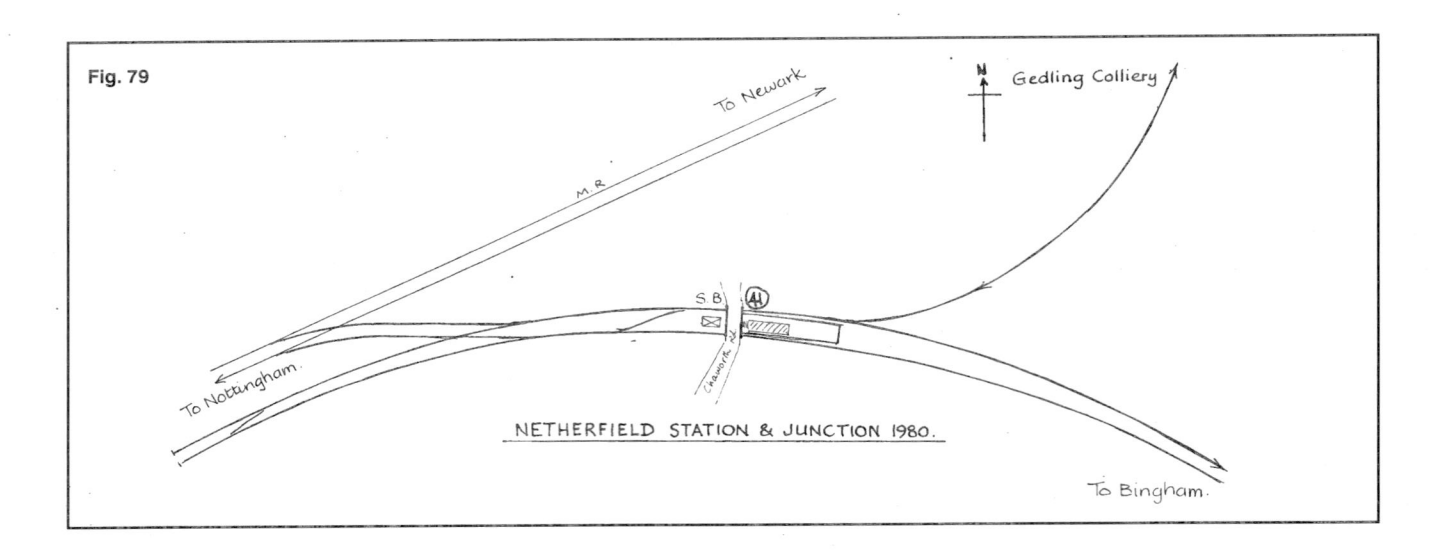

Fig. 80
Seen from bridge 41 facing west the scene has changed considerably. A new signal box - still named Netherfield Junction - stands at the end of the ramp to the platform controlling a single crossover and connection to the Midland lines in the distance, as the Ambergate Line from Grantham had originally been built in 1850. A new factory building stands behind the Station House (itself out of the picture) on the right.
March 1991 A Henshaw

Fig. 81
The Colwick West junction as seen from the east end of the station platform which shows the relief cabin for train crews to advantage, and the cast iron notices not to trespass, and that the footpath round the branch left to Netherfield Lane is private for the use of the company's servants only. On the down main line from Colwick East Junction an ex LNER Class K2 2-6-0 is heading a three coach train from Grantham to Nottingham Victoria into the station. Note the high sky arm of GNR origin above the cabin roof. The disc or ground signal on the right to control movement across the crossover is of later date being the LNER standard type which replaced the original one. Bourne's factory is on the left, with the public footpath behind the sleeper fence.
August 1953 H B Priestley

Fig. 82

NETHERFIELD LANE. 1903.

Fig. 83

NETHERFIELD LANE. COLWICK

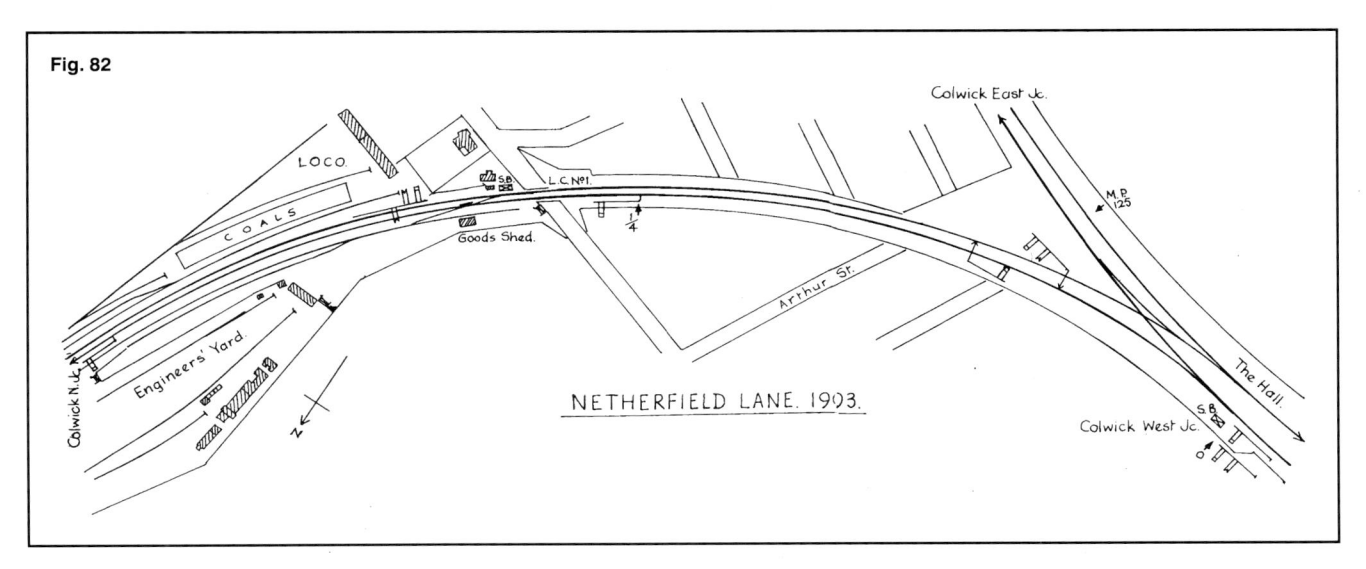

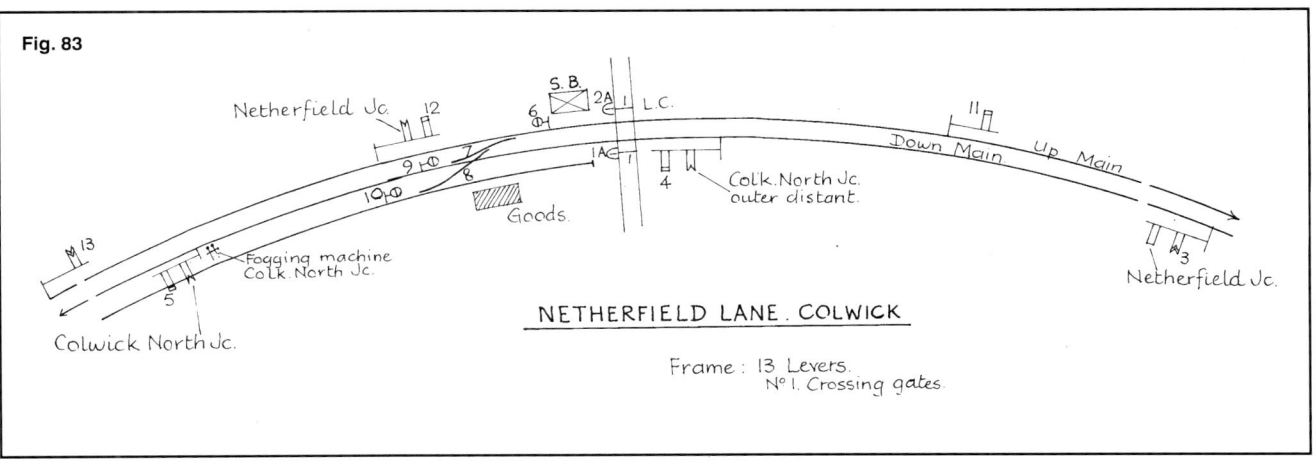

Frame: 13 Levers.
N° 1. Crossing gates.

Fig. 84
The approach to Netherfield Lane from the south which shows the foot of the Home signal lattice post beside an overgrown private footpath to the station. The house behind the signal box is more evident here, and the brick Goods Shed is still standing across the road.
May 1981 A Henshaw

NETHERFIELD LANE 0 m 23 1/4 ch from Colwick West Junction

The signal box controlling the Level Crossing of Netherfield Lane, later Victoria Road, opened in August 1875. The gates were wheel-operated. The access to and from the Goods Yard was controlled from here also. Between May 4th 1968 and April 12th 1970, the Signal box was closed; a block post reopened as a gate operating box for a short time for the Up Branch (then out of use) to be re-used as part of the Single Line from Netherfield Junction through to Gedling Colliery, and connections to the Goods Yard were recovered. The Up distant was fixed at caution, and the Up Home signal slotted from Netherfield Junction. Similarly treated were the Down Branch distant and Home signals. From 22nd November 1971, the box was no longer manned. The gates were closed to rail traffic, and operated by a shunter travelling on the Gedling Colliery train until May 1981 when they were replaced first by auto lifting barriers. The signal box was abolished when the crossing was converted to Automatic Operated Colour Lights on 14th June 1981.

Fig. 85
Looking east along Netherfield lane at the level crossing and signal box which controlled the gates just before its demolition. The large building beyond was the Railway Institute with a little of the houses of Traffic Terrace showing further along. The Up Line nearer the signal box is the single line branch from Netherfield Junction to Gedling Colliery. *May 1981 A Henshaw*

Fig. 86
A more recent view from the same spot shows the line to Gedling Colliery *in situ* and the house behind the site of the signal box renovated and looking very attractive. The unprotected crossing with warning lights has seen occasional accidents. The colliery was closed in November 1991, but the track has not been lifted because of the possibility of using it as part of Nottingham's proposed Light Rapid Transport scheme. The Railway Institute building has been converted to a Social Club named Carolines. *March 1991 A Henshaw*

3. NETHERFIELD & COLWICK - NOTTINGHAM LONDON ROAD

NETHERFIELD AND COLWICK 125 m 12 3/4 ch

When the Ambergate Company made the junction with the Midland at Colwick there were only six cottages and two farmsteads in this straggling parish, with Colwick Hall and Park near its western border with the Town of Nottingham. Netherfield passenger station came later when the creation of the new parish of Netherfield arose from the building of Colwick Yards and Locomotive Depot, which brought a large influx of workers to this rural area. The station opened in May 1878 and was called Colwick, but was nicknamed 'Rags and Tatters' by which it is still known by the older people. It was so named because during the building it was surrounded by scaffolding draped with tarpaulins and this remained in position for so long that the tarpaulins became tattered. Shortly after opening a refreshment room was provided, the station being a changing point for passengers travelling to and from stations to the west of Nottingham, and this survived until the first World War. It was renamed four times - May 1st 1883 Netherfield & Colwick, August 1891 Netherfield, July 13th 1925 reverting to Netherfield & Colwick, and once again Netherfield on 6th May 1974. It only catered for passenger and parcels traffic. The buildings were of wood on an island platform. Access was originally from Meadow Road which crossed the line on the level at the west end of the station. Colwick West Junction signal box stood on the Up side and was opened on 23rd August 1875 when the double line to Colwick North Junction was completed, and the line from Colwick to Pinxton opened. The West Junction signal box remained in this position until it was closed in April 1909 and workings were transferred to the centre of the wooden buildings on the island platform, It was then renamed Netherfield Junction. In 1885 powers were obtained to divert the main road from Colwick to Netherfield over a bridge to be built at the west end of the station. With the rapid increase in population, a number of houses called Balmoral Grove and Woodland Grove had been built in Colwick adjacent to the level crossing. It was the intention of the GN to widen the road here to make room for the approaches to the intended bridge. To do this would have involved demolition of some of these houses, but the owner, a Mr Wagstaffe, refused to sell the property to the GN. To overcome the difficulty the road was diverted some three hundred yards to the east, and crossed the line by a two span girder and brick bridge at the west end of the island platform. A covered flight of steps led down from the east side of the bridge to give access to the station. A stationmaster's house was erected on the Upside close by the old level crossing, and this is now in use as an office by a hosiery firm. Two water cranes of the parachute tank type were erected, one at each end of the station, and these were fed by pipeline from the Colwick MPD water tower.

The timber buildings of the station were demolished in 1958 and replaced by prefabricated concrete structures (Fig. 78 p35). In 1964 the GN line here was once again connected to the MR's Nottingham-Lincoln line and a new signal box built at the west end of the station. Gas lighting was replaced by electric, and a parcels lift installed connecting the overbridge entrance to the platform below. At the same time the old Ambergate crossing keeper's house at this site was demolished. The new junction was brought into use with the Grantham-Nottingham passenger service on Sunday 10th January 1965 being rerouted into the Midland Station at Nottingham. Weekday services followed this route on 3rd July 1967. The station was reduced to an unstaffed halt on 6th October 1968.

The Goods Yard facilities were situated at the west side of the double line between Netherfield Station and Colwick North Junction, 29 1/2 ch from Netherfield Junction. The facilities were opened in May 1878 and closed in 1968. In the goods yard were also the workshops of the District Engineer, comprising tool store, blacksmith's shop and forge, and joiner's shop. The entrance to the goods yard was on Netherfield Lane alongside the point where the line crossed on the level protected by gates worked from the adjacent signal box. Collected and delivered traffic from here was covered by Nottingham London Road from 1st April 1929, usually by lorry driver Burroughs.

CARLTON JUNCTION MR

At the level crossing here the Ambergate Company erected a Junction Keeper's house in the same style as those provided for crossing keepers at Bottesford. Opened on the 15th July 1850 the junction was with the MR Lincoln to Nottingham line. It was situated some 350 yards to the west of the present Netherfield station, and was in daily use until the double line Colwick to Nottingham London Road was opened by the Ambergate Company on 3rd October 1857. The junction was not used after 1860 and was severed in 1866. The Junction Keeper's house was demolished when the GN line was again connected to the Midland at the end of 1964 The double line from Colwick to Nottingham London Road was closed in 1969 and lifted as far as Nottingham Trent Lane Junction. Colwick Station Signalbox (see Fig. 88 p40) situated at the site of the original Level Crossing was superceded by a new one on the platform which also allowed closure of the West Junction Signalbox, and was named Netherfield Junction (1905 GNR Sectional Appendix)

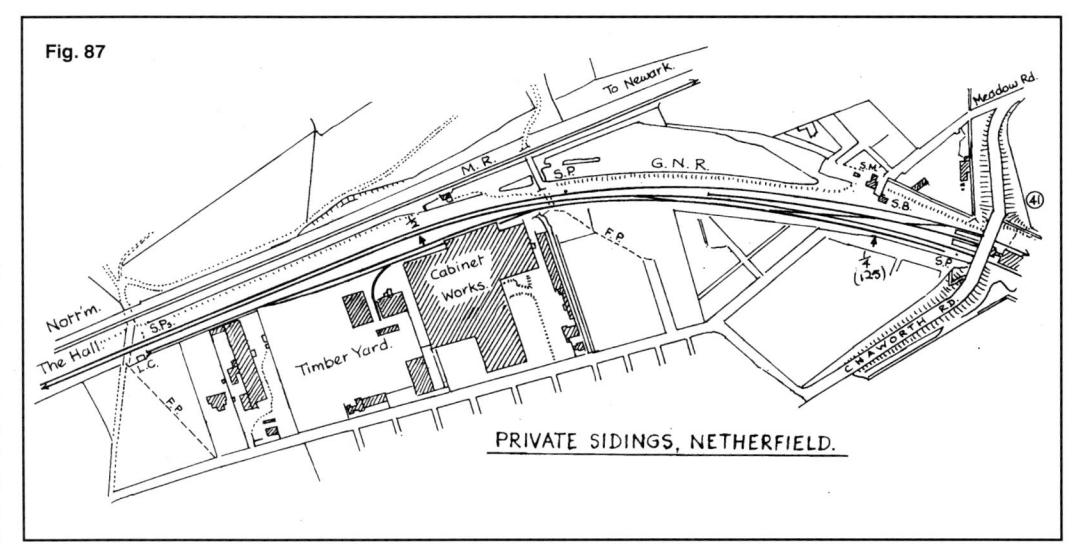

Fig. 87

PRIVATE SIDINGS, NETHERFIELD.

Fig. 88
This interesting view labelled 'Colwick Vale' is taken from the ramp up to the bridge at Netherfield & Colwick station, facing west. The footpath in the foreground led to the Station House, and the track layout is the same as in the 1904 scale plan (Fig. 87 p39). Note the separate posts for the Up Home signals with the West Junction's distants beneath, and lampman's platform in between. These posts remained separate after the closure of the signal box, holding the distant signal arms only, at a lower level until the 1940s. Colwick Station Signalbox and adjacent lamp cabin are on the right.
1905 Authors Collection

Fig. 89
Taken from beside the Midland lines and looking across them can be seen the approach to Netherfield & Colwick Station from the west, with the new connection to the lines in the foreground leaving the original GN route to Nottingham opposite the new factory building. To the left of that are the buildings of an older hosiery factory above which is the tower of the coaling plant at Colwick MPD. On the right are the ends of terraced houses, the further one being where the road to Carlton crossed on the level in 1850. The new signal box between the Main lines is immediately in front of bridge 41, the chimney of Britannia Mills showing above the roofs of the houses.
July 1969 A Henshaw

Fig. 90
Savells Crossing in the foreground crossed both the Midland lines and those of the GNR which are seen here facing east towards Netherfield. This occupation crossing marked the end of the Private Sidings line on the right, on which can be seen the 'Pilot' engine opposite the Cabinet Works. This working, although serving all the works along the siding was called 'Lawrences Man' by the railwaymen.
September 1959 John R Bonser

Fig. 91
To the west of the station, the lines curved away to run adjacent to the earlier Midland Railway's track towards Nottingham, and alongside the Down Main was a long siding serving a few private connections to such firms as Lawrences (furniture makers) and Jno Sands who produced steel girders etc. Access to these private sidings was gained by working a ground frame near bridge 41, which was released from Netherfield Junction. Before the construction of this bridge the road from Colwick to Carlton crossed the line on the level about where the old station house seen on the right was. Beside the Up Main is a Platelayer's hut with tool chest, beyond which is the Up home signal 38, where during the 1930s an adjacent signal for the branch to Colwick North Junction stood.
August 1953 J P Wilson

Fig. 92
This is the scene from the rear of a Basford-bound passenger train as it approaches Netherfield & Colwick station further to the right beyond the Lombardy poplar trees. It shows the first of the Private Sidings to the west of the station and some buildings of Messrs Lawrences Furniture/Cabinet-making works on the right. The buffer stop on the short middle siding (Fig. 87 p39) is just visible in the distance beyond the fence.
1954 C A Hill

Fig. 93

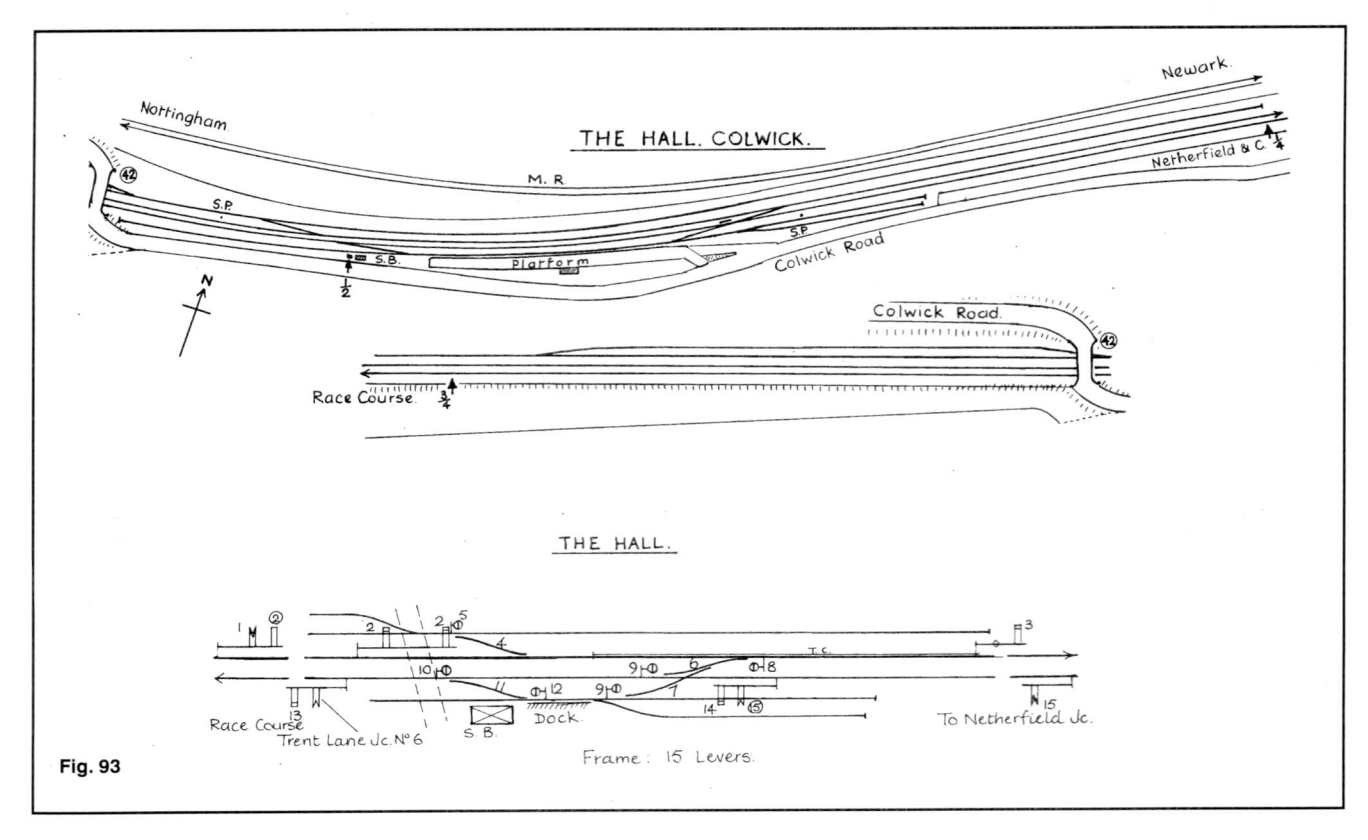

THE HALL SIDINGS 126m 39 1/4 ch

These were laid down to serve the adjacent Nottingham Racecourse and opened in 1892 together with a timber constructed horse dock furnished with timber cabins for the horse attendants and railway staff. Lighting was by oil lamps until closed on 1st March 1954. The signal box remained as a block post until 23rd May 1965, when it was closed and subsequently burnt down. When not needed for race meetings during winter months spare old coaching stock, usually six-wheeled and four-wheeled varieties were stabled in the Up sidings here. Such vehicles were needed during the summer months for strengthening excursion and special trains

Fig. 94
This shot from the Up passenger train about to pass beneath bridge 42 at The Hall shows a fine example of GNR somersault signals on a lattice post, the upper one showing clearly against the sky to the driver approaching from a curve. These sky arms were not always provided with a spectacle plate with a red or green aspect, illuminated from behind with an 8-day oil lamp as is this one. In the distance is the horse-loading dock with its wooden shelter. On the left is the abutment of the first bridge, which crossed the railway at right angles at this point. After a serious accident occurred because of the sharp turns in the road to be negotiated, the bridge was rebuilt on the skew to ease these curves.
1954 C A Hill

Fig. 95
This embracing view of the signal box and layout at The Hall is taken from bridge 42 which carried the Nottingham-Colwick road over the GNR at this point. A Nottingham to Grantham passenger train hauled by an ex LNER Class J6 0-6-0, number 64257 is speeding past, and the sidings on both sides are full of stabled wagons awaiting repair or demolition. The brick platelayers' hut on the right has the 126 1/2 milepost in front of it, and the lamp room is immediately behind. Left of the signal box roof is the wooden shelter on the long platform where the racehorses were unloaded to be walked to the nearby racecourse.
April 1956 F A Quayle

Fig. 96
A view from such a train as seen in Fig. 94, but bound for Basford & Bulwell *via* Netherfield and Daybrook, which shows the two short sidings beyond the horse loading platform. Platelayers are at work beside the Down Main line, with a look-out man on the right. The Down Home signal, 14, is 'off' for the passage of a train, but the Race Course Distant arm has been removed from beneath it, which was normal practice between race meetings. The building on the extreme right beside the stone retaining wall is a Platelayers' hut.
1955 C A Hill

Fig. 97 & 98
Two detailed shots of the lower somersault arm 2 at The Hall.
This type of semaphore signal was designed by Edward French and used throughout the GNR after the serious accident which occurred at Abbots Ripton during freezing blizzard conditions in January 1876. The Up distant signal was frozen in the 'off' position allowing the Up express passenger train to collide with a coal train which was being reversed into a siding. Wreckage from this spread across the other lines, and was hit by a Down passenger train adding to the casualties and wreckage. The one of the rear shows the spectacle plate, oil lamp and back plate or blinder. This obscured the small light from the back of the lamp showing whether it was still alight, for in strong winds oil lamps frequently needed to be re-lit. The back plate obscured this aspect when the arm was in the 'off' position as shown. The hole in the bottom of the back plate was fitted with a purple glass where it was necessary to avoid confusion with other lights, but in this case a white light would show.
(B) The side view shows the spacing of the various cranks and adjustable levers which operated the balanced arm.
October 1953 A Henshaw

NOTTINGHAM RACECOURSE PASSENGER STATION
126 m 68 1/2 ch'

This was built at the same time as the Hall Sidings. The platforms were opposite and constructed of timber as were the booking office and waiting rooms on the Upside. There were no buildings on the Downside platform. A small signal box was erected at the west end of the Down platform and opened on race days only. When the signal box was not in use the relative signal arms were removed from their posts. The station and signal box closed on the 9th December 1959.

Fig. 99
This shows the platforms taken from the down track near where the signal box stood looking east towards Netherfield. The shelters on the up platform are more visible than the booking office which is largely obscured by a bush. In the distance is the bridge 42 carrying the Colwick Road. The tall signal post with repeater arms (Fig. 96 p43) has been lowered to hold one upper quadrant arm with a white board behind.

The station was opened and manned only for race meetings, and a friend of the author who was sent as booking clerk on one such occasion was reluctantly persuaded to place bets on the races, as the rest of the staff were in the habit of doing, using messengers or tick-tack means of communication with the course. Being young and impecunious, against all advice he placed a small bet on the rank outsider for one race. It won! Having more money than he started with, less persuasion was needed for a second wager. Again he chose the one with the greatest odds, and again it won! This happened a once more until the last race, when the rest of the staff envious of his accumulating wealth put their money on his choice. It came nowhere!
August 1959 H B Priestley

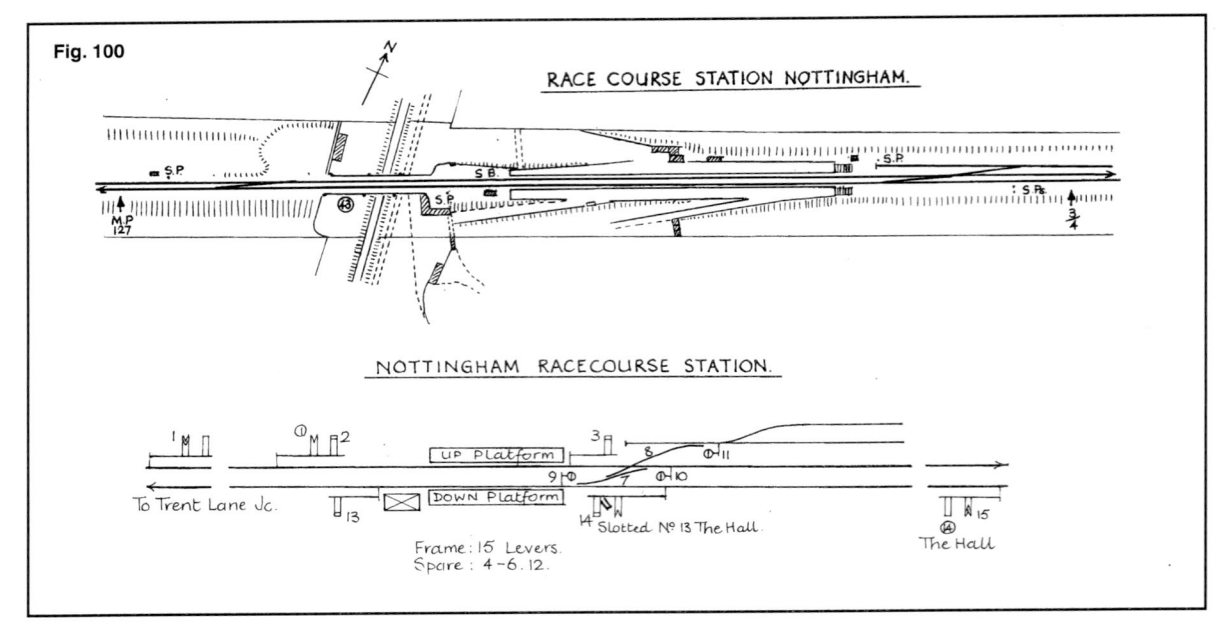

Fig. 101
Bridge 42 has now gone, as has the railway, to be replaced by road improvements between Nottingham and Colwick which here follow the curve of the track and occupy much more ground! On the right can be seen the remains of the loading platform, minus its wooden shelter.
March 1991 A Henshaw

Fig. 102
Another glimpse from the carriage window of the Nottingham Victoria to Basford train which is here passing Nottingham Racecourse station. The Down side platform and shelter are seen with the foundations of the signal box at the near end of the ramp.
1954 C A Hill

MEADOW LANE JUNCTION

When the Amber Gate Company built the double line from Colwick to Nottingham London Road at Eastcroft, Parliamentary sanction was obtained to construct a junction with the Midland Nottingham to Lincoln line in the parish of Sneinton. The short connection was some 500 yards to the east of the London Road terminus. Signal boxes were erected at either end; the Amber Gate one being named Meadow Lane, and that on the Midland, Sneinton Junction. This connection was made for the exchange of goods and coal traffic. Meadow Lane Junction closed on the opening of Nottingham Goods Yard GN signal box, and the Exchange Sidings on the 23rd September 1889. The Nottingham Goods Junction as the first signalbox was called, was moved to a site alongside Trent Lane some 550 yards to the east upon the opening of Manvers Street Goods Depot LNWR.

Fig. 103
Looking east along the main lines from Nottingham to Netherfield this view includes much more than the signal box and platelayer's hut on the left. Note the heavily-laden telegraph post, needed when the block instruments and telephones connected with six other signal boxes, namely The Hall, Thorneywood, Manvers Street (LNW), London Road (High Level), London Road Low Level Goods Yard and Passenger. Beneath the Up home signal can be seen the bracket which held the Race Course distant arm, and beyond the bridges in the centre are the three arms of the Down home signals. The bowstring girder bridges and the one on the right carried the Up Suburban line from Thorneywood. The Midland Railway from Nottingham to Newark passed beneath the one on the right, also beneath the girders on either side of the track just beyond the signal box, and steam from a train on the Midland Line shows above the platelayer's hut on the left. The single connection to Manvers Street Goods depot on the left was originally a double line junction.
August 1954 J P Wilson

TRENT LANE JUNCTION
127 m 23 ch

During the latter half of the 1870s, the LNW Railway entered the scene, being granted running powers over the GN lines to collieries, and jointly contibuting to construction of the line from Bottesford to Welham. It ran a passenger service from London Road to Market Harborough and Northampton, and after initially using a warehouse at London Road for goods traffic, opened its own large Goods Station close by at Manvers Street in 1888.

For access, a junction was made above Trent Lane replacing the earlier Meadow Lane signal box, and called Trent Lane Junction. Within two years the Nottingham Suburban Line from Daybrook made an extra connection. Authority for a line from a junction at Meadow Lane to Weekday Cross to connect with the Great Central Railway for access to Nottingham Joint station was granted on 30th May 1895. However the proposed route would have involved demolition of much property and a very severe climb and curve. So the route was built from Trent Lane Junction at a higher level, along an embankment and brick arched viaduct between the lines to London Road Station to the south and Manvers Street Goods depot to the north. This line was opened on 15th March 1899.

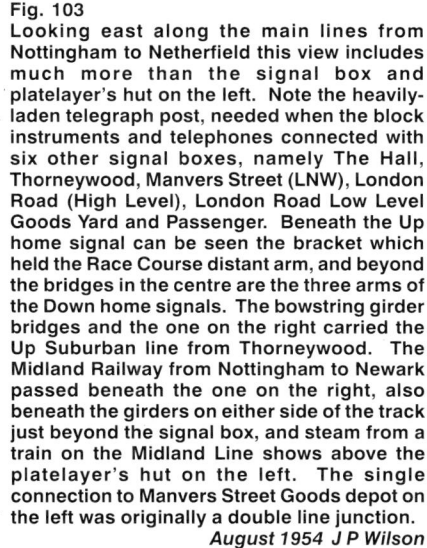

After 1900, Trent Lane Junction was a very busy place, dealing with trips of goods traffic from the Low Level station to Colwick, and LNW workings into and out of Manvers Street Goods station, to both Colwick and London Road for exchange with the Midland railway at Sneinton Junction. Passenger services from Low Level were reduced to LNWR trains to Northampton *via* the GN and LNWR Joint Line through Melton Mowbray, but the GNR services from Grantham, Newark, the Leen Valley and Basford were then routed via the High Level station at London Road into Nottingham Victoria station. Finally came the traffic and passenger trains over the Suburban Line from Daybrook.

In 1967 when trains from Grantham and the east were routed into the Midland Station from Netherfield Junction the line was closed to passenger traffic. But this was not the end for after the closure of the GC line to the south from Nottingham Victoria, traffic to and from the British Plaster Board works at Hotchley Hill (Rushcliffe Halt) travelled via Weekday Cross Junction over a single line into Victoria Street tunnel and back to Trent Lane, and London Road to be exchanged to the Midland lines at Sneinton Junction, movements which involved much to-ing and fro-ing! What a good thing there was little other traffic about at that time. These arrangements ceased with the opening of the spur at Loughborough to connect the GCR line to the Midland Railway in 1974, after which the track was lifted at the Nottingham end. Parts of the viaduct remain but the bridge over London Road has been removed.

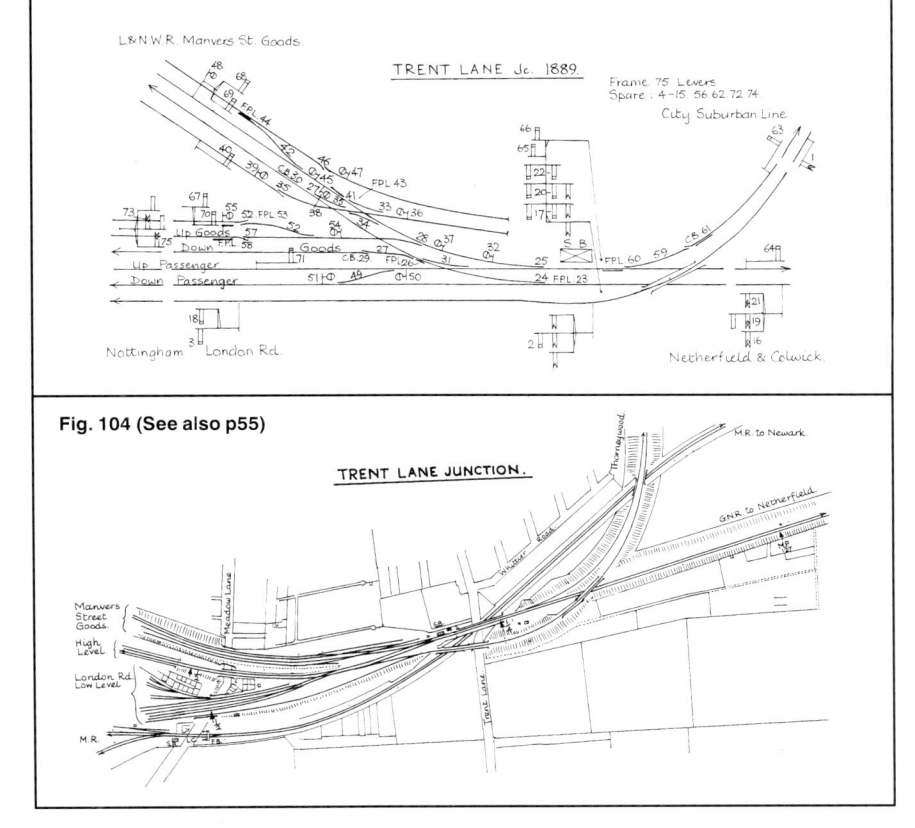

Fig. 104 (See also p55)

At Trent Lane Junction a facing crossover also connected the Up Suburban line to the Down Main line for passenger trains to use the new station. The bridges across Meadow Lane are still there, together with part of the brick arched viaduct to the former London Road High Level station. However, these arches are severed just beyond where the entrance to the coal yard and cattle pens was, off Sneinton Hermitage, for a new trunk road, which now connects Manvers Street to Meadow Lane, and climbs to cross the River Trent by the Midland Railway's Melton line bridge.

Fig. 105
Here we see a typical train of mixed goods wagons from Colwick into London Road passing Trent Lane Junction, and taking the Goods Line points as indicated by the signal in Fig. 133 (p55). The locomotive is an ex LNER Class J52 six-coupled saddle tank, a type which served for most of the 'Pilot' turns worked from Colwick. On the right is the Up Suburban line into the Passenger station.
J F Henton

Fig. 106

Fig. 107
The main buildings and entrance to the passenger terminus at London Road is showing the stone porte-cochère which allowed passengers to alight from carriages and cabs under cover. The clock face is unfortunately missing from its place above the centre, the story being that the works were sent to Doncaster for repair, but lost in transit before arriving back! Note the more recent steel fire escape beneath the bay window of the original Boardroom on the left.
June 1981 A Henshaw

Fig. 108
Viewed from the High Level station the approach to the original terminus of the Ambergate company's line from Grantham is seen crossing the Nottingham Canal on the right. The buildings were designed by T C Hine and built in 1857. The original elegant but not too ornate buildings have been extended as traffic grew, as can be seen from the awning along the front of the offices at the ends of the platforms. The fish dock was beneath the three gables to the right, and in 1913 a traffic control office was built on the end of the upper storey of offices, spanning the platform concourse, and certainly not blending with T C Hine's buildings!

For Control purposes, the GNR Western Division was split into three sections, each with a table, headphone and mouthpiece telephone connected to every signal box, and backed by a vertical board showing a diagrammatic plan of the line under supervision. Each signal box or block post had a hole, as did sidings or yards, into which a peg was placed to represent a train or light engine. The peg was spring-loaded to carry a small card with relevant information about the train such as engine number, length in wagons, time and place the crew signed on. Number one section worked the Derbyshire Extension lines from Basford westwards. Number two section controlled the Leen Valley and its Extension line as far as Shirebrook South and Colliery from Colwick. Number three table worked from Nottingham London Road and Colwick eastwards to Barrowby Road at Grantham, north from Bottesford West Junction to Cotham, and south from Bottesford to Marefield Junction and Leicester Belgrave Road.
June 1967 the late R W Sheppard

Fig. 109

NOTTINGHAM LONDON ROAD
LOW LEVEL STATION.

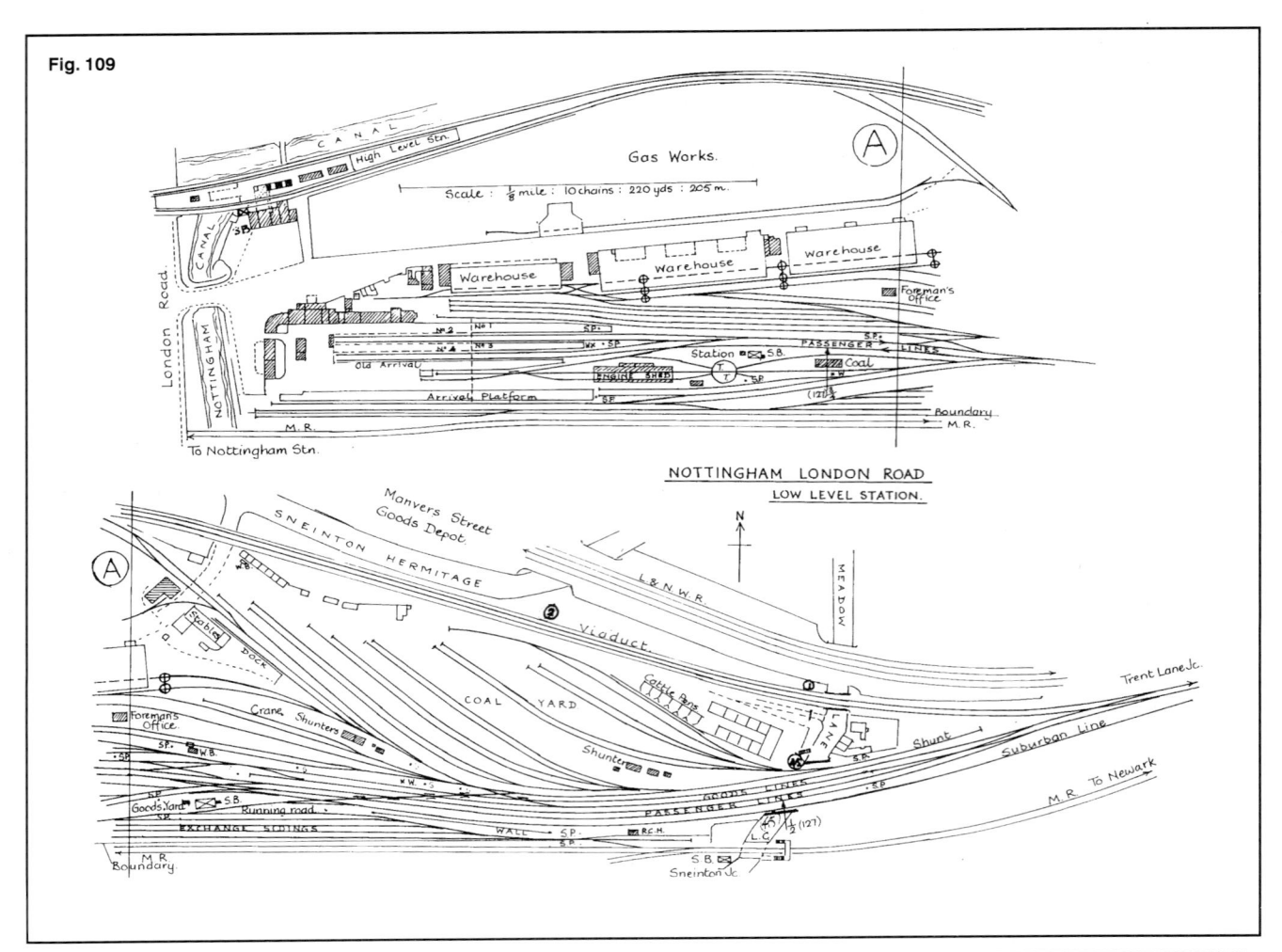

Fig. 110
This shows the buildings along the end of the platform lines in elevation as seen from across the Nottingham Canal. The awning seen in Fig. 108 (p47) has been removed, and through the opening beneath the control office on the right can be seen the long arrival platform added to the original station at a later date. The station was used as a parcels concentration depot at this time, evidenced by the two strings of parcels barrows
June 1981 A Henshaw

Fig. 111
An ex-Midland Railway rebuilt Kirtley 2-4-0 number 20002 is ready to leave with a short train to Northampton from platform 2. Platform 1 at this time was used for goods traffic and known as the Peterborough road. Behind the wagons is the first of the warehouses to be built which was used by the LNWR before their Manvers Street depot was opened. After that the GNR took possession again and during the 1930s it was used by the Signal & Telegraph department for storing equipment.
April 1939 J P Wilson

Fig. 112
This shows the three roof spans covering the platforms from a little further away than Fig. 111, shortly after the station closure as a Parcels depot. Inside the centre span the extension to the original roof can be seen reaching towards the camera. The left-hand span was originally a carriage dock, alongside which a long new arrival platform was built with an awning. The passenger train beyond this is bound for Lincoln from the Midland station.
June 1981 A Henshaw

Fig. 113
A GNR 0-8-0 (LNER Class Q1) 'Long Tom' with Class B headlamps is seen arriving in the transfer road with a train of cattle wagons, probably bound for Ireland whence cattle were regularly shipped, and frequently transferred to the LNER at Nottingham. H A Ivatt designed the locomotives which were built between 1901 and 1907 and had 4 ft 8 in wheels for hauling mineral trains of up to 60 wagons from the Yorkshire, Nottinghamshire and Derbyshire coalfields to London. Behind the engine is the awning over the long arrival platform, and the higher extension roof to the original terminus.
pre-1923 the late F H Gillford

NOTTINGHAM LONDON ROAD 127 m 73 1/4 ch

The original buildings of the Ambergate Company were enlarged and extended by the GN over a period of many years following the opening on 3rd October 1857. The Goods Depot consisted of warehouses, offices and extensive sidings and was the busiest of all the four goods depots in Nottingham handling the bulk of the fruit, vegetable and flower traffic from Covent Garden together with that from the growing areas of the Fens, Lincolnshire, East Anglia, Bedfordshire and Huntingdonshire, all destined for sale in the Nottingham Sneinton Wholesale Market. There were heavy forwardings of John Player's cigarettes and tobacco to all parts of the country, particularly to the Metropolis and Manchester, and one shed and warehouse was set aside exclusively for this and known as the 'Tobacco Shed'. Similarly there were very heavy forwardings of The Boots Company to their branches everywhere and particular days were set aside for despatches to different areas every week. This world-famous firm had sidings and loading sheds alongside the Poplar Arm of the Nottingham Canal served from the Goods Yard layout. Close by was the works of the Nottingham Corporation's Gas and Coke Depot receiving daily trains of coal and despatching quantities of coke and chemical by-products. A large fleet of collection and delivery vehicles of all kinds was maintained covering not only the City and suburbs, but many villages in the outlying area.

The passenger station was built on the East Croft of the Town of Nottingham to the design of the notable architect T C Hine close to the Nottingham Canal and opened on the 3rd October 1857. It was named Nottingham London Road, the words Low Level being added when a station was built at higher level and opened 15th March 1899 on the extension line to Nottingham Victoria. The original station covered two main platforms and four intervening lines with office accommodation above the main entrance. There was an adjoining engine shed and stationmaster's house. The working of the station was controlled from a small signal box at the east end of the platforms. Many alterations took place over the succeeding years. A new platform from the Ticket Office covering a length of 322 feet was completed in May 1874 and in 1881 a central platform was installed to deal with the Goose Fair traffic. Separate new booking offices were added for GN and LNW which opened 6th August 1883, the LNW having obtained running powers into the station on the construction of the GN and LNW Joint Line. The telegraph office opened when the station was built. It was closed on 20th February 1932 and combined with the one at Nottingham Victoria, messages being sent from there to the various offices at London Road by telephone. A refreshment room was added about this time. New buildings were erected over the west end of the station to accommodate the Nottingham District Control which came into being at 6.0 am 10th November 1913. These operations were transferred to an office of the District Superintendent at Nottingham Victoria in 1923. At various times up to 1923 the offices over the station were occupied by the Engineer, Medical Officer, Mineral Agent, and Goods and Passenger Manager for the Nottingham District of the GNR. The Nottingham District Manager's office staff were also transferred at the same time. The Nottingham and Grantham Railway & Canal Company which had been taken over by the GNR and received regular dividends from them also had their office here until 1923. The Medical Officer and District Engineer's office remained at London Road until the 1950s when it was absorbed into the LM Region of British Rail. After the opening of the High Level station the District Mineral office was transferred to a room on the platform there facing the stairs, J H Cain being designated as Mineral Agent.

49

Fig. 114
A stone retaining wall separates the GNR lines on the left as they climb away from the level exchange sidings beside the Midland lines on the right at Sneinton Junction. Semaphore signals are still in use but the gantry across the sidings has had the loading gauge removed, and the Railway Clearing House cabin from which all exchanged traffic between the GNR (LNER) and Midland (LMSR) was monitored prior to nationalisation on January 1st 1948 has also gone. The Midland line to Newark and Lincoln was opened in 1846 when road traffic was horse-drawn, and it crossed Meadow Lane on the level as the crossing gates show. At the time of writing in 1992, the signal box was still there; the level crossing had automatic lifting barriers and closed circuit TV cameras to the Trent Power signal box, and the signals were all colour lights. *August 1967 A Henshaw*

Fig. 115
This is the signalman's view towards Trent Lane Junction from the Goods Yard signal box, and it shows some of the signals, all upper quadrant, and disc, or ground shunting signals of which a column of three can be seen in the centre. The point rodding in the centre and to the right is of standard LNER channel section, with small rollers beneath. The exchange sidings are right, holding wagons of sleepers and a train of coaches beyond which, and partially obscured is Sneinton Junction signal box. *August 1967 A Henshaw*

Fig. 116
The road access on the north side of the Goods Offices and warehouses facing east. The first warehouse used by the LNWR for a short time is on the right, and was used by the Signal and Telegraph engineers in LNER days. Next is the office block where all traffic was invoiced and cartage traffic waybilled on the two upper storeys. Joined to this with two matching arches of later date is T C Hine's brick warehouse, beyond which is the large four-storey goods and grain warehouse built a few years afterwards. The road continued beyond the last warehouse, where it turned left to a gateway into Manvers Street, and also gave access to the coal merchants' yard and cattle dock further east. The Corporation Gas Works stood on the ground behind the fencing on the left. *June 1981 A Henshaw*

On the recommendation of Harold Mather the LNW passenger service was transferred to Nottingham Victoria on the 2nd May 1944 as a war economy measure, the GC having previously declined to give the LNWR running powers over the GN & GC Joint line extension Trent Lane to Bagthorpe Junction. The GN passenger trains had already ceased to operate into the station from the 15th March 1899. The station was also used throughout the first World War for ambulance trains bringing the wounded from Belgium and France. Passenger traffic ceased on the transfer of the LNW services to Victoria station in 1944; the goods station was closed to livestock and cartage traffic on the 5th September 1966, and coal traffic on 6th November 1967. The passenger station was re-opened a year later as a parcels concentration depot and was a hive of activity until BR ceased to deal with parcels there after the 1st June 1981.

Despite the buildings being listed as of historic importance the disused site was invaded by vandals, for no one buyer could be found. The station buildings were somewhat restored and cleaned up by the Manpower Services Commission during the late 1980s but again became disfigured and damaged. However in 1991, Nottingham City was given a Government grant under the City Challenge scheme for the redevelopment of derelict sites. Part of this is to be used for the restoration of the Sneinton Railway Lands - ie, London Road Station to Trent Lane. Already a new road has been built across it, linking Manvers Street to Meadow Lane and the eastern outer loop road, which opened on 29th June 1992. The embankment needed to lift this road over the Midland Railway lines divides the land into two. Plans were proposed for the western half with the warehouses and station buildings to be developed as a Museum of Industry and Transport with the transfer of exhibits at present housed at Wollaton Hall. The Goods Yard signal box standing close beside the embankment of the link road has been dismantled by volunteers from the Main Line Steam Trust at Loughborough, to be re-built within the site but the roof slates have been stolen (January 1994). The large warehouse at the east end was used by a firm for a paint store, and subsequently severely damaged by fire.

Fig. 117 NOTTINGHAM STATION. LONDON ROAD. 1895

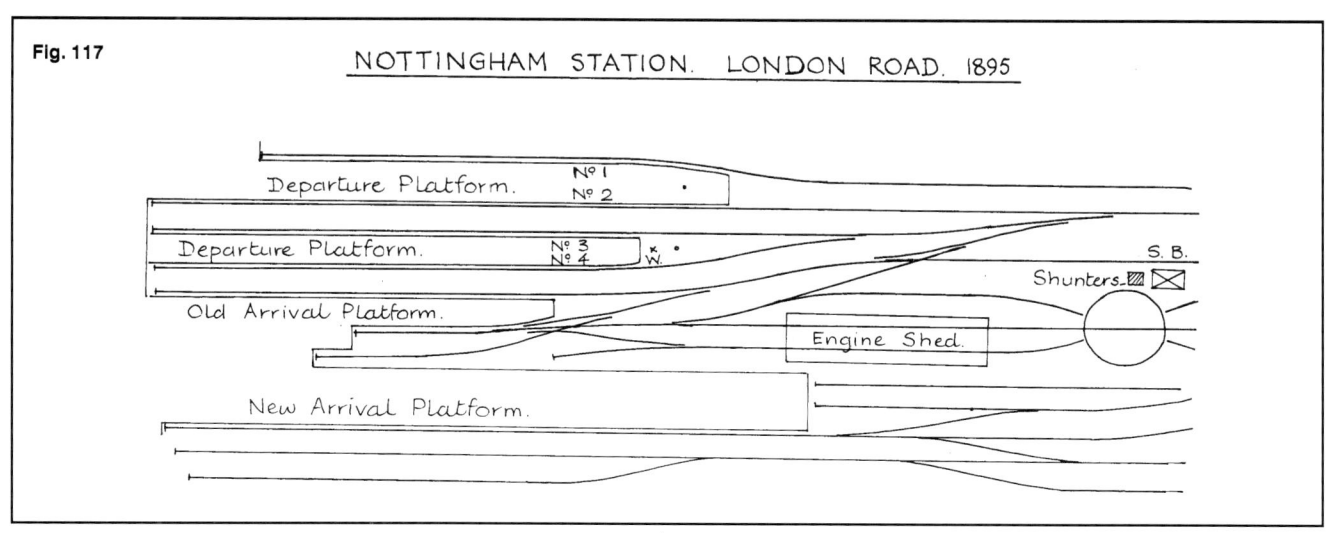

Fig. 118
The already vandalised station signal box seen shortly before its demolition. There is plenty of coaching stock about, but track lifting has begun on the left. The large Boots building on Station Street stands clearly in the distance, whilst behind the roofs of the warehouses on the right can be seen the framework of a gasholder.
1963 J W D Miller

Fig. 119
Another side of the station signal box as seen from the end of the arrival platform with the Goods Yard signal box further to the right and bisected by a telegraph pole. A train of wagons stands in the Peterborough road on the left behind which can faintly be seen the gantry crane and the Foreman's office. After the transfer of passenger services to Nottingham Victoria, no signalmen were appointed at this signal box, which was used as required for shunting purposes. The starting signals for platforms 1 and 2 were worked from Goods Yard box. When it was necessary to work the points connected from the box for shunting or to shunt a passenger/parcels train into the station or to the old arrival platform or for trains departing from platforms 3 and 4 the foreman porter worked the box.
1963 B Elliott

Fig. 120 NOTTINGHAM STATION. LONDON ROAD (LOW LEVEL).
Frame: 25 Levers.
Spare: 1.5.6.8-14. 20-25.

Fig. 121
This shows the other two roof spans and the shortened bay between platform 4 and the old arrival platform which gives a large area for road vehicles to manœuvre. The earlier carriage dock (right) has been filled to platform level and a ramp built beyond the trailer. Behind the trolley-lined wall right is the new arrival platform.
June 1981 A Henshaw

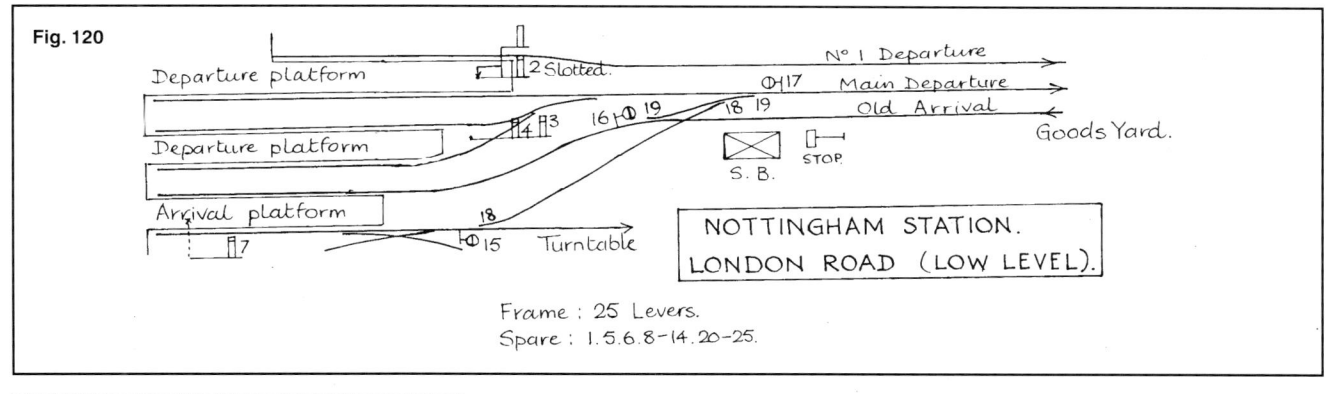

Fig. 122
The interior of the station looking east along the site of the original departure lines. These have been removed and the bay between them filled in level with the two platforms for use as the parcels depot. The entrance was also screened off with corrugated sheeting as a protection from the weather, but wind and rain could still be felt from the open right-hand side, where the parcels vans were loaded. The scene is quiet, with one caretaker railman in charge of the closed depot.
June 1981 A Henshaw

Fig. 123 *June 1981 A Henshaw*
This is a closer view of the first brick warehouse of the 'Ambergate Company' facing west along its north side. It has a graceful exterior with four large doorways for road traffic (originally drays) to use, but the circular upper storey windows have been bricked in. A very unusual feature of its design which allows open space all over the ground level is the upper floor. This is suspended from the roof, and unsupported from beneath. As can be seen the warehouse has been connected to the larger warehouse from the upper floor, and had an office built on at the nearer end. The western end has also been joined to the office block with an attempt to emulate T C Hine's arches and continue the design.
June 1981 A Henshaw

Fig. 124
An interior view of the northwest corner of the station buildings at the time of cleaning and partial restoration by Manpower Services. The excellent quality of the woodwork and panelling of the earlier refreshment room in this corner has been revealed here, but alas it did not last. Many of ground floor windows were boarded up and painted to represent frames and glass from the outside, but access from the east end of the station could not be closed to exclude youths and children who seem to delight in defiling and sometimes destroying property whose history and value has no effect on their moronic behaviour. A development scheme was once afoot to use these buildings and the warehouses as an Industrial Museum.
May 1985 A Henshaw

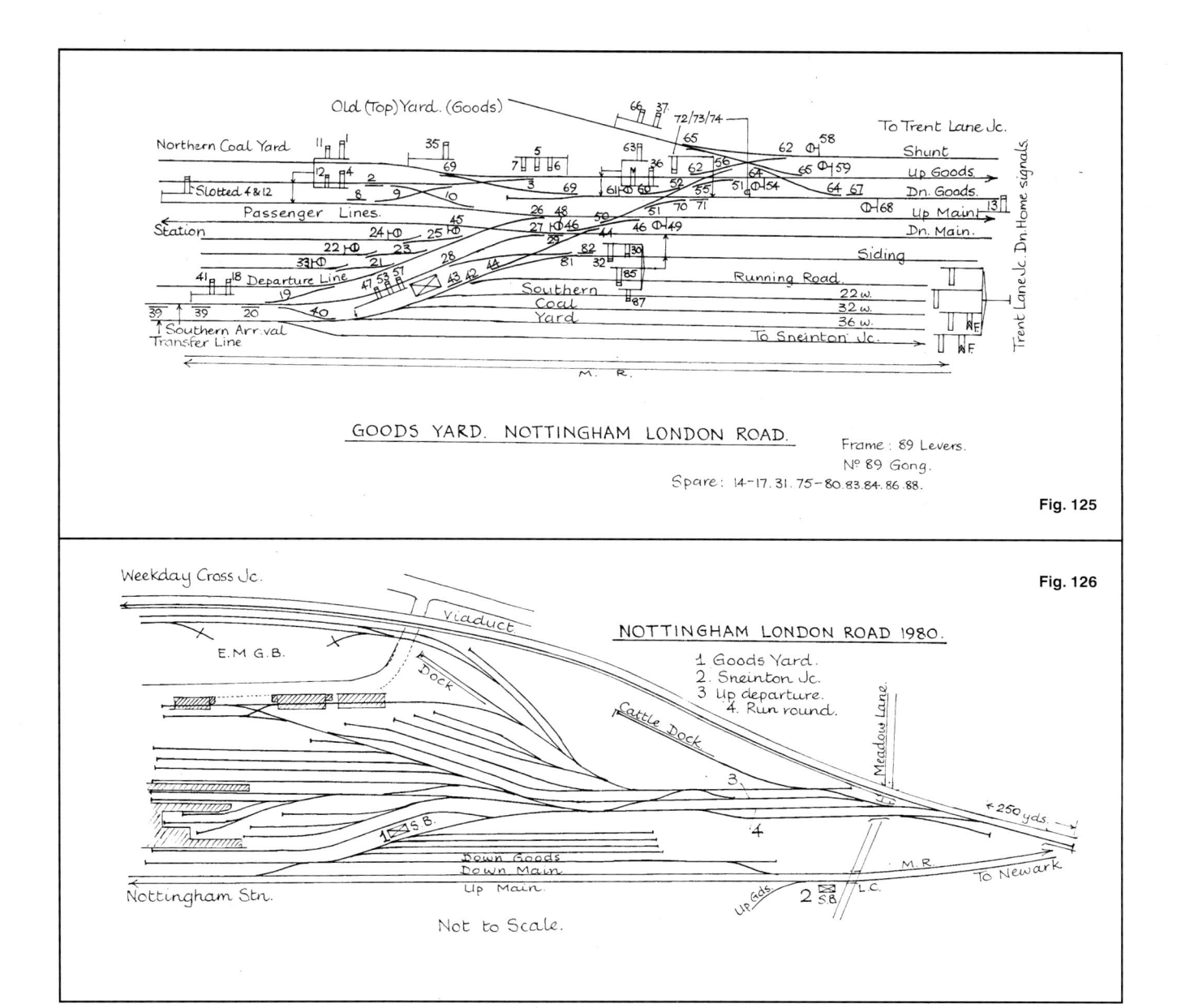

Fig. 125

GOODS YARD. NOTTINGHAM LONDON ROAD.

Frame: 89 Levers.
No. 89 Gong.
Spare: 14-17. 31. 75-80. 83. 84. 86. 88.

Fig. 126

NOTTINGHAM LONDON ROAD 1980.
1. Goods Yard.
2. Sneinton Jc.
3. Up departure.
4. Run round.

Not to Scale.

Fig. 127
The south side and east end of the very large goods and grain warehouse built by the GNR. Later additions to the original building are the steel fire escapes and the covered chute passing through the central grain elevator to the container below. The trackwork has been removed from inside the door above the wagons and along the side but one or two wagon turntables were still there when the photograph was taken. Track simplification is evident in the foreground for the Parcels depot at the station had recently been closed. The apparent blemish at the top corner window is card and paper bundles being thrown out for scrap! It was intended to preserve and use the warehouses in the development scheme for this part of the goods yard, but it was severely damaged by fire on 4th December 1993. It now stands roofless.
June 1981 A Henshaw

Fig. 128
This scene across the now derelict northern coal yard and cattle dock shows the construction of a new bridge over the Midland Railway lines to Newark on the left and the embankment being built to meet it from the right, to carry the new link road from Sneinton to Colwick. Left of the embankment is Goods Yard signal box, which it was hoped to dismantle and rebuild as part of the Industrial Museum on the station site. Peeping above the bank the three gables of the passenger station can be seen, and furthest right are the large warehouses. The High Level viaduct was severed for this road construction.
March 1991 A Henshaw

Fig. 129
The signalman's view of things at Trent Lane Junction, which shows an LMS Stanier Class 8F 2-8-0 No 48507 with a train of iron ore from Belvoir to Stanton *via* Nottingham Victoria waiting at the Down Home signal. Working hard up the gradient from Low Level Station Stanier Class 5 4-6-0 mixed traffic engine is returning to Colwick with an engineers' train. Between the two locomotives the Up Suburban line can be seen on the left, whilst the line branching right in the foreground leads into Manvers Street Goods Depot.
December 1965 A Henshaw

Fig.130
The Colwick breakdown crane and engineers are seen here at work on bridge 45 over Meadow Lane on a misty frosty morning. The jib was being raised at the time and the cables round the pulley wheels have caught the mass of telegraph wires above, lifting and stretching them somewhat! Fortunately this was noticed in time, and the crane was moved to avoid any damage. The train is standing on the Goods lines, and Trent Lane signal 70 on the bracket is obscured by steam from the crane. The small signal arm beneath the steam is the Up Home 64 on the line from High Level. The bridge (No 1) carrying this line over Meadow Lane is framed between the lifting chains.
December 1965 A Henshaw

Fig. 131
A scene to compare with Fig. 130 at Meadow Lane showing bridge 1 which carried the lines into High Level Station, and the trackbed where the breakdown train was standing. Above the bridge stands the recently restored Green's Windmill at Sneinton, now a prominent landmark of the area.
November 1992 A Henshaw

Fig. 132
This shows the scene approaching the Low Level terminus from Trent Lane Junction near Meadow Lane. The girders and parapets of bridge 45 over Meadow Lane are spread along the trackbed in the middle, and beyond them are the embankments and recently opened bridge which carry the link road from Manvers Street to Meadow Lane and Colwick. On the extreme left is the Midland Railway's Sneinton Junction signal box at the level crossing with the automatic barriers raised, and behind that is the city's Eastcroft incinerator plant where household rubbish is sorted and consumed to provide heat for various parts of the city. To the right above the embankment and behind it are the large Boots factory and the three gable ends of the GNR warehouses which were hopefully to be preserved and used in the development of the site.
November 1992 A Henshaw

Fig. 133
Facing west towards Nottingham at the Up Suburban Line bridge can be seen the Down Home signals on their bracket post, with the route set for the Goods lines into London Road Low Level indicated by the centre arm being 'off'. When there was a facing double line junction into Manvers Street Goods Depot, the bracket supported another post on the right. An ex LNER Class K2 2-6-0 is hauling an express from Nottingham Victoria to Skegness beneath the bridge.
July 1954 J P Wilson

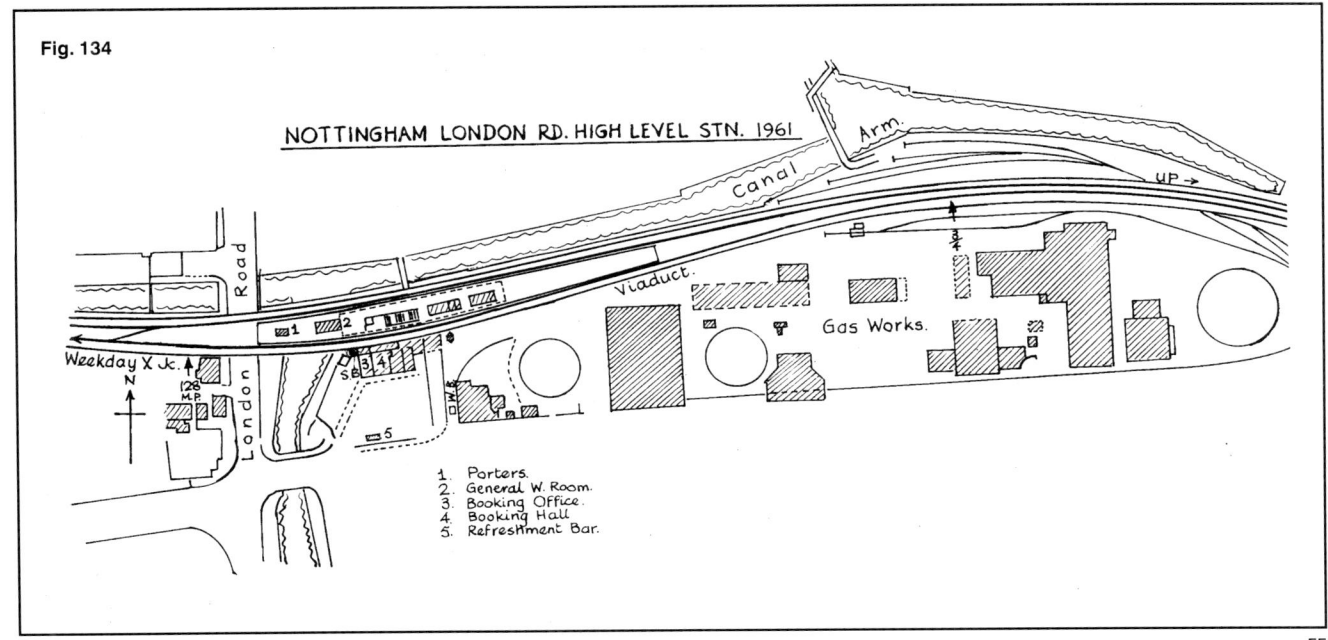

55

NOTTINGHAM LONDON ROAD HIGH LEVEL
127 m 75 3/4 ch

This station was built on the viaduct between Trent Lane Junction and Weekday Cross Junction because the GNR transferred its passenger services from the terminus at London Road to the newly opened Joint station. It opened for passengers on 15th March 1899, and boasted a small signal box. The single island platform had wooden buildings with slate roofs, and both sides were covered by glazed canopies supported on cast iron columns. At street level were the Booking Hall, Booking and Parcel Office of red brick, and a wide stone stepped staircase with white glazed brick walls led up to the platform. A 30-hundredweight hydraulic lift connected the Booking Hall to the platform for the parcels traffic.

The station served as an exchange point for both passengers and parcels to the nearby Midland Station. Fish traffic was unloaded at the Low Level terminus on the south side, and distributed from the High Level station by local passenger trains to GNR stations in Nottinghamshire and Derbyshire.

The signal box was closed and demolished in 1930; the station itself remained open until 3rd July 1967.

Fig. 135
The cobbled approach to the High Level station seen from the bridge spanning the Nottingham Canal from London Road itself. The street level buildings included a booking hall, booking and parcels offices. Above the roof of these buildings is the awning over the island platform on the viaduct behind which is the Boots Island Street factory with extensive building work being added. Note the stone-capped pillar with iron lamp post above and billboards on its sides. To the right of this is part of the end of the refreshment room which replaced the original one incorporated in the Low Level buildings (Fig. 124 p52).
April 1956 John R Bonser

Fig. 136
This fine view of bridge 36 spanning the Nottingham Canal has the Down line upon it. On the island platform is the general waiting room centre, and the porters' room left. The signal box stood in the brick-walled corner on the right before its removal, its sentinel telegraph pole still *in situ*. There is a T-junction on the canal here, the main canal turning left towards Castle Boulevard, and the short Poplar arm, now bricked off, going right. The girders supporting the Up line are longer because of the skew abutments, and their greater depth can be seen beneath those in the foreground. The two girder bridges were removed and cut up in 1997.
September 1962 John Marshall

Fig. 137
Although not widely used by commuters to the city after the 1930s, the passenger service between Basford & Bulwell and Nottingham Victoria *via* Gedling seemed to consist of five or six coaches to the end. By the 1960s the service to Derby Friargate was reduced to three coaches. Here is an unidentified ex LNER Class J39 six-coupled locomotive leaving London Road High Level station with a Basford train travelling towards Trent Lane Junction along the viaduct. The buildings of the gasworks are on the right, evoking memories of pungent sulphurous smoke and coal gas which pervaded the area, particularly in foggy wintry conditions, before the advent of North Sea gas and demolition of these works. There were private sidings beneath the viaduct serving the gasworks.
1957 C A Hill

Fig. 138
A view from the west end of the platform which shows the station name board with original type of metal letters and exhortation to 'alight here for Trent Bridge Cricket and Football Grounds'. An unidentified ex LNER J6 is running towards the up side with a short train for Grantham. Note the GNR-type milepost 128 on the left; the small L beneath the figures indicating distance from London Kings Cross. Between the posts of the name board is an engineers' caution sign, which would be illuminated at night, to indicate a speed restriction.
November 1957 H B Priestley

4. GEDLING - LEEN VALLEY JUNCTION - BASFORD & BULWELL

G. N. R.
Derbyshire & North Staffordshire Extensions
Gedling Station

Fig. 139

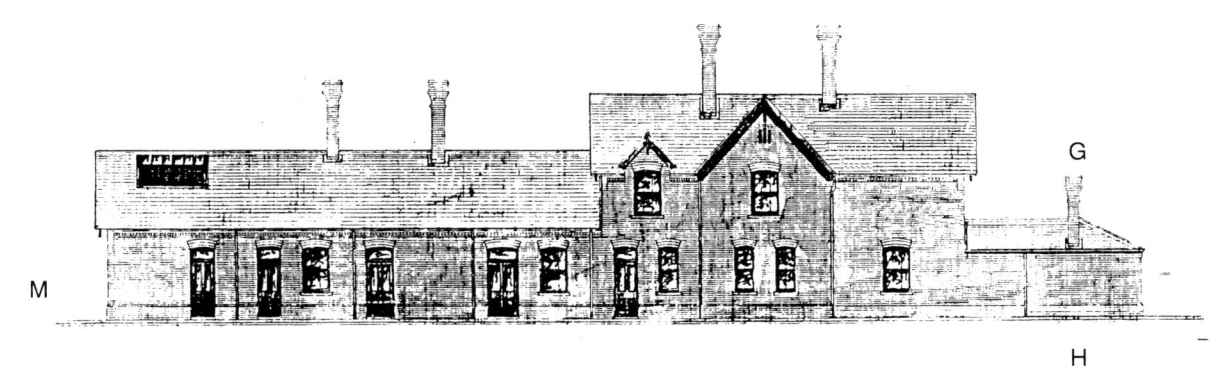

ELEVATION TOWARDS RAILS

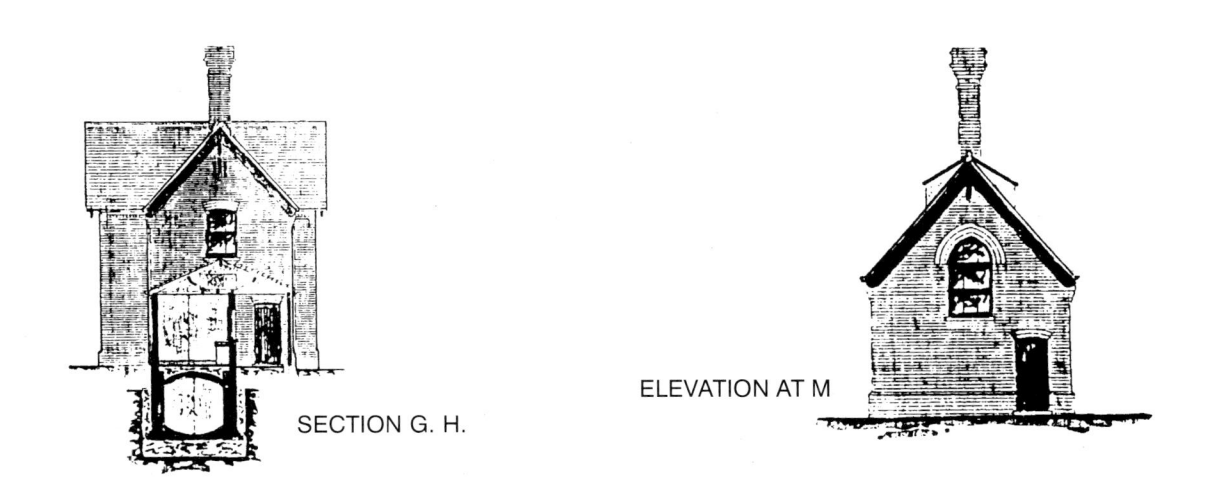

SECTION G. H.

ELEVATION AT M

ELEVATION TOWARDS ROAD

Fig. 140
This is a copy of a colour-tinted postcard of Gedling station. Facing south east along the Up platform the small waiting rooms are largely hidden by trees, but there are passengers at the bench seat in front. Beyond the platform end is an impressive signal gantry holding the Up home signal and four directing distant arms of Colwick North Junction. From left to right they indicated the route to Eastern Reception sidings, Western Reception sidings, Up main line and Up branch to Netherfield station. During 1915 three of these distant signals were removed, together with the gantry, and replaced by a single post with one distant arm (for the Up main line) beneath the home stop signal (Circular No 30,494a - Kings Cross, April 26th, 1915). Behind the signal gantry stands the original signal box, a narrower structure than its successor, seen in Fig. 2 (p2), and right of the gantry is the rear of an Up goods train. There are wagons and a van or two in the small goods yard, but the connections to the Down main line beyond the platform are missing! An oversight of the artist? The loading gauge beyond the dock is shown with a figure, possibly the stationmaster, on the Down platform, on which stand the main buildings and station house.
c. 1910 H H Mather collectionc.

Fig. 141
This scene, looking north west from the Down siding, shows the loading dock and part of the cattle pen on the left, and gives an end elevation of the main buildings, partially obscured by a van body used as a store for building materials. The standard type of timber waiting room used on most of the Derbyshire Extension stations can be seen on the Up platform, and behind it a further wooden shelter with an awning. This was used by the South Notts Hunt when hounds and horses would arrive and depart from Gedling station. Access to the Up platform could be gained from concrete steps leading up from the footpath along the rear.

The closure of Mapperley tunnel meant the end of traffic at the station. The signal box was closed, and access to the siding obtained by a three-lever ground frame, released electrically by Colwick North Junction. Beside the ground frame in the white cabinet is the telephone connecting with the North Junction signalman. Three iron fire buckets hang above the wooden rails at the foot of the ramp on the right.
September 1959 John R Bonser

Fig. 142
A full view of the main station buildings along the Down platform is seen from the end of the Up platform here. From the left the single-storey buildings comprise Gentlemen's toilet, Porters' room, Ladies Waiting Room and Booking Hall/General waiting room. The two-storey section is the Stationmaster's dwelling, but the room adjacent to the Booking Hall was the Booking/Parcel Office. Beyond the two-storey dwelling is another single-storey containing the kitchen and scullery. The heavily corbelled chimneys were a standard feature of these buildings along the Derbyshire Extension. The station nameboard has been changed to an enamelled plate, and the firebuckets are again plainly visible. Idling down the gradient towards Colwick North Junction is a Class B mixed goods train behind Gresley ex LNER Class K3 2-6-0 No 61947.
May 1957 H B Priestley

GEDLING & CARLTON 125 m 60 1/2 ch

Situated north of Colwick Yards, beyond the crossing of the MR Nottingham-Lincoln lines on bridge 10, this pleasant little station had opposite platforms which were planted with various shrubs. The buildings followed a standard design used on most of the Derbyshire Extension to Pinxton and Egginton Junction. The Up side waiting rooms were of timber with a slate roof, the Ladies' being separate from and smaller than the General one. The main buildings were of brick, also slate roofed, and comprised the Stationmaster's house, Booking Office, Booking Hall/General Waiting Room, Ladies' Waiting Room with toilet, Porters' Room, and Gentlemen's urinal. The single-storey section of the dwelling house consisted of kitchen and scullery with a large tank for holding soft water beneath. A hand pump beside the sink lifted the water. Extra bedrooms were provided above the Booking Office.

A small Goods Yard of one siding and a loading Dock was situated on the Down side, and the signal box on the Up. During World War 2 the Ministry of Supply used the Yard for timber storage. Hunt meetings were held at The Kennels, on Kennel Lane before World War 1, and hounds would arrive at Gedling Station in special Hound Vans for such meets.

The station opened for Goods traffic on August 23rd 1875; for Passengers on February 2nd 1876, to and from Nottingham London Road. Livestock facilities were withdrawn 1st September 1960; it was closed to passengers on 4th April 1960, and to Goods traffic on 12th March 1962. The main buildings are now used as a Youth Community Centre, fenced off from the running line to Gedling Colliery.

Fig. 143
Gedling Station House, now almost enveloped in trees, is fenced off from the disused single line leading to the dismantled colliery site. The building, used as a Youth Community Centre, has had extensions added on the left as well as a modern decor! *May 1993 A Henshaw*

Fig. 144
New housing now occupies the site of the Goods Yard, south of the station, a white part of the Station House gable peeping above the trees to the left of the line, which appears less overgrown and better ballasted here. To the right of the wire fence are two pipes which fed slurry from the colliery washing plant to a settling pond east of the Up sidings in Colwick Yard. The line has been left *in situ* for possible future use by a Light Rapid Transport scheme which it is hoped will ease road traffic in and out of Nottingham. *May 1993 A Henshaw*

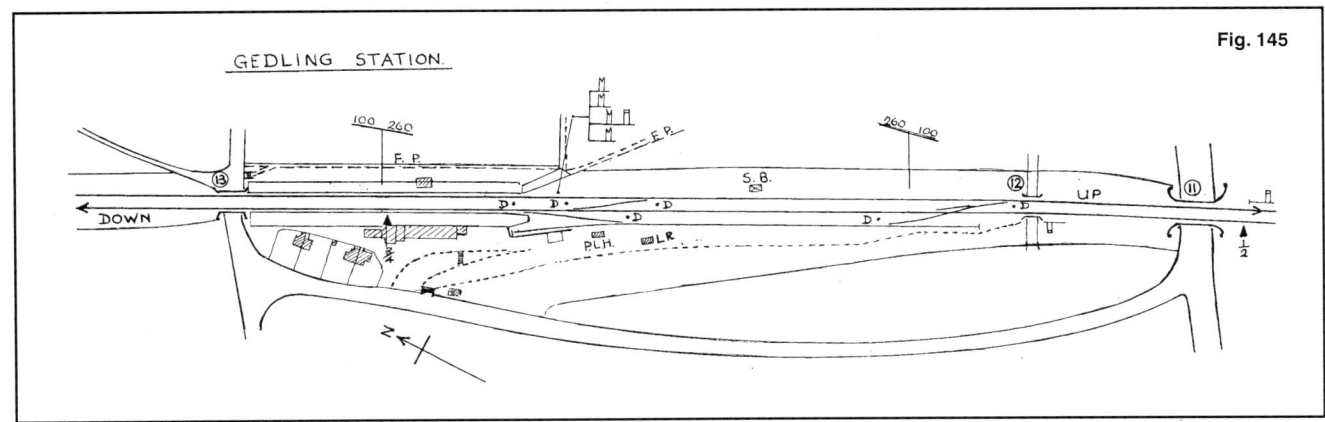

Fig. 145

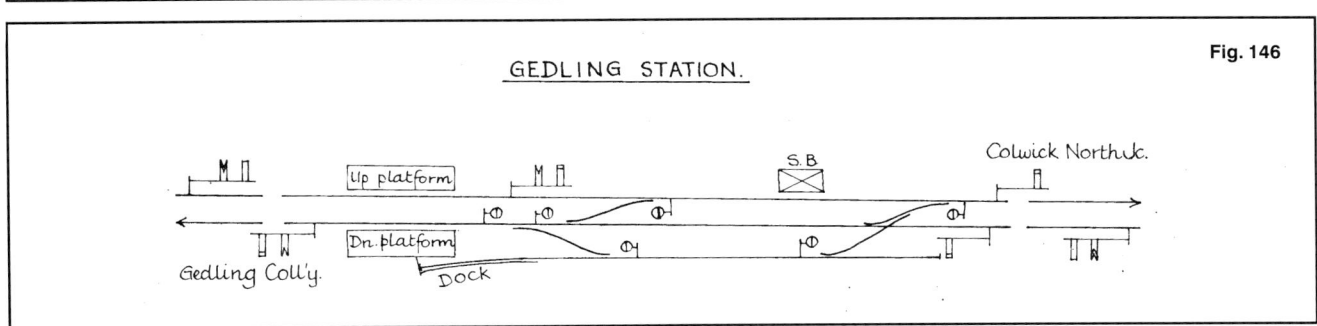

Fig. 146

Fig. 147
An ex LNER Class O4, 2-8-0 hauling a train of iron ore for Stanton is here approaching the Down starting signal at Gedling colliery seen from the overbridge 20. The wooden platforms of the Miners' Halt have been removed from where the train is seen, but the signal box is visible just left of the brake van. Left of the signal post are some wagons standing in the arrival road. Before 1900 this post had the distant signal arm of Mapperley signal box beneath the stop signal, hence the fogman's hut to its right.
September 1959 John R Bonser

GEDLING COLLIERY & Halt 126 m 56 ch - Mapperley Tunnel

Sinking of this new colliery by the Digby Colliery Co was begun in 1900 and by 1902 the Top Hard seam had been reached. The first signal box, opened in December 1882 was built on the Up side and named The Kennels because of its proximity to the South Notts Hunt Meetings, mentioned earlier. Gedling Colliery signal box replaced The Kennels and was inspected in November 1904. A colliery line to a Landsale Wharf in Gedling crossed over the GN lines by bridge 20 a little further north called Cumberlands, and just east of this a Passenger Halt was built in May 1906 (126 m 56 ch) for the use of miners. It consisted of two wooden platforms without shelters, and was lit by oil lamps. An early morning and afternoon weekday miners' train called 'The Paddy' ran between Ilkeston and here calling at the intermediate stations. The stock consisted of old four- and six-wheeled coaches with wooden seats and was frequently hauled by an GNR Class R1 0-8-2 tank engine. With the extension of the colliery and increased output, the layout here was remodelled to allow Down trains to run directly into the Arrival Road, and both Empties and Full sidings increased in number. The rebuilt signal box was renamed Gedling Colliery. This pit was in production until November 1991, but after the closure of Colwick Yards was served with a Single Line branch from Netherfield Junction. At its height, it had a continuously manned pilot working trips into Colwick, returning with empties as required. The Colliery Halt was closed before 1940.

Fig. 149
An official view of Cumberlands occupation bridge 20 which was rebuilt in 1908, facing south-east towards Gedling. This bridge also carried the colliery line to Gedling Landsale Wharf beside Arnold Lane. The signal box in the distance is The Kennels and the double armed somersault signal designed to show above the bridge parapet to approaching trains is the Up home signal.
c. 1910 courtesy British Rail

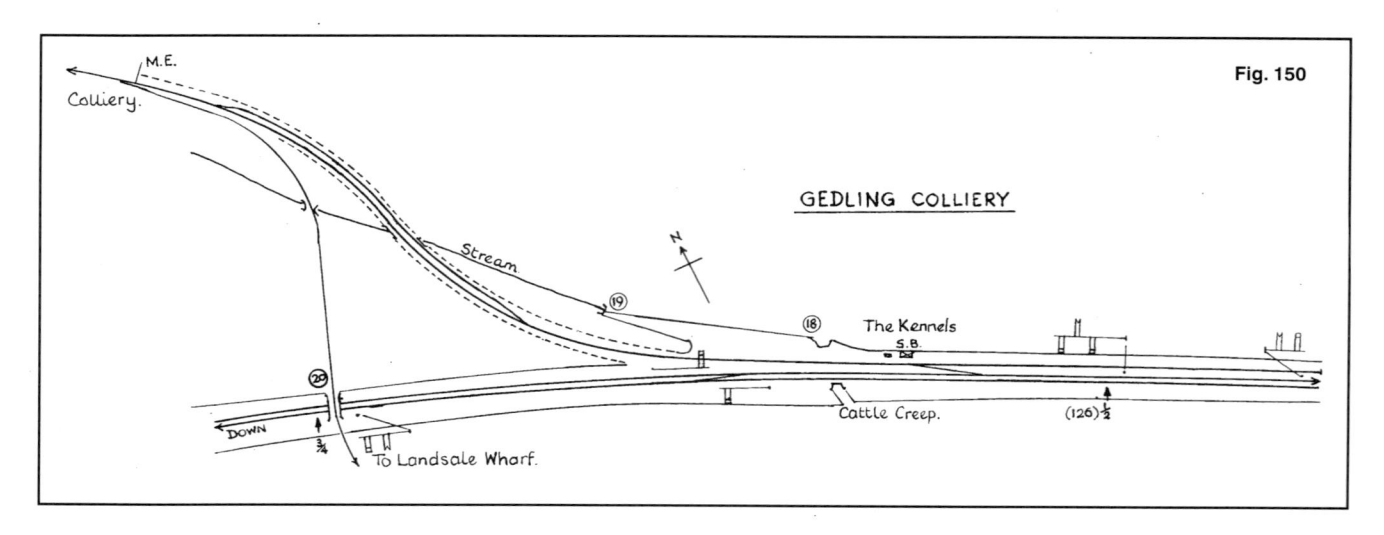

Fig. 150

Fig. 151

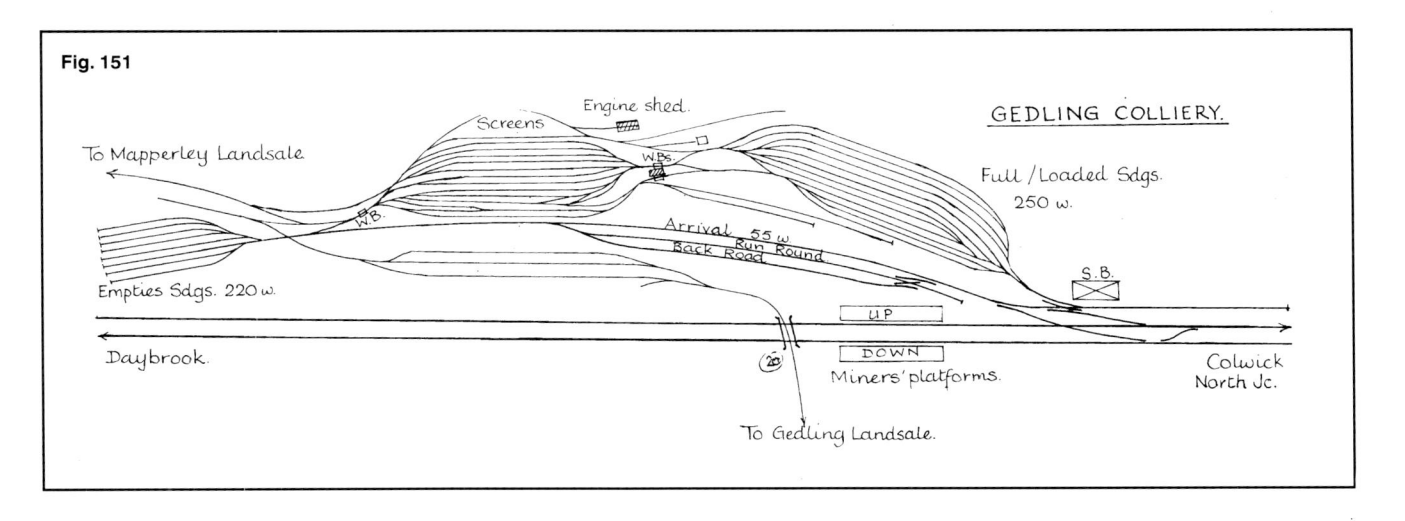

GEDLING COLLIERY.

To Mapperley Landsale

Screens
Engine shed.
W.Ps.
W.B.
Full/Loaded Sdgs. 250 w.
Arrival 55 w.
Run Round
Back Road
Empties Sdgs. 220 w.
S.B.
U.P
DOWN
Daybrook.
Miners' platforms.
To Gedling Landsale.
Colwick North Jc.

Fig. 152

W.B
Colliery Halt
Gedling Coll'y. S.B.
Culvert
Arnold Lane
Lambley Lane

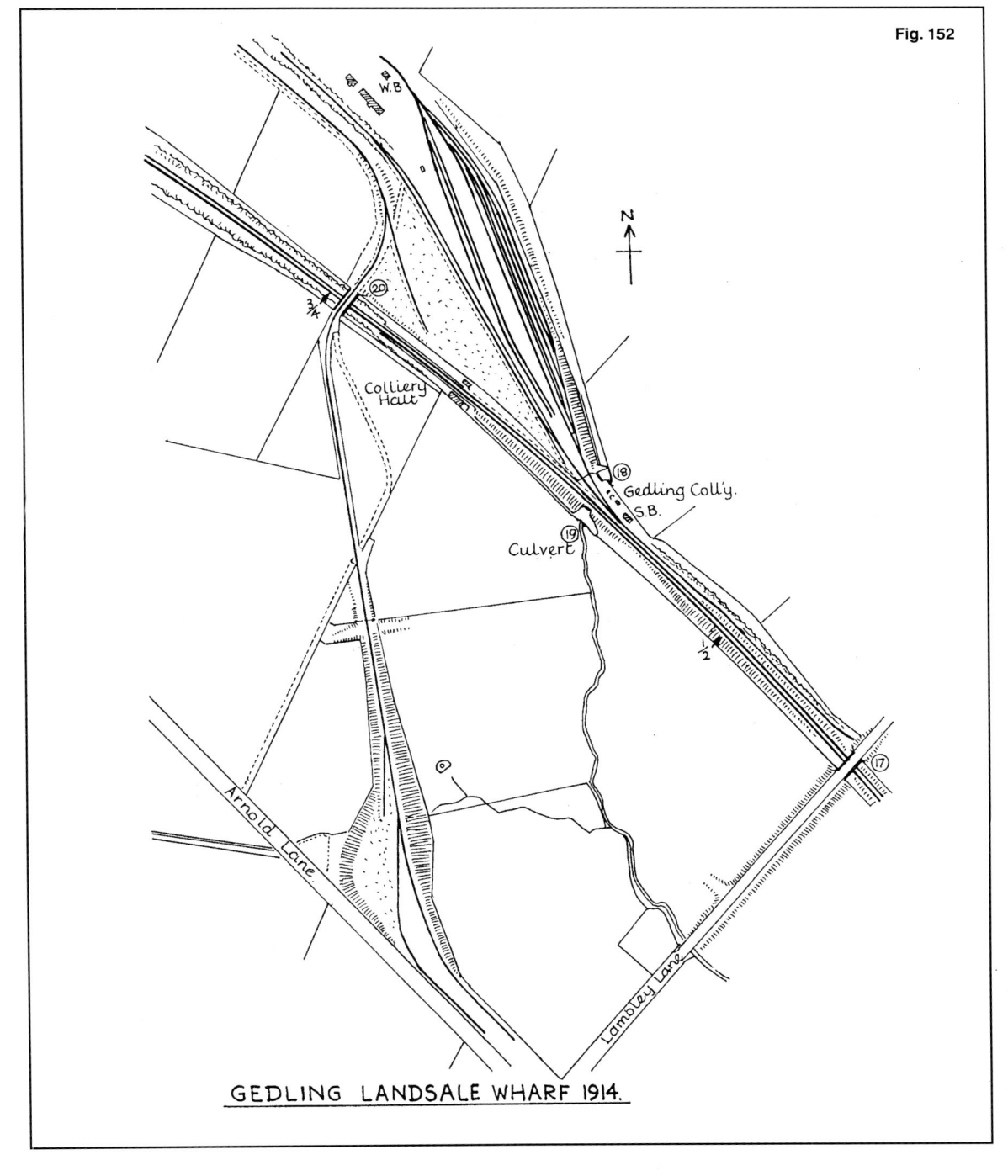

GEDLING LANDSALE WHARF 1914.

At the east end of Mapperley Tunnel at 127 m 18 3/4 ch the GNR built a small signal box named Mapperley to signal Down trains only, and serve as an intermediate Block Post on the long climb from Colwick to Arno Vale. This was opened in December 1882 and replaced with a new signal box in 1900. Having but two levers for a Home and a Distant signal they were affectionately known as 'Mild & Bitter'. After World War 1 it is shown 'switched out', the block being from Gedling Colliery to Arno Vale.

The line still climbs at 1 in 100 through the 1132 yard long Mapperley tunnel. On 23rd January 1925, twelve yards of roofing fell in, burying both lines under some 150 tons of bricks and clay. Until this was removed, and repairs completed, passenger trains were diverted *via* the Nottingham Suburban Line from Daybrook to Nottingham (p84).

Mapperley tunnel continued to prove unsafe, requiring regular monitoring by the engineers and by 1959 plans were made for the lines through it to be reduced to one located down the centre of the bore. The installation of this alteration, together with new signalling and track circuits between Gedling Colliery and Daybrook was to be shared betwen London Midland and Eastern Regions of British Rail, the boundary between these Regions being 127 1/4 milepost. The double tracks from Gedling Colliery were to converge at overbridge no 21, the spring catchpoints at the east portal to be transferred to the Down line east of the bridge. At the western side of the tunnel the single line was to be swung back to the existing Down side where a facing crossover would join it to the Up line. This single line section was to be worked by direction lever and track circuit; the Up direction lever in Gedling Colliery signal box and the Down lever in Daybrook signal box. Each direction lever would release a plunger at the other signal box proving the track clear. To release the signal at the opposite signal box, the direction lever would be reversed and the plunger operated. Only one direction lever could be reversed at a time. Colour light proving signals were to be installed at both ends of the single line section. However the tunnel was finally closed for safety reasons on 4th April 1960, and the plans never implemented. The passenger service from Basford to Nottingham through Daybrook was replaced by a bus service which called at each station until 27th May 1968, when it was withdrawn.

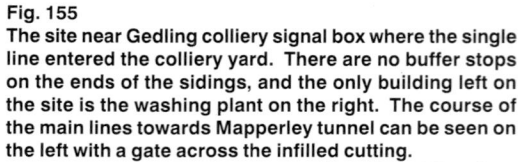

Fig. 153
A six-coupled goods engine of Patrick Stirling design is here seen blasting away up the bank at Gedling towards Mapperley tunnel with the 2.50 pm train of iron ore from Colwick to Stanton.
c. 1910 the late F H Gillford

Fig. 154
The scene at Gedling Landsale Wharf alongside Arnold Lane, which shows a Hunslet six-coupled saddle tank engine 'King George' shunting internal user wagons into the sidings. The roadway from Arnold Lane is behind the train, and the tall spire of Gedling church can be seen faintly in the distance on the left.
1971 C A Hill

Fig. 155
The site near Gedling colliery signal box where the single line entered the colliery yard. There are no buffer stops on the ends of the sidings, and the only building left on the site is the washing plant on the right. The course of the main lines towards Mapperley tunnel can be seen on the left with a gate across the infilled cutting.
May 1993 A Henshaw

62

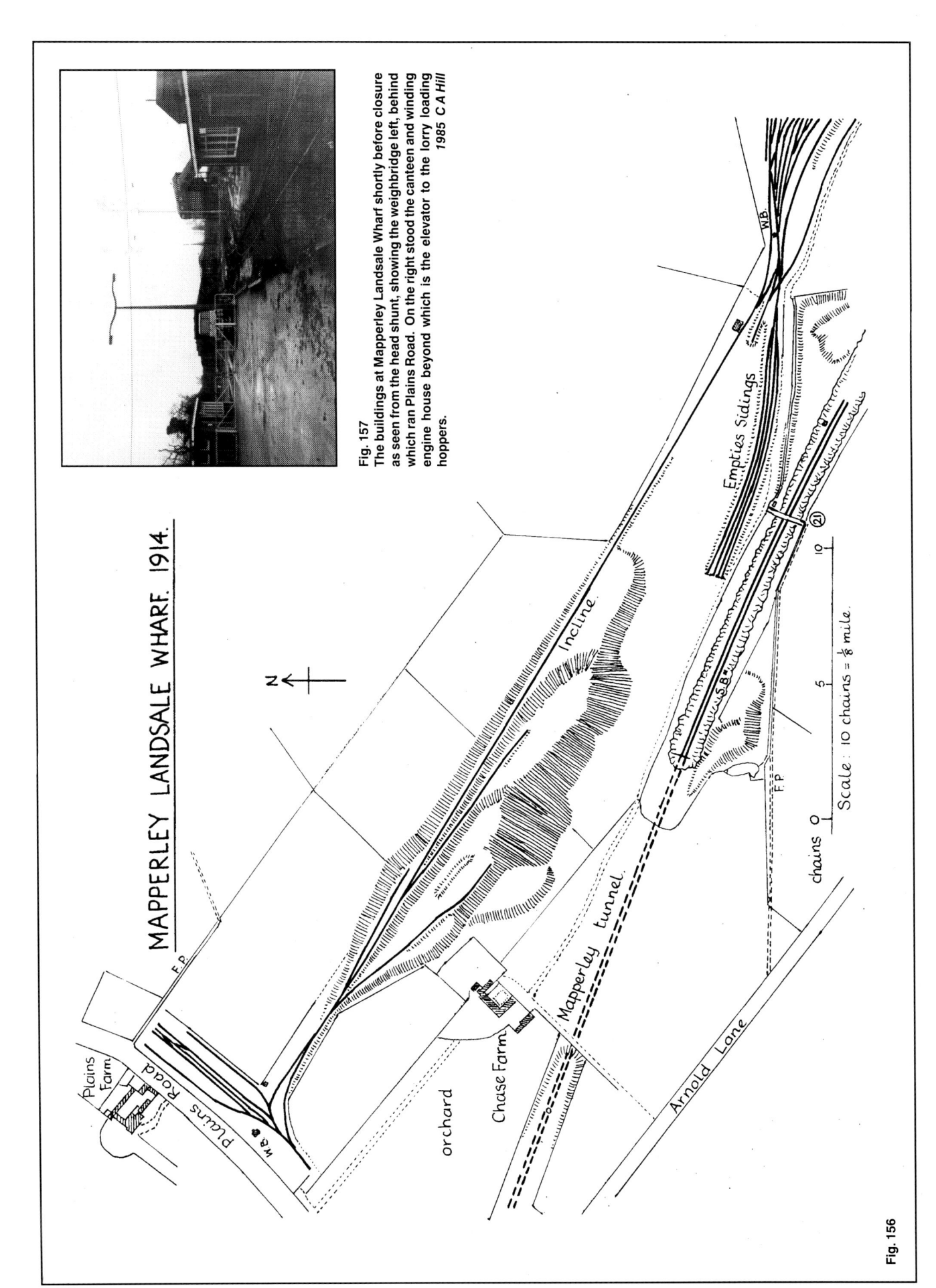

Fig. 157
The buildings at Mapperley Landsale Wharf shortly before closure as seen from the head shunt, showing the weighbridge left, behind which ran Plains Road. On the right stood the canteen and winding engine house beyond which is the elevator to the lorry loading hoppers.
1985 *C A Hill*

MAPPERLEY LANDSALE WHARF. 1914.

Scale: 10 chains = ⅛ mile.

Fig. 156

63

Fig. 158
Looking north-west from between the screens and the empties sidings at Gedling colliery, the steep incline to a large landsale wharf on Mapperley Plains can be seen on the right. Between the two sets of internal user wagons with bright yellow corner plates lie the empties sidings which could hold 220 wagons. *May 1967 D G Birch*

ARNO VALE 128 m 27 1/4 ch

This signal box marks the summit of the climb from Colwick with a short stretch of level track. It was opened in December 1882 and shunt sidings on both Up and Down sides were provided. When the Nottingham Suburban Railway between Daybrook Junction and Trent Lane Junction was singled in 1930, the only passenger trains to use this stretch of line apart from Summer Excursions and holiday traffic for the East Coast resorts not using Nottingham Victoria station, were five Suburban services which ran a shuttle between Basford & Bulwell and Nottingham Victoria *via* Netherfield until the closure of Mapperley tunnel. In 1937 both Mapperley and Arno Vale signal boxes were closed. The latter signal box and its shunt sidings were removed in November 1950. Intermediate Block signals (colour lights) replaced the signal boxes.

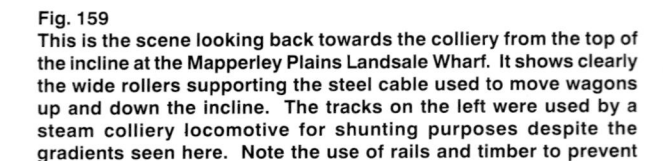

Fig. 159
This is the scene looking back towards the colliery from the top of the incline at the Mapperley Plains Landsale Wharf. It shows clearly the wide rollers supporting the steel cable used to move wagons up and down the incline. The tracks on the left were used by a steam colliery locomotive for shunting purposes despite the gradients seen here. Note the use of rails and timber to prevent the track on the left from slipping. *September 1958 John R Bonser*

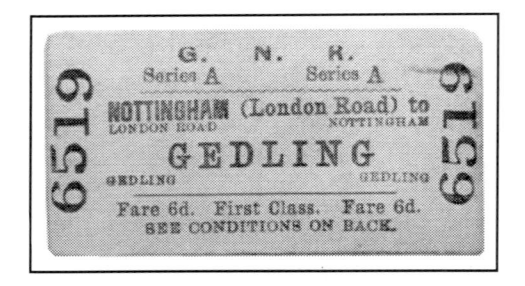

Fig. 160
This shows the wagon tippler with an internal user wagon inside. Part of the bunker is visible on the right behind the stairway. The incline to the colliery led from the track on the left where the shunter holds his pole. *September 1958 John R Bonser*

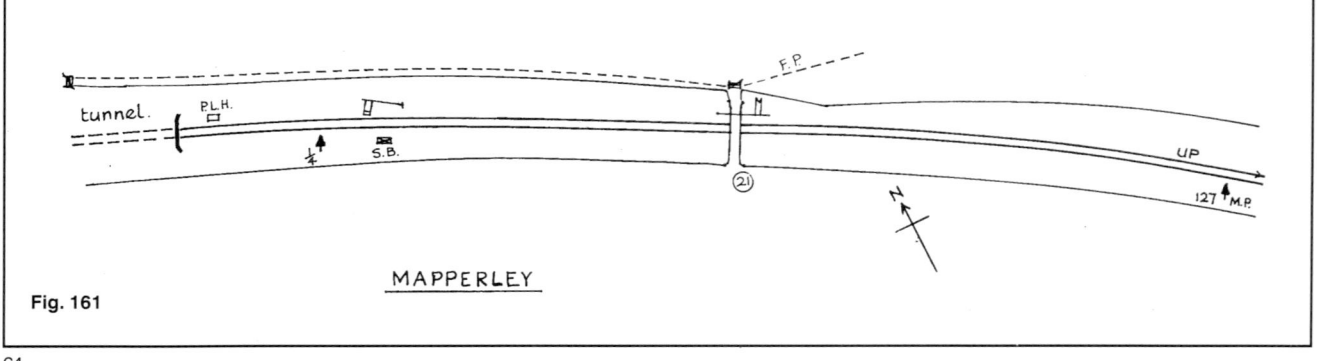

Fig. 161

Fig. 162

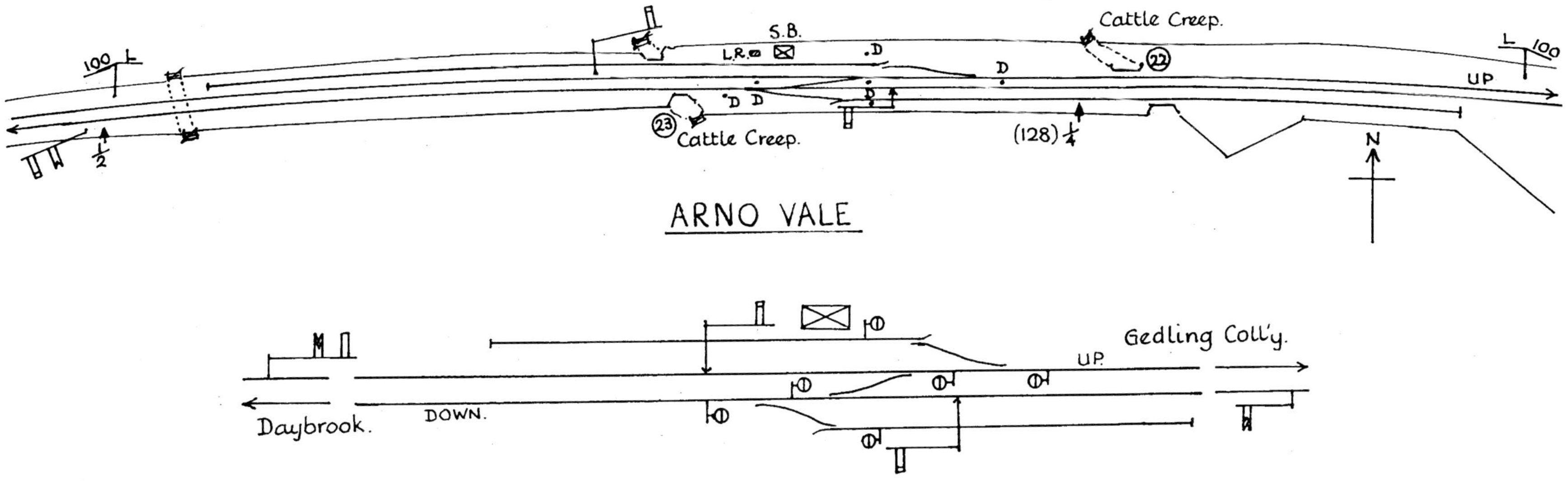

ARNO VALE

Fig. 163
The western portal of Mapperley tunnel showing clearly the straight bore and the nameboard stating the length of 1132 yards. Pointing on the brickwork of the abutments and coping over the entrance indicate subsidence but that can hardly be the reason for the missing stone on the right? Perhaps frequent work inside the tunnel necessitates a second Engineers' hut on the left. The one nearest the camera shows no windows facing the rails like the further one. Note the very long ladder on the left.
c. 1905 Courtesy *British Rail*

Fig. 164
Ex LNER Class K3 2-6-0 No 61833 having climbed from Daybrook is here idling downhill towards the tunnel and Gedling with a mixed goods train. The intermediate colour light block signal which replaced Arno Vale's semaphores shows up clearly, and the stone above the right hand abutment is back in place.
1955 *C A Hill*

Fig. 165
This fine view from above the west end of Mapperley tunnel well illustrates the hilly nature of the route taken by the Derbyshire Extensions out of Colwick, a route which incurred heavy civil engineering as it cut through hills and crossed intervening valleys. A short train of mostly coal filled wagons headed by an Austerity 2-8-0 and bound for Colwick is about to enter the tunnel.
July 1957 J Cupit

Fig. 166
Ex LNER Class L1 2-6-4 tank engine hauling a short train from Nottingham Victoria to Basford & Bulwell is passing the site of Arno Vale signalbox which stood on the far side of the tracks. The ground in the right corner held the Down shunt siding, which together with a similar one on the Up side would frequently be used to shunt goods trains for passenger trains to pass during the early part of this century and before the Joint station (Victoria) was built in Nottingham.
1959 C A Hill

Fig. 167
Working a train of coal from Babbington Colliery to Colwick is an ex LNER Class J50 tank engine 68967, seen between bridge 24 and Arno Vale. These engines together with J52 saddle tanks of similar ex LNER Class 0-6-0 wheel arrangement were used for shunting and pilot duties, making occasional trips with trains into Colwick from nearby yards and depots.
1959 C A Hill

Fig. 168
H A Ivatt's GNR class A (LNER J6) was a real maid-of-all-work, seen regularly throughout the Nottingham area on goods and passenger trains, including East Coast excursions in summer time. Here is 64183 returning to Colwick with a train of mineral empties having passed beneath Hallam's Lane bridge 24 between Daybrook and Arno Vale.
1956 C A Hill

Fig 169
This photograph of the wooden signal box standing beside the Up shunt line is the only one the author has been able to locate. It is an early one possibly taken around 2 pm when the signalmen were changing shifts, unless one of the men is the lampman whose cabin was to the left of the steps.
Notts County Library

Fig. 170
Mapperley tunnel is now filled in, and this is all that can be seen at the west end, which is well obscured by vegetation. The cutting behind the photographer is filled in level with the original land, and has a large brick Scout hut near to the road which crosses over the infill. However the filling dips down to the track level just before the tunnel mouth (see Fig. 163 p65).
August 1992 A Henshaw

Fig. 171
When accident or failure caused delays on the Great Central main lines between Sheffield and Nottingham, important trains were diverted *via* Killamarsh Junction and Shirebrook to the Leen Valley line to reach Nottingham or Colwick. Here is an example of such a diverted special for Cambridge carrying its working number between the headlamps on the buffer beam. LNER Class B1 4-6-0 61367 is climbing towards Arno Vale from Daybrook.
1956 C A Hill

67

Fig. 172
When this station opened for traffic in 1875 it was similar to Basford & Bulwell in 1880 (Fig. 196 p77), but the opening of the Leen Valley line in 1881 and the Nottingham Suburban Railway in 1889 necessitated alterations and additions. This is the east end of the station taken from an enlargement of a photograph of the whole footbridge. It shows Daybrook Junction signalbox and the junction to the Suburban line swinging to the right beyond bridge 26 over the Nottingham-Mansfield road, with the roofs of buildings alongside that road appearing above the wooden fencing on both sides of the track. The Up home signals on the gantry have repeater 'sky' arms to show above bridge 27 west of the station, and the Down home signal which protects the junction has also a tall post. Its arms are obscured by the right hand side of the gantry, but the lower spectacle plates can be seen beneath it.
c. 1904 Courtesy British Rail

Fig. 173
This superb all-embracing view of the passenger station shows how clean and tidy things were maintained quite near to its closure. The standard type of building as seen at Gedling is on the Up platform with the addition of a brick lean-to on the west end of the Gentlemen's toilet. Peeping above the footbridge is the upper quadrant arm of Up starting signal No 16 standing where the gantry at Daybrook station formerly was. The rising gradient of 1 in 100 is noticeable along the track beyond the platforms and parapets of bridge 26. The wooden waiting rooms on the Down platform are partially blocked by the water column and its brazier with stove pipe, needed in severe winter weather on this elevated location. Note the GNR gaslamps along the platforms and on the footbridge together with the buffer stop on the Down shunt, right.
May 1960 John Marshall

Fig. 174
After the Suburban line was singled in 1930 access was gained from the Down main line by means of a Ground Frame released from Daybrook signalbox and signalled with a miniature or shunting arm, well pictured here. Note the telephone box and cupboards on the right and the block instrument above the levers, for communication with the signalman some 300 yards away.
October 1954 the late A G Cramp

DAYBROOK   128 m 79 1/2 ch

On the opening of the line on 23 August 1875 this Station was named Bestwood & Arnold, but after the commencement of passenger services, was renamed Daybrook for Arnold and Bestwood Park in March 1876 and by 1st August of that year simply reverted to Daybrook. The two platforms were opposite, and connected by a lattice wrought iron girder bridge (26A at 129 m 0 ch) on cast iron columns and staircases.

The station buildings were of standard pattern used for most of the Derbyshire Extension, with the Stationmaster's House on the Up platform, and the smaller wooden waiting rooms on the Down side. The goods yard had a brick-built goods shed with adjoining office, two coal roads for retail merchants, a brick-built office and cart weighbridge, and dock. The yard crane had a lifting capacity of 10 tons. With the transfer of the R1 0-8-2 tank engines (Baltics) to Colwick for working coal trains around 1913 a water crane was fixed at the end of the Down platform. The limited water capacity of these locomotives' tanks would not always guarantee sufficient water to last as far as Newstead, Eastwood or Ilkeston, where the next supply was available.

Fig. 175

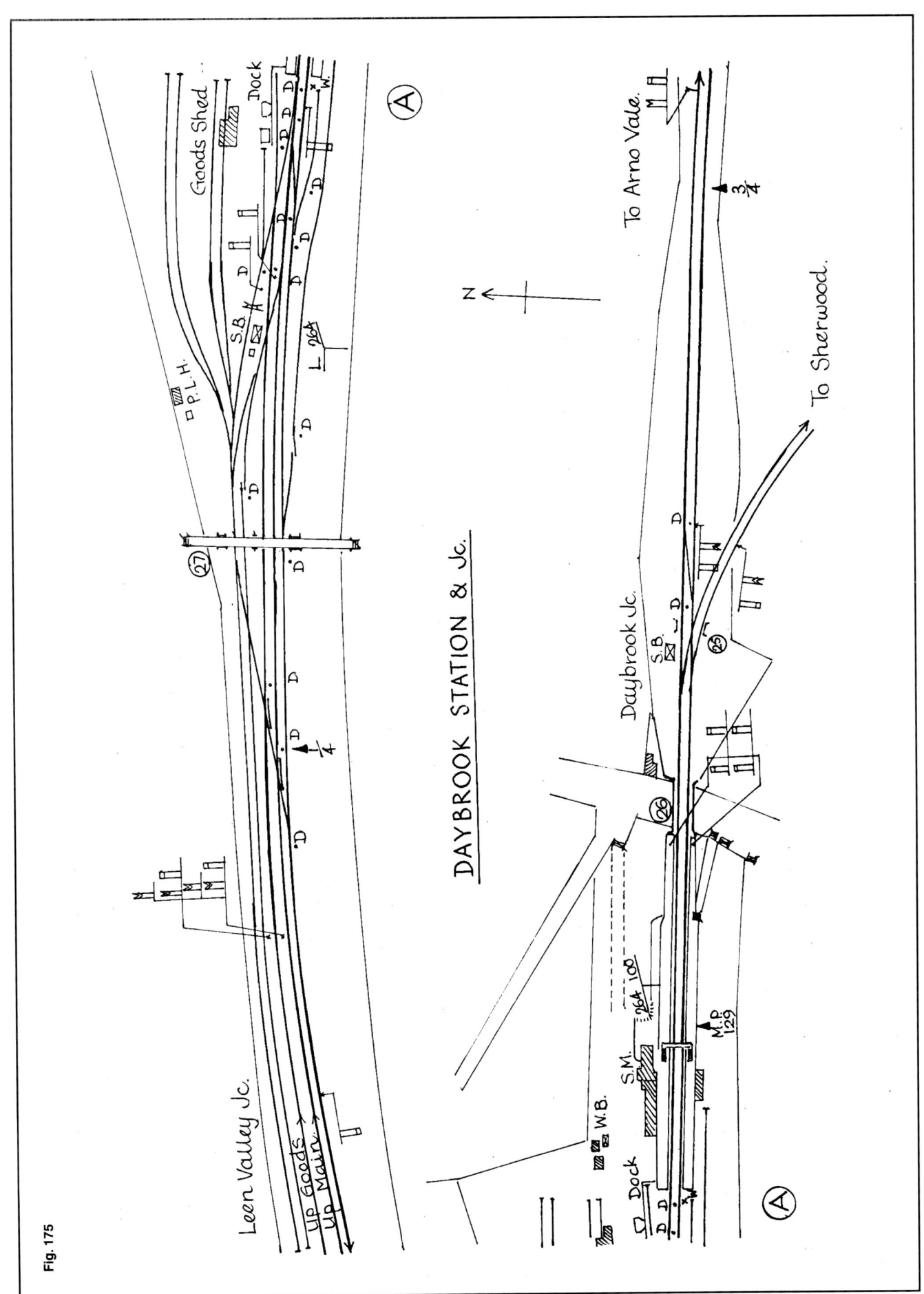

DAYBROOK STATION & Jc.

Fig. 176
Another overall view, now of the west end of the platforms which shows the layout, signalbox and Goods yard clear of trains to fill in the details of the plan at Fig. 175. From left to right across the scene are a) the Down shunt siding beyond which is the abutment of bridge 27, b) the water column, for use by the GNR Class 0-8-2 'Baltic' tank engines and pilot engines chiefly, and the Down home signal with Leen Valley Junction's distant arm beneath it, c) the signalbox and the Up home signals either side of the Up Goods line, d) the dock and cattle pen, beyond which are the yard sidings and a Platelayer's Hut, e) the brick Goods shed and office with the typical hand crane close by. Finally come the station buildings with the 'Way Out' sign at the double-door entrance to the Booking Hall, and a bedroom window above the entrance to the Booking/Parcels office. To the right of this doorway are three gaspipes connected at the top to valves for reducing pressure and dimming lights during air raids in wartime. A removable key controlled this operation. *May 1960 John Marshall*

Fig. 177
This scene, looking east from bridge 27, embraces the layout and buildings of the goods yard and station itself, with little encumbrance from wagons or trains as it might have appeared on a Sunday. A few wagons stand in the coal sidings, left; the next pair serve the goods shed, seen behind the signal box. The line immediately behind the latter passed beneath the loading gauge and to the dock/cattle pen. On the right is the Down shunt siding, with the adjacent main lines and slow line which joined the Up main line near the end of the platform.
May 1960 John Marshall

Fig. 178
This photograph of the west side of bridge 27 shows up the earlier type of ballasting the track with fine material covering the sleepers. There are many wagons in the Goods yard, seen through the left span, and the line behind the signalbox to the Dock. The wider span bridges the Up Goods line and both Main lines with the Down shunt branching off right just beyond the abutment. The lamp room is partly visible behind the middle pillar, and a passenger train stands in the Up platform, beyond which are the tall signals on the gantry at Daybrook Junction.
c. 1904 Courtesy British Rail

Daybrook Junction, just east of bridge 26 over the Mansfield Road was built at 128 m 71 1/4 ch to connect the Nottingham Suburban Railway from Trent Lane Junction in 1889. The inauguration of electric tram, and later, bus services effectively stifled passenger traffic from its three stations, but the local brickworks provided much traffic in addition to the basic coal and goods traffic of local merchants. The Junction signal box closed on 14th September 1934, when the Suburban line was singled. Private Sidings dealt with by Daybrook station included Wm Wright's Wagon Repairs, Nottingham Corporation Hospital (now called City Hospital), and Nottingham Guardians' Workhouse.

The passenger station closed on April 4th 1960 with the closure of Mapperley tunnel, but two private excursions to Cleethorpes started from Daybrook on 21st May 1961, and 10th June 1962, running via the Leen Valley line and Annesley. A bus service calling at the stations from Basford & Bulwell to Netherfield and Nottingham Victoria replaced the passenger trains, tickets still being obtained from the station Booking Office! Goods traffic continued until 1st June 1964, being worked via Basford & Bulwell along a single line, and the lines beyond the station towards Mapperley tunnel were used for storage of unwanted cripple wagons for a time. The track was lifted by June 1966.

East of Edwards Lane bridge 29 which is now packed with earth, a new school occupies the ground, and further still towards Daybrook are more new houses. Bridge 26 over Mansfield Road has gone and a Car Park/Supermarket occupy the east side of the road. From here it is possible to walk to Woodthorpe Park along the trackbed as far as Arno Vale where a new road and housing estate cut across the line to reach down to Arno Vale Road. This latter cuts through the line of the GNR to climb up to Plains Road at Mapperley, above the tunnel, which is now filled in.

Fig. 179
This view of the main buildings and Station House shows the rear side facing east from the access to the Goods yard beside Station Road. This design was used for most of the stations between Gedling and Egginton Junction along the Derbyshire Extension. The private yard to the Station House is behind the dark fencing on the left. The door which is boarded up gave access to the Parcels/Booking Office without the need to go through the nearby Booking Hall to the platform.
October 1965 B Walker

Fig. 180
The end of Daybrook station is imminent now the rails have been removed, together with bridge 27 which carried an occupation road over the railway. However an unobstructed view of the buildings is given beyond the north abutment on the left which includes the yard crane and Goods shed as well as the footbridge spanning the platforms and the water column.
October 1965 B Walker

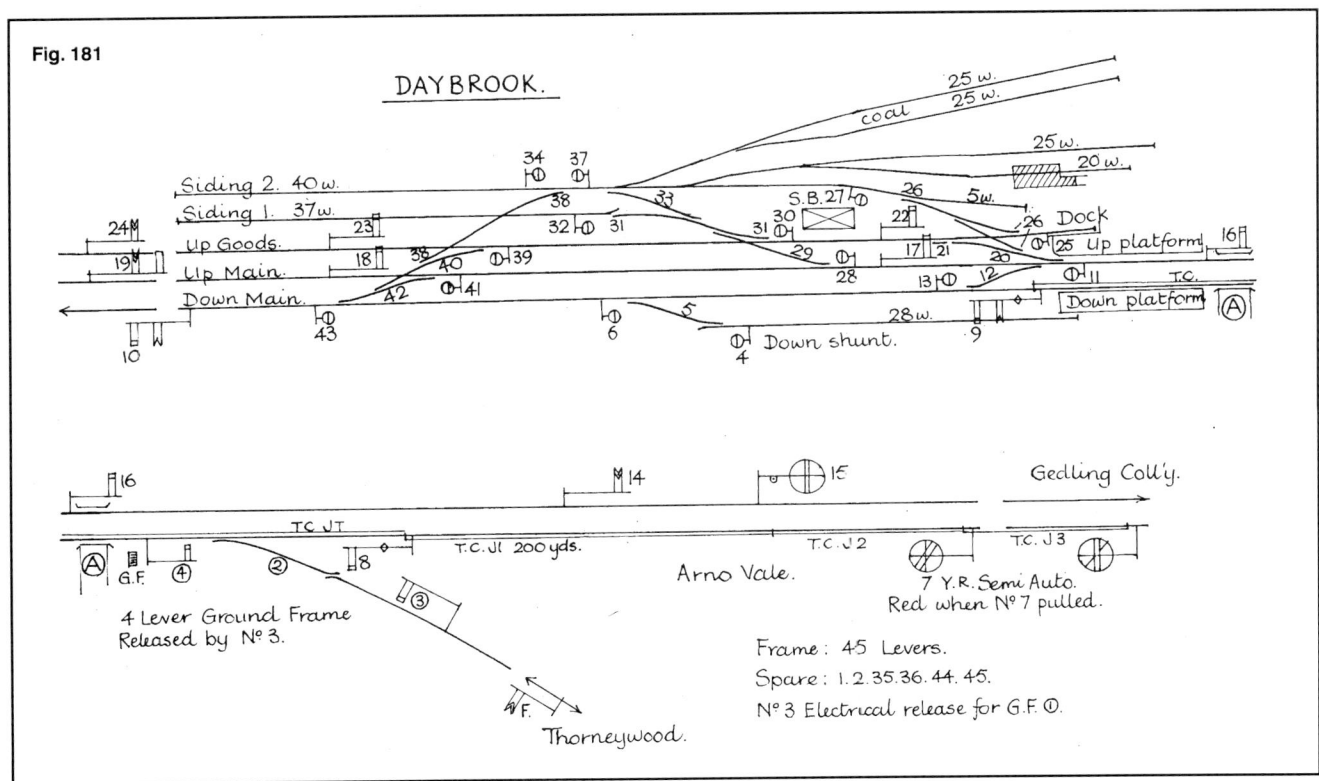

Fig. 182
A close view of the signalbox facing east Towards the Goods shed and station which shows the circular platform holding the yard crane, Right of the station buildings and straddling the line behind the signalbox is the loading gauge.   *May 1960 John Marshall*

Fig. 183
This detailed shot of the base of the Yard crane has the doors of the Goods Shed in the background. The crane was hand-operated, had a wooden jib, and a capacity of 10 tons. Similar cranes were provided at most of the stations along the Derbyshire Extension. They were made by Kirkstall Forge Company. The makers plate at the base of the jib bore the legend 'To lift not more than 6 tons single chain and 10 tons double chain'.
October 1965 B Walker

Fig. 184
Daybrook station has gone and bridge 26 over the A60 to Redhill and Mansfield demolished for that busy road to be widened there. The footpath from bridge 29 at Edwards Lane (now filled in) follows alongside the trackbed, passing a new school and playing field and further along some modern houses until reaching the A60. On the east side of the road is a Superstore and car park as shown in this view.
August 1992 A Henshaw

Fig. 185
Inevitable increase in road traffic necessitated widening bridge 29 in the 1930s, and this view of the west side shows the newer widened section with the original arches beyond. The signals on the left are Leen Valley Junction Up Main starter and Daybrook's Up distant signals, the left hand arm, partly cut off is an upper quadrant type. The fog signalman's hut is also included. On the right can be seen the entrance to the Down Loop put in in 1940 as an extension of the existing Down shunt.
September 1953 the late R W Sheppard

LEEN VALLEY JUNCTION 129 m 74 3/4 ch

This important junction was not part of the Derbyshire Extensions, but opened on 9th May 1881 for coal from Bestwood Colliery via a single line at first, and for passenger traffic to and from Newstead on October 10th 1882, by which time the lines were doubled. An Up loop or Goods Line between here and Daybrook was laid, along which coal trains could stand nose to tail awaiting acceptance for marshalling at Colwick, between the passenger services to Nottingham London Road. The junction was sited at 129 m 76 ch from King's Cross. Seven sidings for marshalling and storage with a capacity of 420 wagons were built on the Up side around the turn of the century, when William Wrights established a wagon repair works here. On the Down side was a shunt siding, transfer road, and Private Sidings to the Hospital and Workhouse mentioned under Daybrook Station's responsibility. During the 1940s the Down shunt siding was extended as far as bridge 29 carrying Edwards Lane over the railway at 129 m 43 ch, and electrically operated facing points laid to make a Down Loop. All train movements except Stopping Passengers were reported to Control by Leen Valley Junction.

A train was booked from Colwick at 7.15 am for Leen Valley on weekdays pre-1939, and the engine performed pilot (shunting) duties during the morning, and worked at Bulwell Forest wagon works in the afternoon. The engine which shunted at Daybrook during the morning worked traffic from Leen Valley Junction over the Suburban line to London Road, and returned to Colwick with a train from Nottingham. This working ceased after the air raids on Nottingham on 8/9th May 1941 which damaged much property around Sneinton and in particular the embankment near bridge 4 (which was closed) over Colwick Road. Thereafter traffic was worked over the Single Line branch as far as Thorneywood, then back to Leen Valley Junction, and into Colwick.

Fig. 186
Edwards Lane crosses the line by this bridge (29) between Daybrook station and Leen Valley Junction. Originally the one segmental arch spanned the two running lines which continued through to Basford & Bulwell, then on to Pinxton, but with the building of the Leen Valley line and the Junction signalbox traffic for Colwick increased rapidly, and resulted in the building of an additional Goods Line alongside the Up Main between Leen Valley Junction and Daybrook along which goods trains were allowed to proceed with caution nose to tail under Permissive Block regulations. The brickwork of the additional arch on the left shows clearly here. Note also the tall bracket signal holding two Down Distant arms of Leen Valley Junction.
c. 1905 Courtesy British Rail

Fig. 187
This view, facing west from Edwards Lane bridge shows LNER Class O1 2-8-0 63768 hauling a train of ironstone from Colwick to Stanton, and includes the four running lines, signals and fogman's hut seen in Fig. 186.
1956 C A Hill

Fig. 188
From the footpath parallel to the line of the railway on the right can be seen the houses beyond the school playing field. This new estate reaches as far as the old station itself, where the footpath descends to Mansfield Road at Fig. 179 p71.
August 1992 A Henshaw

73

Fig. 189

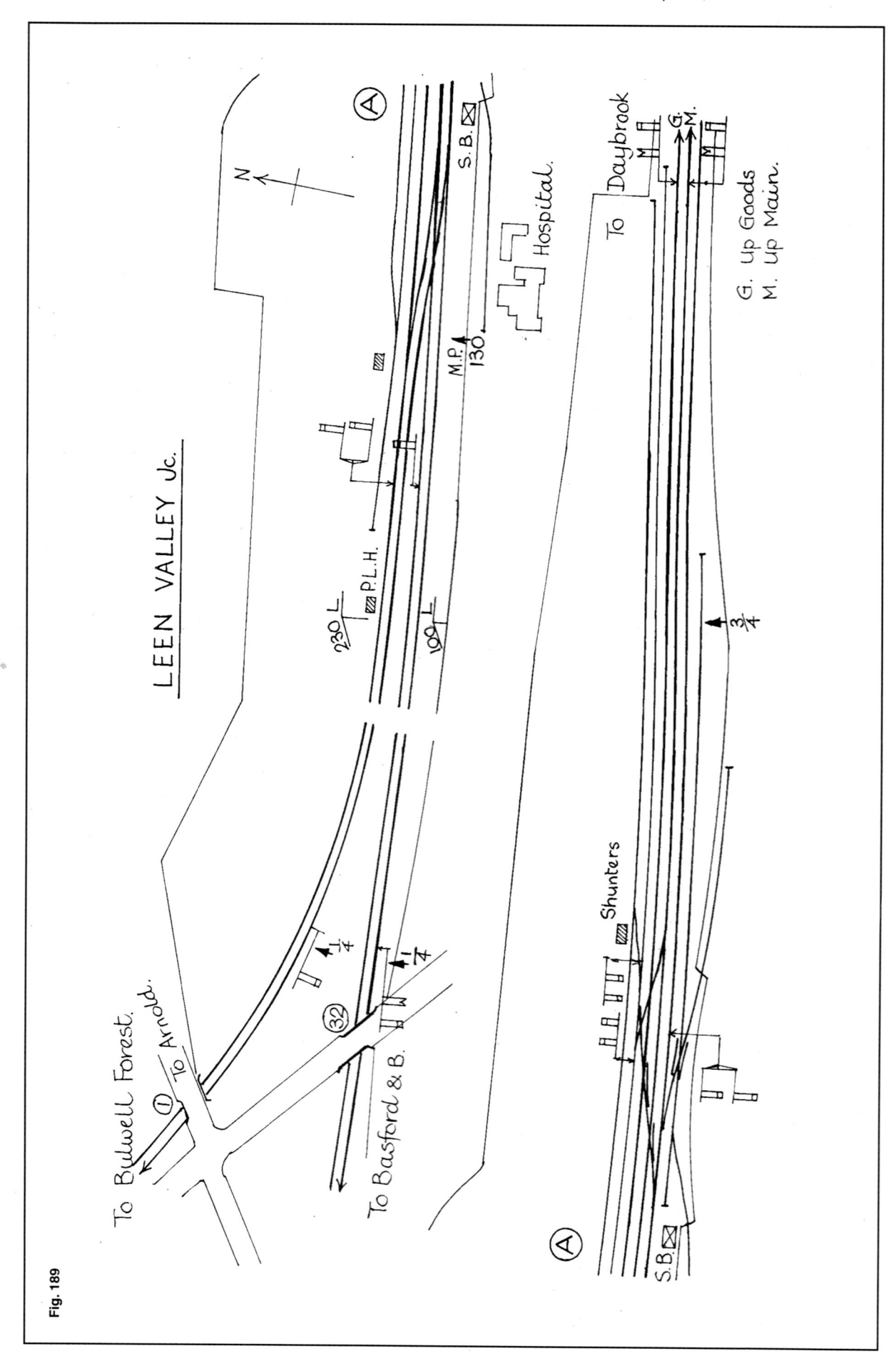

Fig. 190 — LEEN VALLEY Jc. 1942.

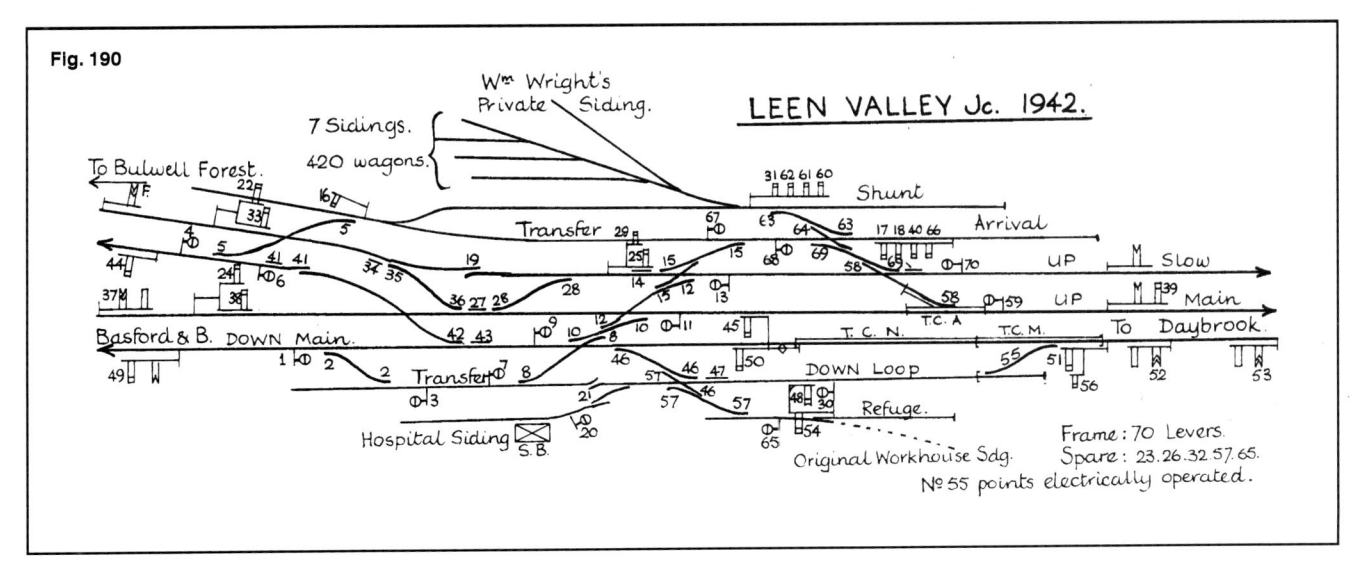

Fig. 191
A view of the scene at Leen Valley Junction shortly before the track was lifted and the site cleared, looking west and showing the signals, signalbox and shunters' cabins (right). The line in the middle foreground is the headshunt for the yard sidings in the distance. Beside it to the left is the yard arrival road, followed by the Up slow or goods line. Then came the Up and Down main lines with the Down loop already removed from between the two bracket signal posts holding the Home signals. The miniature shunting signals on the right were much more clearly seen by drivers and yard staff than ground or disc signals frequently used for short movements.
April 1965 A Henshaw

The line to Daybrook was closed on 1st June 1964, and that from Bestwood Junction through Bulwell Forest on 3rd December 1964, apart from a single line operated as a siding, between Leen Valley Junction and William Rigley's, who were cutting up locomotives which had been withdrawn for scrap. After Rigley's closed on 6th March 1966 the line was lifted and the land sold to Nottingham City Corporation who have made a pleasant footpath along its route. Bridge 33 carrying Hucknall Road over the trackbed near Leen Valley Junction is filled in with earth and fenced off on the east side. From here eastwards to Edwards Lane bridge 29, three-storey flats and more houses have been built, but it is possible to walk along footpaths through these near to the course of the line. To the south, extensions to the City Hospital are encroaching, making the course of the railway difficult to recognise.

Fig. 192
This shows the lampman's view of the junction and sidings facing east from the platform of the Up Main Home signals. One wonders if the diamond crossing from the Up Transfer and Arrival roads has been recently renewed from the new ballast there!
April 1965 A Henshaw

Fig. 193
On Saturday 19th September 1959, the Railway Correspondence and Travel Society organised a special Rail Tour of Nottinghamshire and Derbyshire from Nottingham London Road Low Level station *via* Netherfield & Colwick, Daybrook, the Leen Valley line and Extension to Shirebrook North where the train reversed, to return south down the Erewash Valley lines of the Midland Railway. Here the special train is seen taking the junction at Leen Valley. On the right, a mineral train stands on the arrival road to the yard awaiting the Special's passing to follow it. There are plenty of wagons in the distant yard sidings beyond the engine of the mineral train.
September 1959 John Marshall

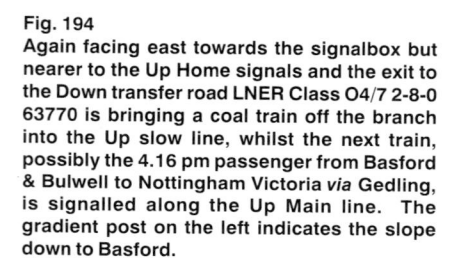

Fig. 194
Again facing east towards the signalbox but nearer to the Up Home signals and the exit to the Down transfer road LNER Class O4/7 2-8-0 63770 is bringing a coal train off the branch into the Up slow line, whilst the next train, possibly the 4.16 pm passenger from Basford & Bulwell to Nottingham Victoria *via* Gedling, is signalled along the Up Main line. The gradient post on the left indicates the slope down to Basford.
March 1960 the late A G Cramp

Fig. 195
This shows a more normal scene of activity around Leen Valley Junction during an afternoon period. The difference in level between the branch newly ballasted, and the Main lines to Basford shows clearly. A Thompson rebuilt LNER Class O1 2-8-0 63768 is approaching on the Down main line with a train of mineral wagons, and the yard sidings on the left have a variety of wagons in them.
March 1960 the late A G Cramp

Fig. 196

BASFORD & BULWELL 1880

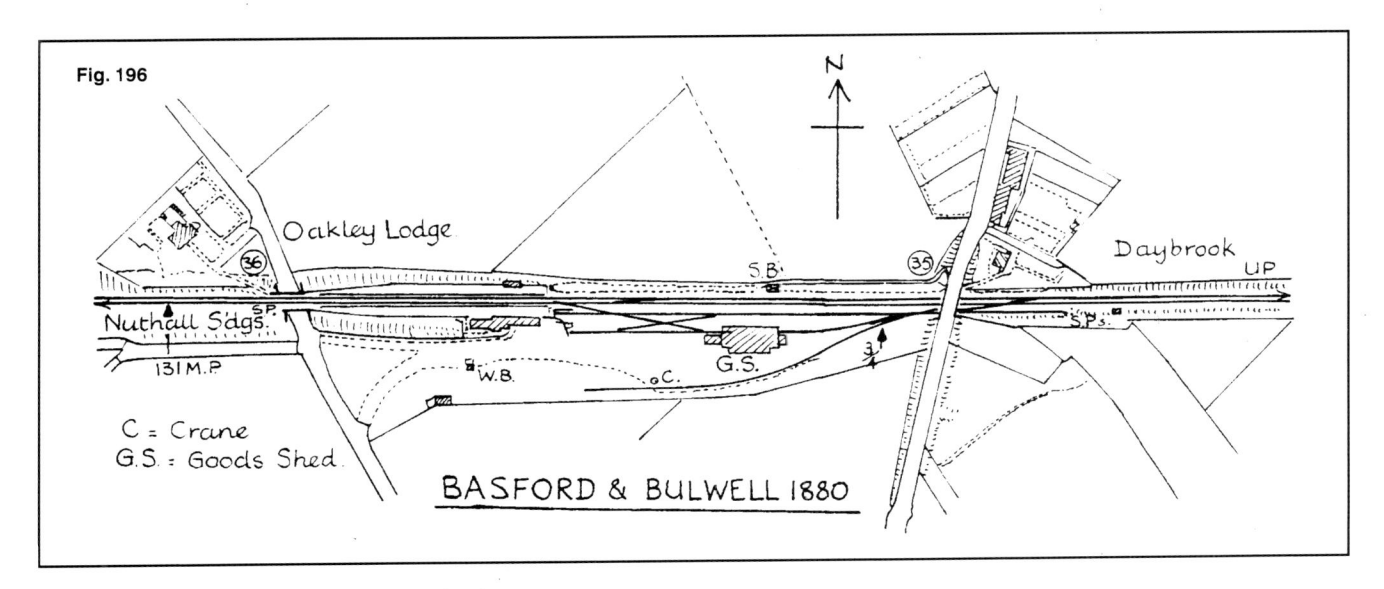

C = Crane
G.S. = Goods Shed

BASFORD & BULWELL 130 m 71 3/4 ch

When opened for Goods traffic on 23rd August 1875 this station was named New Basford for Dob Park and Bulwell. Bridge 35, east of the station carries Park Lane over the rails. Passenger services began 1st February 1876, and by August of that year the station was renamed Basford & Bulwell. Initially it was the usual type of through station with the main buildings on the Down side, the smaller wooden waiting rooms, including a miners' room, on the opposite Up platform. There was a spacious Goods Yard with a crane of 10 tons capacity, a large Goods shed with upper storey and adjoining office, and a cart weighbridge. A unique feature of these buildings is that they were of local limestone, with corner stones alternating between dark gritstone and lighter limestone. A large house named Oakley Lodge, after Sir Henry Oakley, the General Manager of the GNR, was built on the Bulwell (north) side of the line west of bridge 36. This house, to the same design as the one at Colwick for the Locomotive Superintendent, was for the Superintendent of the Line. After much alteration and modification it still stands and is used as a Social Club.

Considerable alterations and extensions were made in 1898 with the Great Central Railway's London Extension coming through Bulwell to Nottingham Victoria, which station was shared with the GNR.

A double line junction from the east end of the platforms curved away to the left to Bulwell South Junction and immediately east of bridge 35 was a Down side branch from Bagthorpe Junction, The Up connection burrowed beneath the GN main lines to Leen Valley Junction, passed through a 90-yard long tunnel, and joined the GC Up main line at Bagthorpe Junction. This short stretch was known as the Rat Hole. In the triangle of sandstone between the GC embankment and the Down curve from Bagthorpe a large turntable (54ft 10 in) was built with an ash pit road and run round, and between Arnold Lane and the GC lines were the GNR carriage sidings.

The GCR was granted running powers over the south to west curve to the Derbyshire Extension collieries. Basford now became a busy junction, and, being the first station on the Control section to Burton reported all train movements to Control except Stopping Passengers.

The Goods Yard was altered also. Two roads were extended behind the Down platform forming a bay platform used for the Basford-Nottingham Victoria passenger trains which served the Back Line and Netherfield. A shunting spur extended beyond bridge 35 curving round beside the Down curve from Bagthorpe Junction. M/s Whiteley Read had a Private Siding reached from the Back road in the Goods Yard and protected by a gate. The Down shunt siding held 38 wagons with engine and brake van.

Fig. 197
How clean the locomotives, stock and properties were kept in the early days, when traffic was abundant and competition for it came only from rival railways! Here is a very smart-looking LNER Class D1 4-4-0 designed by H A Ivatt, built in February 1903, and withdrawn in October 1949. It is standing in the platform to the rear of the main buildings, sometimes called the bay, although there were other sidings on the south side (foreground) and no platform. The train is bound for Nottingham Victoria via Gedling and the stock is of Gresley design. The crew is obviously aware of the photographer.
c.1920 S L S

Fig. 198
This is the south face of bridge 36 spanning Vernon Road, Basford, in the foreground, and Highbury Road, Bulwell, beyond the arch, with fencing at the end of the Down platform on the right. The rails and overhead wires for the recently introduced electric trams feature here, and the notice on the arch reads: 'Keep your seats. It is dangerous to touch the wires'. The upper deck of these early trams was uncovered.
c. 1904 courtesy British Rail

After nationalisation, to avoid confusion with Midland Railway names, the Goods Depot was called Basford North from 1st July 1950, the Passenger station following suit on 21st September 1953. After the closure of Mapperley tunnel and withdrawal of passenger trains in 1960 some track recovery took place resulting in Daybrook Goods being served by a 'One Engine in Steam' arrangement from Basford using the Up Main line only.

The Sunday passenger services to the west were withdrawn on 11th November 1962, and all passengers withdrawn on 7th September 1964. Final closure to all traffic was on 2nd October 1967. Track was lifted in 1969-70 and taken to Derby Road Depot of M/s T W Ward, on the Stanton branch.

The station site west of Park Lane (bridge 35) is a new housing estate, and this continues to the other side, obliterating all traces of the railway.

Fig. 199
This early picture of the station is taken from bridge 36 over Vernon Road A 611 looking east along the Up platform. Standing in the Down platform is a stopping passenger train of Howlden coaches with flattish roofs which were in use through the 1930s particularly for strengthening or duplicating excursion and special trains which were overbooked. Here the train is headed by a GNR Class 0-4-2 tender engine designed for mixed traffic working by Patrick Stirling and built in 1893. Note the wooden ramp in the foreground - the platform surfaces were of asphalt. The three home signals on the bracket post behind the footbridge are somersault arms, and were replaced by upper quadrants in the 1930s. In the background beneath the footbridge is bridge 35 carrying Park Lane over the railway, and from which good views of the Goods yard and carriage sidings were available.
c. 1912 F H Gillford

Fig. 200
A good view of the station from the Down platform facing east. The wooden fence with posters on the right surrounds a small yard round the single-storey kitchen/scullery whose original stone chimney has been lengthened by a brick addition. The man on the extreme right is at the pedestrian entrance from Vernon Road, and the wooden building behind the Way Out sign is the Stationmaster's Office. Entering the station hauled by ex GCR (LNER Class A5) 4-6-2-T is a late afternoon Nottingham Victoria - Pinxton Train.
September 1951 V R Webster

Fig. 201
Here can be seen the Goods shed, loading dock and loading gauge, behind which is the cattle pen, looking west from Park Lane bridge. Although not covering all of the yard layout, the scene is full of atmosphere with the platelayers on the left, their trolley on the rails before the van at the dock and the yard being shunted by an ex GCR 0-6-0 (LNER Class J11 nicknamed Pompoms). The wagons behind the engine hold a consignment of steel plates for Whiteley Reads factory which is out of sight to the left (Fig. 212 p81). The shunting spur for movements in the yard passed under the bridge and curved round beside the Down line from Bagthorpe Junction, and connections to the carriage sidings, turntable and ash pit roads were controlled by the five miniature somersault arms on the lattice post in the foreground. A good view of the large signal box with a soft water butt at the east end is obtained from this point. Note the miscellany of tools, chairs, ramps and wheelbarrows on the left.
August 1959 John Marshall

Fig. 202

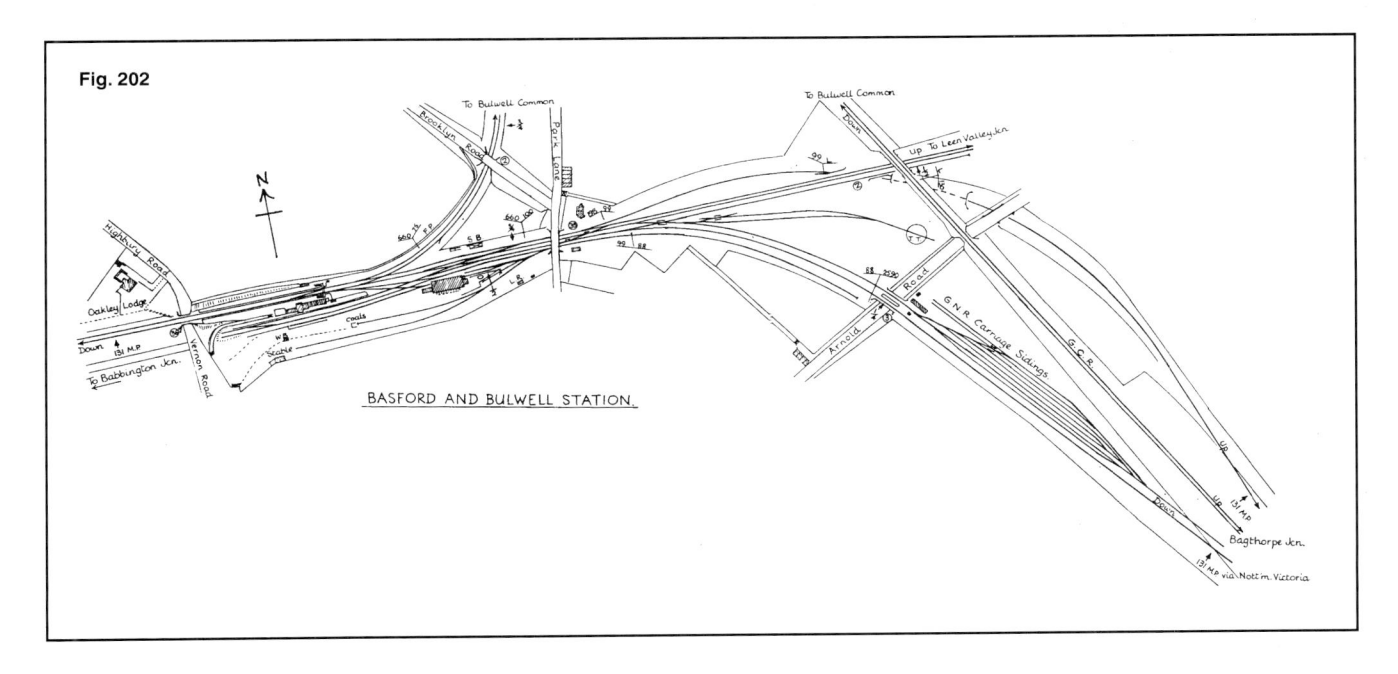

BASFORD AND BULWELL STATION.

Fig. 203
A splendid view of the layout and Goods yard east of the station is obtained from the footbridge which includes LNER Class B1 4-6-0 61281 awaiting departure from the bay with the 4.15 pm passenger train to Nottingham Victoria *via* Gedling. Strictly speaking the locomotive should not be beyond the signal post on the platform! The stone warehouse and goods office show up well beyond the engine, and several wagons of coal for the local merchants stand in a siding on the right. A gang of workmen, possibly platelayers, are making their way to the station after a day's work. The three on the left are walking along the Up branch to Bulwell Common. This signal box was built after the Great Central Railway came through Nottingham in 1898, when connections were made to Bagthorpe Junction and Bulwell South Junction, forming a triangle which was used to turn locomotives too long for the turntables at Victoria station and Basford & Bulwell itself. The main lines to Colwick, passing in front of the signal box were slewed from their former position (1880 map Fig. 196 p77) to accommodate these alterations, the straight line of the Down main becoming the curve from Bagthorpe Junction beyond Park Lane bridge 35. The former Up main became the Down main and joined the line of the Bagthorpe curve (points 46 p81), and the Up main was slewed further left towards the signal box.
March 1960 the late R W Sheppard

Fig. 204
Another splendid shot from Park Lane bridge, this time facing east towards Leen Valley Junction, and including a wealth of detail. An ex-GCR six-coupled Class J11 643691, is running round the curve from Bagthorpe Junction with a Nottingham Victoria to Derby Friargate train, and showing a good head of steam which will be needed to climb the three mile stretch up Basford bank to Kimberley. The tall bracket signal with somersault arms has a concrete post, some of which were made at the Engineers' depot at Derby Friargate to replace wooden posts when necessary. To the right of this post and the train is the shunting spur with a coach at the far end. Above the second coach, waiting at the Down main home signal is a train of empty wagons for one of the Erewash Valley collieries, with more coaching stock standing in the Down shunt alongside. The line on the extreme left is the Up curve to Bagthorpe Junction which burrowed beneath the main lines, which are spanned by the former GCR, seen in the background. Note the well-kept allotment gardens and sheds beyond the footpath along the top of the cutting.
July 1955 J P Wilson

79

Fig. 205
A more distant but overall view of the station buildings is seen from beside Brooklyn Road bridge over the sharp curve from Bulwell South Junction. WD Austerity 2-8-0 90447 is on the way to Stanton, judging from the empty wagon at the front of the train. Such wagons, designed by the LNER to carry spun pipes from Stanton Works at Ilkeston or Staveley Works had a 12-foot wheelbase and were 24 feet 11 inches long over buffers. Those wagons fitted with vacuum brakes were code-named 'Longfit'. There are coaches stabled behind the main buildings, and a corner of the Up side waiting room appears behind the telegraph pole on the right. The steelwork behind the open wagons in the goods yard is a factory under construction. The overhead crane gantry of the constructional steel company Whitely Read appears on the left of the view.
May 1962 John R Bonser

Fig. 206
This shot was taken from a Derby Friargate - Nottingham Victoria passenger train as it was taking the curve to Bagthorpe Junction shortly before the service was finally withdrawn. A brake van stands on the Up main line, but goods services ceased on 1st June. An unobstructed view of the layout and signals is seen although weeds are obscuring the shunting spur beyond the wagons on the right. The semaphore arm of the Down main home signal 43 has been lowered to drivers' eye level, and the plate with a hole in it just beneath the arm indicates that there is a telephone to the signalman in the cabinet at the front of the post. The wagon standing between the two posts of miniature shunting signals is on the road to the turntable, and behind it is the embankment of the ex-GCR main line into Nottingham, its falling gradient clearly apparent. The gradient post on the right refers to the Down curve from Bagthorpe Junction only.
1964 R Garton

Fig. 207
After the outbreak of World War II on 3rd September 1939, precautions against air raids were taken at railway stations, yards and sidings. These included blacking out lamps, except for the name, and the fitting of a valve in the gas supply, usually on the platform, to lower the pressure and illumination. Sandbag blast barriers were erected at the entrance to the booking/parcels office, as is seen here facing west along the Down platform, which also shows the separate stationmaster's office; a unique feature most likely erected after the developments around 1900.
1939 C H Eggleston

Fig. 208
A similar viewpoint to Fig. 204 which shows a detail of the morning shunting operations in the yard. The shunter is watching operations beside a rake of high sided wagons with a variety of contents as a train of empty mineral wagons from Colwick to a local colliery rolls down the main line from Leen Valley Junction. The gradient post left of the locomotive refers to the Up curve to Bagthorpe Junction only.
April 1959 John R Bonser

Fig. 209
Weak winter sunshine illuminates this scene of an unidentified Austerity 2-8-0 rolling through the station with an Up class B mineral train. The usual type of waiting room buildings is clearly shown here; wooden construction upon a brick foundation, but these are longer than the ones at other stations along the line. Note also the standard bench seats, which had the station name inset at the centre of the top back rail. The two sets of fire buckets were not kept filled ready for use, and the small enamelled name plate of British Rail design shows the 1953 title *Basford North* which distinguished it from Basford Vernon on the Midland line.
c 1964 R Garton

Fig. 210
One of the regular traffics to Basford & Bulwell during the 1930s was Jacobs' biscuits which were consigned by rail from Walton-on-the-Hill, Liverpool, and invariably loaded in a hifit (a high sided wagon fitted with vacuum brakes) and sheeted over. Here is the rear side of the Goods shed with its ample canopy over the two bays, one of which is occupied by a delivery van. The wagon was shunted into the Goods shed for unloading the three locked containers which it held, and the centre one lifted out with the hand crane before loading the tins of biscuits into the road vans for delivery to local stores, shops, restaurants, etc. The smaller road van usually delivered to surrounding villages. Empty tins would be returned the day after delivery, loaded into the three containers, and returned sheeted down to Walton-on-the-Hill, the wagon being moved out of the Goods shed by pinch bars and manpower! Note the two hinged plates at the end of the dock, seen above the radiator of the van in the bay, and the large office behind the van on the left.
1938 C H Eggleston

Fig. 211
During the late 1920s many steam railcars were built by Sentinel Cammell for the LNER for use on Branch line off-peak passenger services, and these continued to work during the 1930s and '40s, occasionally strengthened by a 6-wheeled coach! Here is 51913 'Rival' having worked the 7.53 am Nottingham Victoria to Basford *via* Netherfield, Gedling and Daybrook, which brought schoolboys for the Grammar School in Bulwell, newly opened in 1929. Standing on the Bay road, its next working was from Bulwell Common to Newstead as the 'Dido' for company's workmen, but as a train is already signalled to Bulwell South Junction the railcar will await its clearance before proceeding. 'Rival' entered traffic in August 1929 and was withdrawn in January 1946.
1938 C H Eggleston

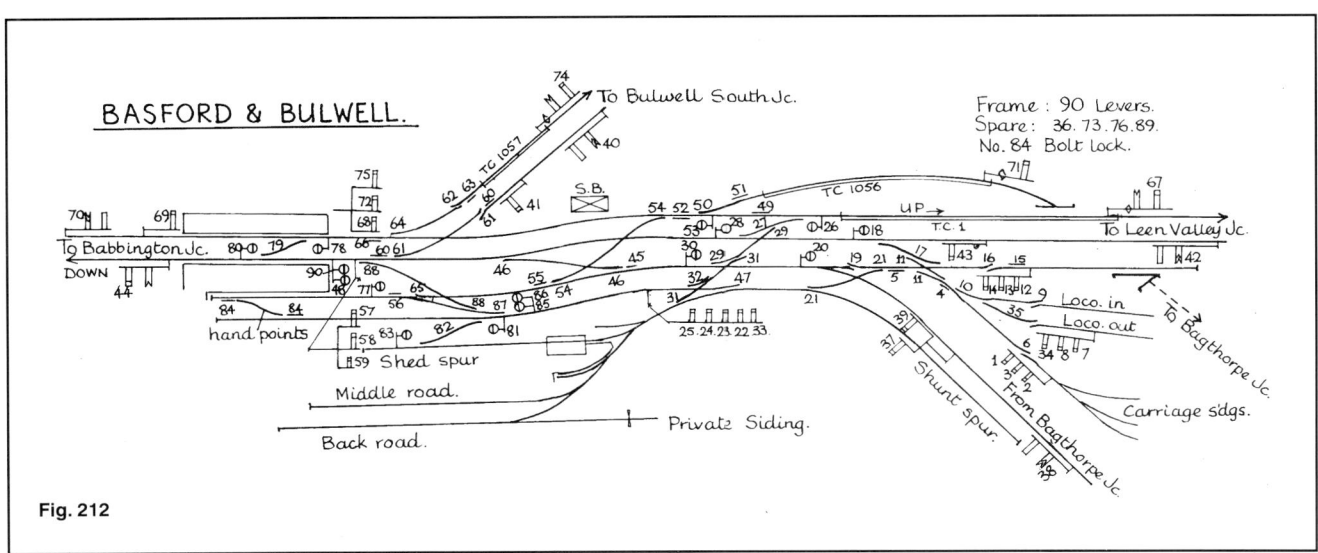

Fig. 212

Fig. 213
Facing west from above the Rat Hole along the Bagthorpe curve towards Park Lane bridge with the station beyond, a heavy special express train bound for the east coast is climbing the gradient towards Daybrook headed by a Gresley-designed LNER Class K3 2-6-0. Such trains from Pinxton and Derby were routed *via* Colwick Yards to miss Nottingham Victoria. Crews would be changed at Carlton Field signal box. Stabled coaches occupy the roads to the turntable and head shunt to the left, overlooked by the tall bracket home signals on the Down curve from Bagthorpe Junction.
June 1956 the late A G Cramp

Fig. 214
A later view of the entrance to the Rat Hole which shows the tunnel name board and the Down branch starting signal 71 against the bridge. Coaches, possibly for weekend excursion and special trains occupy the Down shunt and the turntable road, seen through the gap, and the carriage sidings, above the right hand coach. The tall sky arms have been removed, and Bulwell South Junction's Down distant signal has been placed beneath Bagthorpe Junction's Down starter, right of Arnold Lane bridge. The light engine moving towards Bulwell Common is a Gresley-designed LNER Class J 39 six-coupled type whose tender picks out the gradient post clearly.
May 1960 John Marshall

Fig. 215
The 7.15 am Colwick to Pinxton with a long train of empties hauled by LNER Class J5 0-6-0 3035 displaying class C headlamp above the right hand buffer. This train was booked to detach wagons for Basford, and would stop on the Down main line, draw forward with the necessary wagons clear of points 88 at the platform end, then reverse along the line on the right beneath the bridge into the shunting spur alongside the Bagthorpe curve, where the wagons were left. The engine would then return *via* the same route to the train and continue its journey calling at Awsworth Junction, Newthorpe and Eastwood on the way to Pinxton. The wagons for the Goods yard were moved by the Carriage Siding pilot which shunted the yard.
1938 C H Eggleston

Fig. 216
Charles Eggleston was a probationary clerk in the Goods Depot at Basford & Bulwell during the late 1930s, being conscripted for National Service in the army in May 1940. During his time at work he was able to capture many typical scenes of the working and trains with his camera. Here LNER Class J3 4096 is idling through the station with a train of coal for Colwick, the steam from the safety valve indicating she is ready for the climb past Leen Valley Junction to Daybrook. The building to the right, situated beyond the Up platform, housed the foreman's office and the passenger guards' mess/locker room. There was a hatch in the wall between the rooms to enable guards to answer the telephone in the foreman's office when this was closed. *1938 C H Eggleston*

Fig. 217 (2 Photo's)
In May 1929 the LNER published a booklet titled 'How the LNER Carries Exceptional Freight Loads', in which are diagrams and descriptions of special wagons for such things as boilers, ships' propellors, transformers and stators. One such special wagon was the well trolley, designed to carry self-contained loads of up to 110 tons, but with the application of the cantilever principle, this load could be increased to 150 tons. An exceptional load comprising a Stator Generator set which was out of gauge and moved on Sundays when traffic was light was stabled on the siding next to the turntable at Basford between 17th and 24th November 1946 before continuing *via* Egginton Junction to a destination in the West Midlands. To negotiate tunnels and station platforms, the Down line was temporarily slewed nearer to the Up line for its passage. The two photographs show the sheeted load in close-up, jacked up whilst at rest, and the length of the cantilever girders which balance the load.
C H Eggleston

Fig. 218
Goose Fair was traditionally held in Nottingham from the first Thursday to Saturday in October. Here can be seen a trainload of Fairground amusements in containers being loaded preparatory to despatch as a special to Hull, after the fair had closed. The hand crane on the left is typical of those at stations along the Derbyshire extension of the GNR (See Fig. 183 p72). *October 1938 C H Eggleston*

5. NOTTINGHAM SUBURBAN RAILWAY

This short railway, connecting the existing Derbyshire Extension line at Daybrook in the north to the Grantham-Nottingham London Road line at Trent Lane Junction in the south was completed by 23rd November 1889, and opened for traffic on 2nd December of that year. It was a private undertaking which served brickworks in the area, but was maintained and worked by the GNR until 1st January 1923, when it became part of the London and North Eastern Railway.

The line provided a short cut for passenger trains from Nottingham to Daybrook and stations west, as well as those along the Leen Valley line, but its heavy gradients limited their length, and many continued to use the longer route via Netherfield where connections with Grantham and Newark trains could be made. From January 1890 there were 10 trains to Daybrook, 4 of which went through to Newstead. In the reverse there were 9 trains from Daybrook to Nottingham London Road, 4 of which came from Newstead. There was no Sunday service. The journey time from Nottingham to Daybrook was 13 minutes. On the opening of Nottingham Victoria in May 1900 the service was 4 to Basford & Bulwell and 3 to Skegby. There was an extra train to Skegby on Saturdays. In the reverse direction there were 5 from Basford, and 3 from Skegby. There was an extra train on Saturdays from Basford & Bulwell. The services stopped at all stations. On 1st November 1901 the service was extended beyond Skegby to Pleasley and Shirebrook.

At the beginning of the First World War there were 8 trains to Shirebrook, five of which ran non-stop to Daybrook. In the reverse direction the service ran via Bestwood Junction and Bagthorpe Junction into Nottingham Victoria. First World War economies closed the three Suburban Railway stations to passengers on 1st July 1916. The passenger service using the line then became 2 through trains to Shirebrook with none in the reverse.

When the Company became part of the LNER on 1st January 1923 there were 3 passenger trains daily over the line from Nottingham Victoria to Shirebrook, and one from Basford & Bulwell. In the reverse direction on Wednesdays and Saturdays one from Shirebrook passed over the line into Nottingham Victoria. Later the 1.3 pm from Nottingham Victoria was extended to Chesterfield Market Place LDECR and passed over the Suburban. Following the collapse of Mapperley Tunnel on 23rd January 1925, all the Leen Valley coal and passenger trains had to use the Suburban whilst repairs were carried out. The coal and return empties trains had to reverse in Nottingham London Road Goods Yard.

When the line to the Joint Victoria station was built along the viaduct from Trent Lane Junction to connect with the GCR at Weekday Cross Junction, a facing crossover was constructed between the Up Suburban line and the Down Main line into the High Level and Victoria stations.

Passenger traffic using the three stations was never heavy, for electric trams served the area as housing developed, and on 13th July 1916 passenger services ceased, followed by Goods traffic in January 1931. On 1st August 1951 the line was closed to all traffic.

King George V and Queen Mary visited Nottingham on Tuesday 10th July 1928 when they opened the Royal Show at Wollaton Park, and also the new University. Between these two events their Majesties reviewed a huge gathering of schoolchildren in Woodthorpe Park, and the stations of Thorneywood and Sherwood were cleaned up and opened for the occasion. The children and their teachers were brought to Sherwood in special trains from London Road and Basford & Bulwell.

The branch was converted to single track throughout on Sunday 9th February 1930, when the signal box at Sherwood was closed, and all signalling removed. The line was then worked by a Staff which unlocked the ground frames controlling siding connections.

During the first year of operation, the one goods train from Leen Valley worked through to London Road Low Level Goods during the afternoon, and the Staff was returned to Daybrook with the 5.5 pm passenger train from Nottingham Victoria to Shirebrook via Trent Lane Junction until 14th September 1931, when the connection to the Down line at that junction was removed, together with the crossover from the Up line to the High Level line, leaving access to the Low Level station only.

Fig. 219
A view from track level facing north of bridge 11 which carries Sherwood Vale over the station. On the right is the signal post carrying the Up starting signal and St Ann's Well distant beneath: a detailed view of GNR somersault, or balanced arm signals which includes the slotting balance weights. These ensure that the distant signal which when pulled 'off' means the line is clear through the next station or section, cannot be lowered until the stop signal above is 'off'. Note also the fogman's hut at the base. Although the platforms extend south of the bridge, access to the station was afforded to the Down platform on the left hand side beyond the arch. The short extensions do have a gas lamp each. The main buildings and booking hall are seen together with ornamental brackets and gas lamps through the centre of the arch.
c.1904 G Cawthorne collection

Fig. 220
An official view of the footbridge at Sherwood station which includes the north end of the platforms, signal box and the track layout. The house in the centre is Woodthorpe Farm. On the extreme left, above the notice board is the chimney to the weighbridge office. Reflections at the platform edges indicate a recent shower of rain, but how neat and clean stations were kept in those days!
c.1904 G Cawthorne collection

Subsequently the service along the branch was reduced to the Pick-up Goods running three days a week. Apart from a short section at Daybrook the lines were lifted between June and October 1954. This last 100 yards of track and the connection at Daybrook Junction was finally removed on 24th February 1957.

Daybrook Junction signal box was dismantled in 1934, the double junction to Sherwood being removed, and replaced by a single connection to the Down line worked from a Ground Frame, and controlled by a miniature somersault signal (Fig. 174 p68).

Through working between Daybrook and Trent Lane Junction to London Road Low Level Goods ceased in May 1941. During an air raid on the City on the night of 8th-9th considerable damage was done in the Sneinton area, one bomb hitting the lines north of the bridges over the Midland Railway lines to Newark and Lincoln, and damaging the embankment so much that no repairs were made. Instead buffer stops were placed either side of the bridges. This did not affect the working of the line, which by now was very light, being covered by the Leen Valley pilot making a trip during the afternoon as far as Thorneywood and back. The up track at Trent Lane Junction was useful for storing wagons.

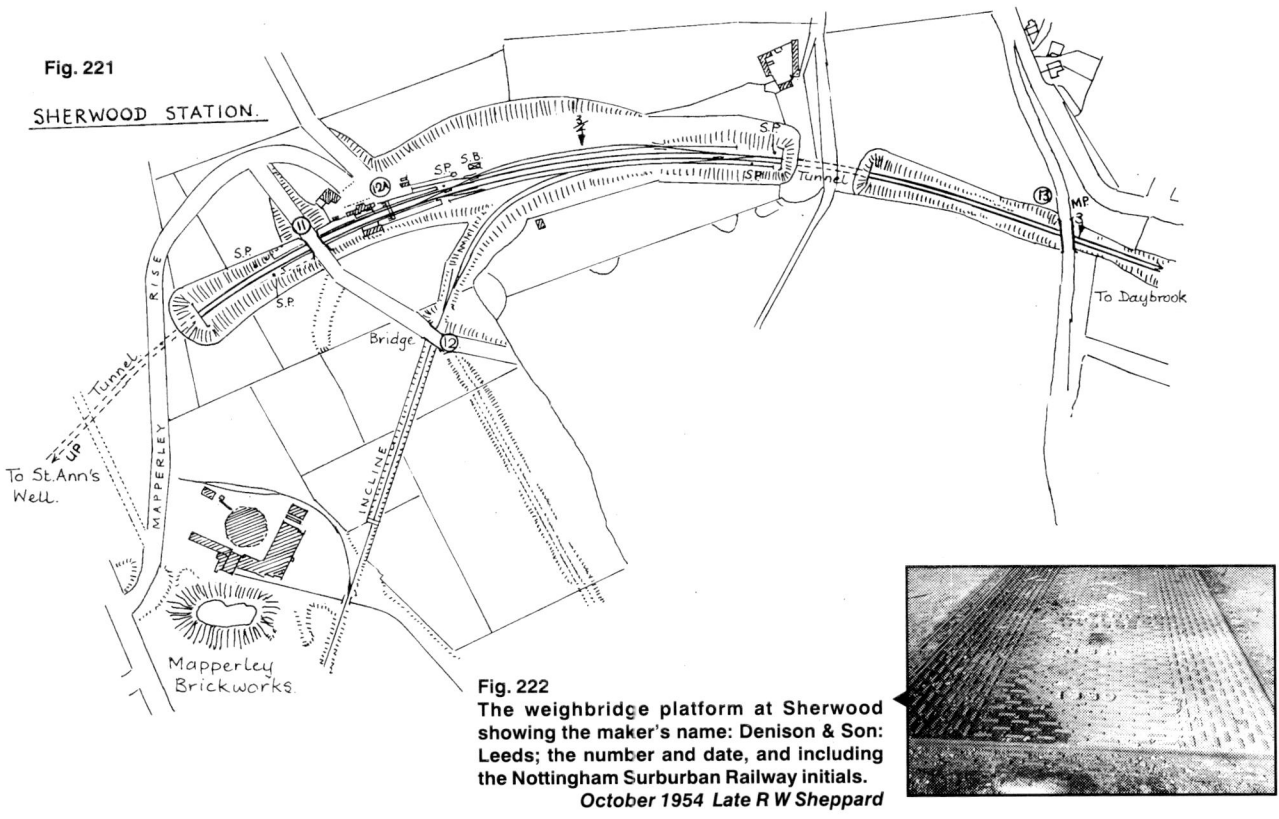

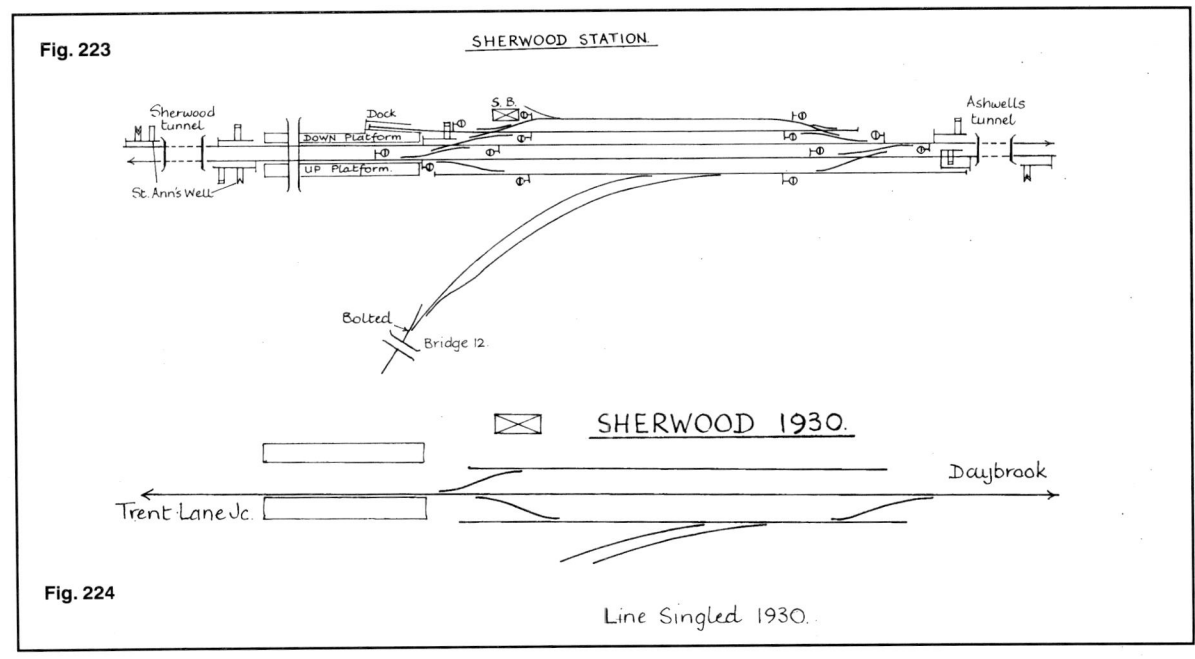

Fig. 221
SHERWOOD STATION.

Fig. 222
The weighbridge platform at Sherwood showing the maker's name: Denison & Son: Leeds; the number and date, and including the Nottingham Surburban Railway initials.
October 1954 Late R W Sheppard

Fig. 223
SHERWOOD STATION.

SHERWOOD 1930.

Fig. 224
Line Singled 1930.

SHERWOOD 2 m 51 1/4 ch

This station had opposite platforms built round a curve and spanned by road bridge, 11, and a wrought iron lattice footbridge at the north end. Access was from Mapperley Rise into the Yard and Station buildings, which were of brick with wooden awnings having a decorative 'fringe' painted in two colours. There was a dock and cattle pen on the Down side, together with a cart weighbridge and office, but no Goods shed. The small signal box was sited on the Down side just north of the platform end. The Station House was a substantial building of quality and elegance, the gable ends being clad in terracotta tiles above the brickwork. From the south end of the short Ashwells tunnel a branch swung eastwards, to pass beneath a high narrow bridge 12 and climb a steep incline to reach Mapperley brickworks of the Nottingham Patent Brick Co. Rope haulage was used to convey wagons up and down the gradient. The station was opened on 2nd December 1889 to all traffic; closed to passengers on 1st July 1916; closed to goods traffic in January 1931, and to all traffic on 1st August 1951.

No trace of the station or buildings can be seen now (1992). The site is occupied with two tower blocks of flats and rows of lock-up garages which follow the curve of the original track. The tunnels at either end are filled in and their entrances fenced off, well obscured with dense foliage. Bridge 11 carrying Sherwood Vale is intact with a new building across where the station house stood. The area of the branch to Mapperley brickworks has been landscaped and bridge 12 removed.

Fig. 225
Looking south at the platforms and bridge 11, on the left is a typical sleeper-built platelayers' hut, and their trolley, usually dismantled when not in use, is at the buffer stop. Immediately behind this is the ground frame to operate points to the sidings. To the right is the dock and cattle pen with the weighbridge office near to the bridge. Part of the station house is seen extreme right.
June 1951 F E Quenby

Fig. 226
In the foreground is the weighbridge office and abutment to bridge 11 from which the photograph was taken. It shows the station house and out-buildings before they were demolished. These were the same at all three stations with ornamental string courses between ground and upper floor, and tiled gable ends. The road climbing left behind the house is Mapperley Rise, and the main approach is Winchester Street further right.
December 1955 John R Bonser

Fig. 227
The north portal of Sherwood tunnel, 442 yards long, built on a curve and a rising gradient of 1 in 70 with steps and handrail on the right.
c.1904 G Cawthorne collection

Fig. 228
This view through Ashwell's tunnel is taken from the north side. Note the steps and handrail on the right for use of the Signal and Telegraph Lineman. The telegraph wires were not taken through the tunnel.
c.1904 G Cawthorne collection

Fig. 229
This is a view of bridge 12 looking down the incline from the Nottingham Patent Brick Company's works east of the station. Note the grooves cut into the guide between the rails in the foreground by the rope which hauled up empties and lowered full wagons to the sidings at Sherwood. The stub points to the trap left of the arch were later replaced with the usual blades. Just beneath the arch are the main running lines.
c.1904
G Cawthorne collection

Fig. 230
This view from the station yard shows the branch and incline to the brickworks through bridge 12 carrying Woodthorpe Vale. Behind the house and a tree stand two of the tall kiln chimneys. Note the tubular point rodding and rollers, commonly used by the GNR leading to where quite obviously British Rail maintenance of the track ends.
June 1951 F E Quenby

Fig. 231
Looking north from Sherwood Vale on bridge 11 along the line of the station showing the curve flanked by garages, and the route to Ashwell's tunnel beyond blocked by the high rise flats of Winchester Court, hidden behind which is a similar block named Woodthorpe Court.
November 1992 A Henshaw

87

Fig. 232
Here is the south portal of the short Ashwell's tunnel, a mere 70 yards in length, beneath the drive to Woodthorpe Grange which is situated a little way to the east. Fencing along the drive can be seen behind the young trees beyond the tunnel. Of railway interest are the earth and sleeper buffer stop at the end of the brickyard branch; the two somersault signals, the right hand one slung beneath the bracket to be visible from inside the tunnel is well blackened with soot. The one on the left has the semaphore arm backed by a white board for better visibility, but the spectacle plate, illuminated in hours of darkness is placed at the driver's eye level. Between the running lines is a disc or ground signal of standard GNR type for controlling shunting movements. At the foot of the cutting on the left can be seen a gradient post indicating a downhill slope to Daybrook Junction.
c.1904 G Cawthorne collection

Fig. 233
A view facing south, of bridge 11 to compare with Fig. 225 p86. No platforms reach beyond the arch where the ground is fenced off and Sherwood tunnel, now filled in, is hidden behind twenty years' growth of scrub.
November 1992 A Henshaw

Fig. 234
A last look at the railway and station site with the recovery train wagons in the platform, and weed-covered dock, cattle pen and platforms together with the small brick goods shed. The embankment of the brickworks branch is seen clearly on the right.
June 1954 John R Bonser

Fig. 235
A rather forlorn view of the station remains through bridge 11 to compare with Fig. 219 p84. The station buildings have gone together with the footbridge, and the main line is singled. At least there is a clearer view of the Lamp room and cattle pen.
June 1951 F E Quenby

Fig. 236

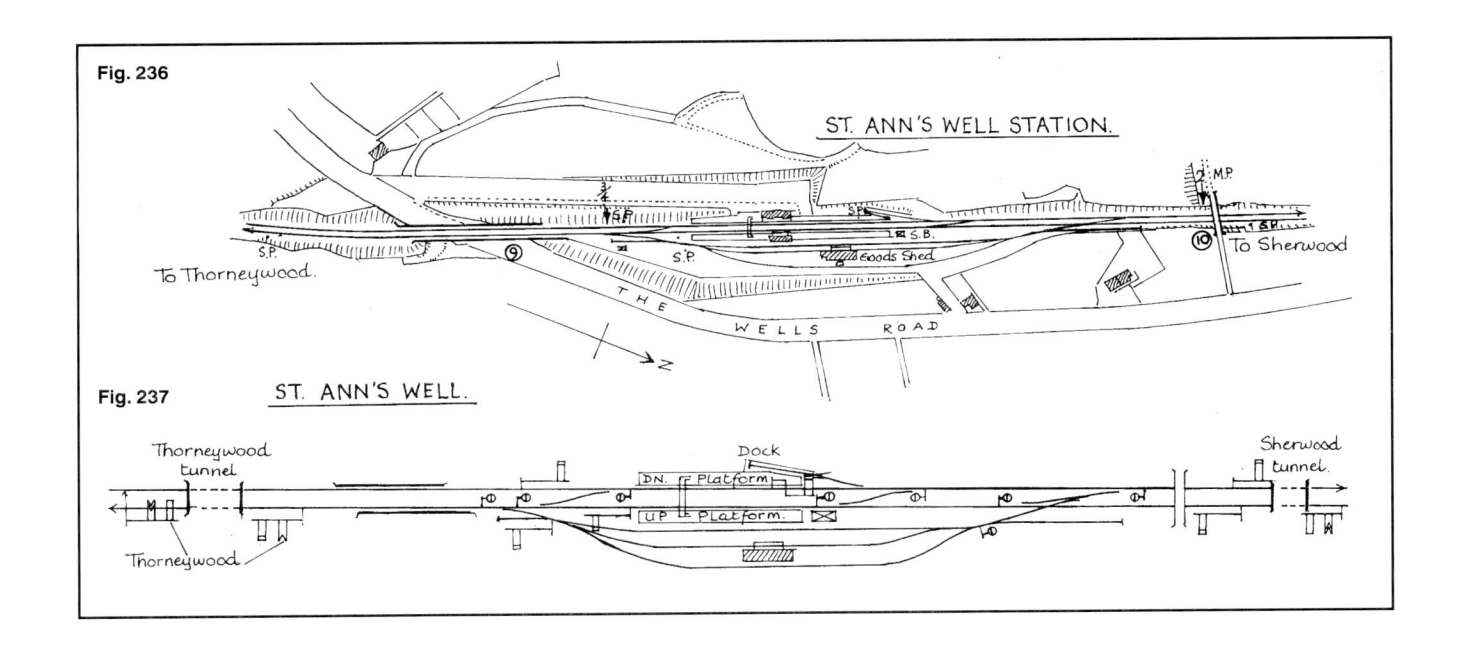

Fig. 237 ST. ANN'S WELL.

ST ANN'S WELL 1 m 66 3/4 ch

The red brick buildings here were of similar design to those at Sherwood, but the opposite platforms were longer and straight. The railway crossed The Wells Road by a substantial skew bridge beside which was the passenger approach to the station. Nottingham City Corporation gave the land for this approach and paid half the maintenance costs. On the Down side was a small dock, and the platforms were spanned by a lattice girder footbridge. The signal box stood at the north end of the Up platform, behind which was the goods yard with a red brick Goods shed and an awning over one track. Access to the yard was from The Wells Road further north than the bridge, and the Station House was situated beside this gated entrance facing the road. No brickworks were served from here, merely local goods and coal traffic together with passengers and parcels.

Opening and closure dates were the same as for Sherwood station, but the signal box was taken out of regular use on 28th October 1904, thereafter being opened and operated by the Stationmaster when required for dealing with traffic.

In November 1992, the only remaining building was the Station House on The Wells Road, beside which is an entrance to a large housing development of terraced brick flats. The bluebrick abutment of the skew bridge 9 remained beside ' The Gardeners ' public house, but the flats development covers the station entrance between Kildare Road and The Wells Road. Beyond bridge 10, which carried the occupation road to a farm, the cutting to Sherwood tunnel, well covered in shrubs and vegetation, was used as a nature site by the adjacent Walter Halls Primary School.

Fig. 238
The impressive skew bridge 9 spanning The Wells Road as yet seemingly unmetalled. The approach to the station was up the slope to the left which has a standard type of excursion notice board above the fencing. Note the gas lamp by the pedestrian 'tunnel' partly hidden behind the tree trunk.
c.1904
G Cawthorne collection

Fig. 239
Technically a view of the lattice girder footbridge 9A, with gas lamps at each end to illuminate the steps after dark, this photograph also gives a first class view of the station at St Ann's Well. The camera is facing north along the Down platform with the main buildings on it. On the Up platform are the waiting rooms with the signal box at the end. Part of the brick Goods shed is visible behind the steps on the right, access to which was from The Wells Road. In the distance beneath the canopy are the two cottages beside that road. The substantial bridge 10 in the distance carried an occupation road (Bentley's) and had No. 2 mile post at its side.
c.1904 G Cawthorne collection

Fig. 240
A view from the carriage window of the enthusiasts' special of the remains of the platform buildings on the Up side clearly showing the ornamental brackets which supported the wooden awning. Beyond this is the line leading out of the Goods yard with the usual trap and buffer stop.
June 1951 F E Quenby

Fig. 241
Much new housing has been built in St Ann's recently as this view from the Goods Yard entrance shows, looking across The Wells Road. The railway side of the Station House is seen here with a new boundary wall.
November 1992 A Henshaw

Fig. 242
A time of demolition facing north through the station site, with little left of the platform buildings, but a good view of the Goods shed and office which still appear intact. Further to the right is the Station House which can be identified from the ornamental tiles on the gable.
June 1954 John R Bonser

Fig. 243

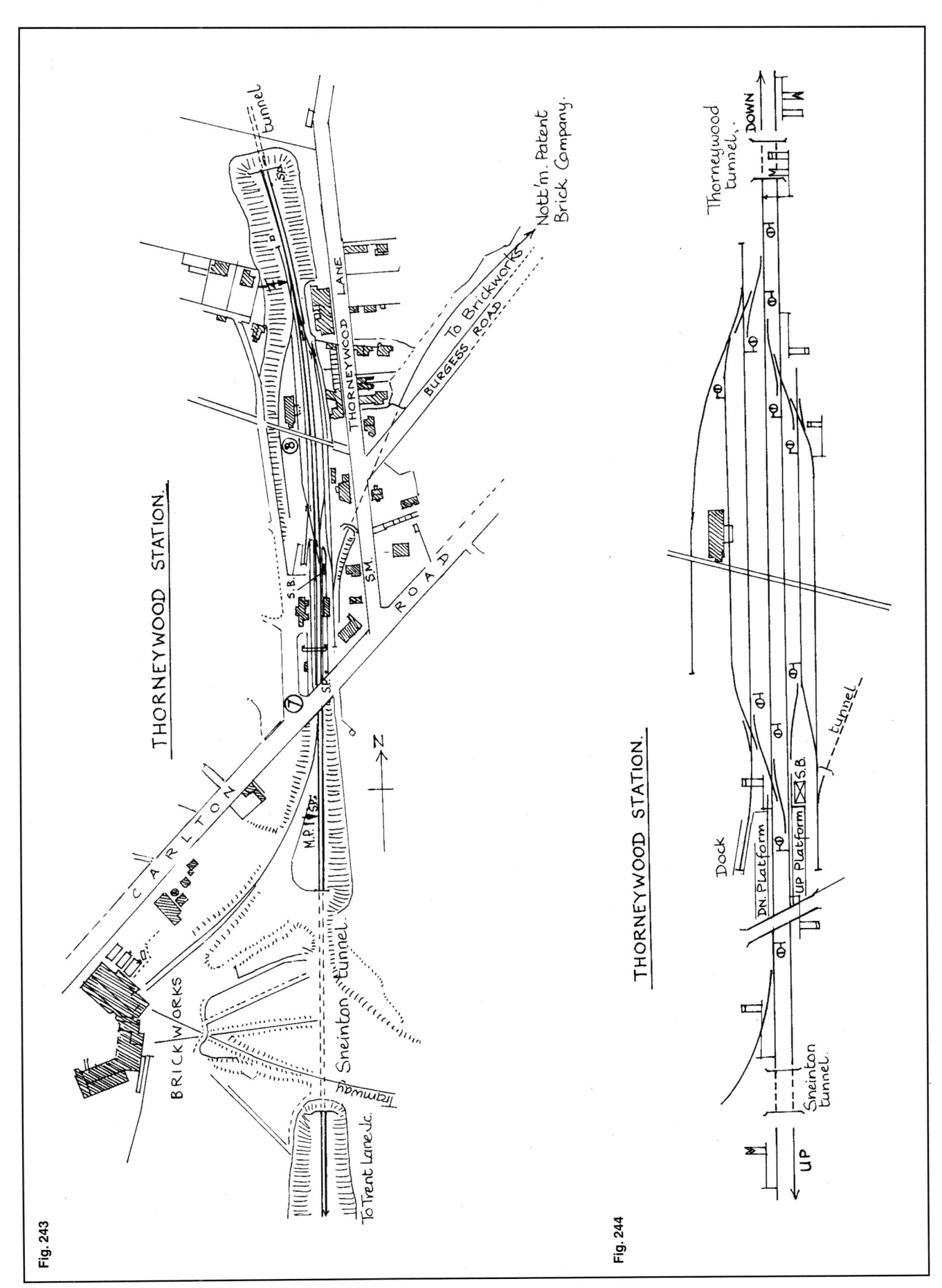

THORNEYWOOD STATION.

Fig. 244

THORNEYWOOD STATION.

Fig. 245
Another official photograph of the station footbridge with the oval number plate clearly visible on the right hand pillar, but which embraces much more detail. Beside the name board on the Down side platform (left) is the gradient post indicating an easing of the climb from Trent Lane Junction of 1 in 49 to 1 in 200, to assist drivers to get away. At the foot of the steps are posts holding the notice board to passengers to cross the line by the bridge. Beyond this the buildings and an enamelled plate advertising one of Nottingham's staple industries - Player's Navy Cut tobacco. Beneath the awning on the left, is part of the Goods shed and its awning, whilst the steps and doorway to the signal box appear on the Up platform. The long footbridge in the distance spans the cutting from Thorneywood Rise (left) to Thorneywood Lane, now Porchester Road on the right. There are two GN lettered wagons behind the Up platform above which is the gable end of the Station House.
c.1904 G Cawthorne collection

Fig. 246
There are alas no wagons in the sidings as the Enthusiasts' Special draws into the station pulled by an Ivatt LNER Class C12 4-4-2 tank engine. Very little coal remains in the merchants' bunkers, but word of the train had got through to some people who line the footbridge to witness its arrival.
June 1951 F E Quenby

THORNEYWOOD 1 m 7 1/4 ch

Between St. Ann's Well and Thorneywood, the line passed through a tunnel 408 yards in length to emerge into a cutting beside Thorneywood Lane (now Porchester Road) where the station and Goods Yard were built. The east side of this cutting was strengthened by a massive blue brick retaining wall at the northern end. The platforms were straight and opposite each other, with the same design of buildings as those at Sherwood. Approach to the station was from Marmion Road on the west side, and a lattice girder footbridge 8 spanned the Goods Yard linking Marmion Road with Thorneywood Lane. The Booking Office was on the Down side, and a lattice girder footbridge connected the two platforms. The signal box was on the Up platform, and there were sidings on both sides of the Main Lines here. The Dock and Goods Yard with its brick Goods shed and coal siding were on the Down side; the siding and run-round on the Up side had a branch to the Nottingham Patent Brickworks leading from the small dead end. This branch immediately entered a low tunnel 110 yards long with a headway of 10 feet 1 inch above rail level, which passed beneath Thorneywood Lane. The line then ran up an incline along which wagons were rope-hauled, parallel with Burgass Road to the Brickworks. After the Brickworks closed it was not then

Fig. 247
A view through the 408 yard long Thorneywood tunnel from the south with the Down starting signal, and St. Ann's Well distant signal beneath it. The crank above the latter would work an indicator in St. Ann's Well signal box to show if the arm was correctly 'off'.
c.1904 G Cawthorne collection

possible to move the winding engine because of its size and weight. The flywheel weighed 25 tons. A public house was built round it and named 'The Engine House'. This has now been rebuilt and the winding engine removed to the Nottingham Industrial Museum at Wollaton Park and restored (1983).

There was another short branch south of bridge 7 into a brickworks beside Carlton Road.

The Station House, of similar elegant design to the others faced Thorneywood Lane at road level above the siding to the tunnel and incline.

The same opening and closing dates for passenger and Goods traffic as those for the other two stations apply here.

On June 16th 1951 an enthusiasts' special train ran over the branch to Thorneywood and back, and three years later the lines were dismantled after removal of any stored rolling stock.

As at St. Ann's Well, the only remaining building in November 1992 was the Station House surrounded by high fencing on Porchester Road. The small plot of land on top of the cutting has a number of sheds where the owner carried out motor body repairs, but apart from the addition of a conservatory on the south side there is little alteration to the original building.

However all traces of railway and buildings have gone from the cutting which, still spanned by the footbridge with additional wire mesh sides, was occupied by British Telecom's Engineering Centre and RMT workshops. Bridge 7 beneath Carlton Road was filled in and to the south, the line of the railway was metalled making a good footpath as far as Sneinton Tunnel. The north portal was boarded up but had an entrance door, for although the south end was filled with earth, this end was used as a rifle range, the refuges being bricked up for safety against ricocheting bullets. The footpath climbs round the western side to reach Skipton Circus where the curving road descends sharply to Sneinton Dale. Here the three-arch viaduct 6 which spanned this now busy road has been demolished without a trace, and on the north side a new Surgery and Medical Centre has been built. The opposite side is the site of a Police Station. The embankment south of here was visible between houses which flank it, but inaccessible, and bridge 5 carrying Sneinton Boulevard has been filled in. A ramp leads down the north side to a depot of Balfour Kirkpatrick-BICC Group, and opposite is a pleasant gravelled footpath along the trackbed as far as Colwick Road. Here again bridge 4 across the road has been removed, and on the south side is a public house with a spacious forecourt car park.

The girders of the bridges between Colwick Road and Trent Lane Junction have all been removed, and only abutments and pillars remain to be seen here. Trent Lane itself is closed to vehicles at its crossing of the Midland line to Netherfield, but pedestrians can cross by opening wicket gates. The large blue brick segmental arch of the Suburban line which spans Trent Lane here is still intact, and a metalled footpath climbs the embankment beside it eastwards. This path, gravelled along the trackbed passes a mock signal post and arm, and continues as far as Colwick Road near the Level Crossing. The land between the old GNR and Midland Railway lines was being developed for new housing in 1992.

Fig. 248
A closer view of the long footbridge 8 and the Goods Yard to the north of the station. Behind the central pillar of the bridge stands the brick goods shed with awnings either side, and office. On the extreme left is a coal merchant's cart backed up to a wagon standing in the coal siding. Between the long string of GN wagons and those to the right are the two Main Lines curving away into Thorneywood tunnel. The two sidings on the right led to the brickworks branch which was behind the camera. Note the arched buttresses to the retaining wall along this side of the cutting.
c.1904 G Cawthorne collection

Fig. 249
Bridge 7, immediately south of the station, and carrying Carlton Road over the railway. The station and footbridge are seen through the opening, and on the left is the siding controlled by the Ground signal 8, leading to another brickworks beside Carlton Road.
c.1904 G Cawthorne collection

Fig. 250
The track removal and recovery train wagons are seen here standing on the original running lines from the long footbridge facing south. On the left is the siding behind the Up platform whence the brickyard branch beneath Porchester Road connected. Part of the Station House with its two string courses of ornamental bricks can be seen above the bushes. The weighbridge platform and office stand near the Dock in the middle distance beyond which is the station approach road and Goods Yard entrance. Much of the hill beyond Carlton Road bridge, and through which Sneinton tunnel was driven has been removed by the brickworks company, which occupied the ground where the house opposite the station entrance stands.
June 1954 John R Bonser

Fig. 251
A detailed shot of the brickworks tunnel mouth in preparation for being bricked up. *June 1966 A Henshaw*

Fig. 252
This is a view of the brickworks tunnel whose entrance is bricked up and gated. The rear of the Coopers Arms above the cutting appears to have little space for the advertised car park! The footbridge and retaining wall were still there in November 1992. *A Henshaw*

Fig. 253
The station site, facing north, then occupied by British Telecom buildings, and used as an Engineering Centre and Road Motor Transport workshops. New housing development is evident on both sides, the only remaining feature was the lattice girder footbridge. *November 1992 A Henshaw*

Fig. 254
A view of the Station House now painted white and numbered 1 Porchester Road which can be seen climbing the hill to the right. Access to the house is down a slope to a wooden gate at the end of the fencing. The Coopers Arms public house which backs on to the cutting can be seen behind the traffic signal in the middle.
November 1992 A Henshaw

Sneinton

Fig. 255
A mere 154 yards (7 chains) south of bridge 7 at Thorneywood was Sneinton tunnel, 183 yards long, and here can be seen the north portal. Evidence of the severe gradient shows over the Down line on the right by the sooty deposit above the arch.
c.1904 G Cawthorne collection

Fig. 256
This photograph shows the scene in November 1992, where a well-maintained footpath from Carlton Road to a housing estate beyond the tunnel leads to Sneinton Dale. The south end of the tunnel was blocked, but this end is only partly filled with earth, and boarded up. It was used by a club for rifle shooting and kept locked when not in use.
A Henshaw

Fig. 247
Facing north across Sneinton Dale in November 1992 at the site of the viaduct which carried the railway was a new surgery and medical centre, then under construction. Behind the photographer was a modern police station.
A Henshaw

Fig. 258
The three-arch viaduct 6 spanning Sneinton Dale facing west towards Nottingham. The gates on either side of the unmetalled road belong to Dale Farm, a name still used on milk and dairy produce in this area. The farm house still stands, but is surrounded by newer housing.
c.1904 G Cawthorne collection

Trent Lane Junction
(See also pages 45 & 46)

Fig. 259
This is where the Nottingham Suburban railway joined the GNR Grantham to Nottingham lines, which run from left to right beneath the nearer of the bridges (No 2). These two spans carried the Up line only, which continued into London Road Low Level terminus. Further to the left is the girder bridge 3 which carried two lines across the Midland Railway's Nottingham to Lincoln lines. The sharp curve and steep 1 in 49 gradient of the Down connection can be traced between the bridges. The lattice parapet girders have already been removed from this bridge, and the embankment cleared from the northern abutment which is shored up prior to the removal of the main girders.
April 1954 John Marshall

Fig. 260
Facing east across the Midland Railway's lines from Nottingham (right) to Newark (left) in November 1992 can be seen the pillars and abutments of the GNR bridges at Trent Lane which crossed the MR on the level. As can be seen from the iron railings the road is closed to vehicles now but pedestrians could cross at the far side. The stone pillars and abutment on the left carried the GNR Nottingham-Grantham lines, and a wide footpath can be seen climbing to the trackbed which leads as far as Colwick Road. On the right is the abutment of bridge 1 on the Suburban Railway whose girders have been removed but whose arch and parapets over Trent Lane were still there. The white central post supports cameras which give a screened image of the crossing in Trent Power Box near Long Eaton. *A Henshaw*

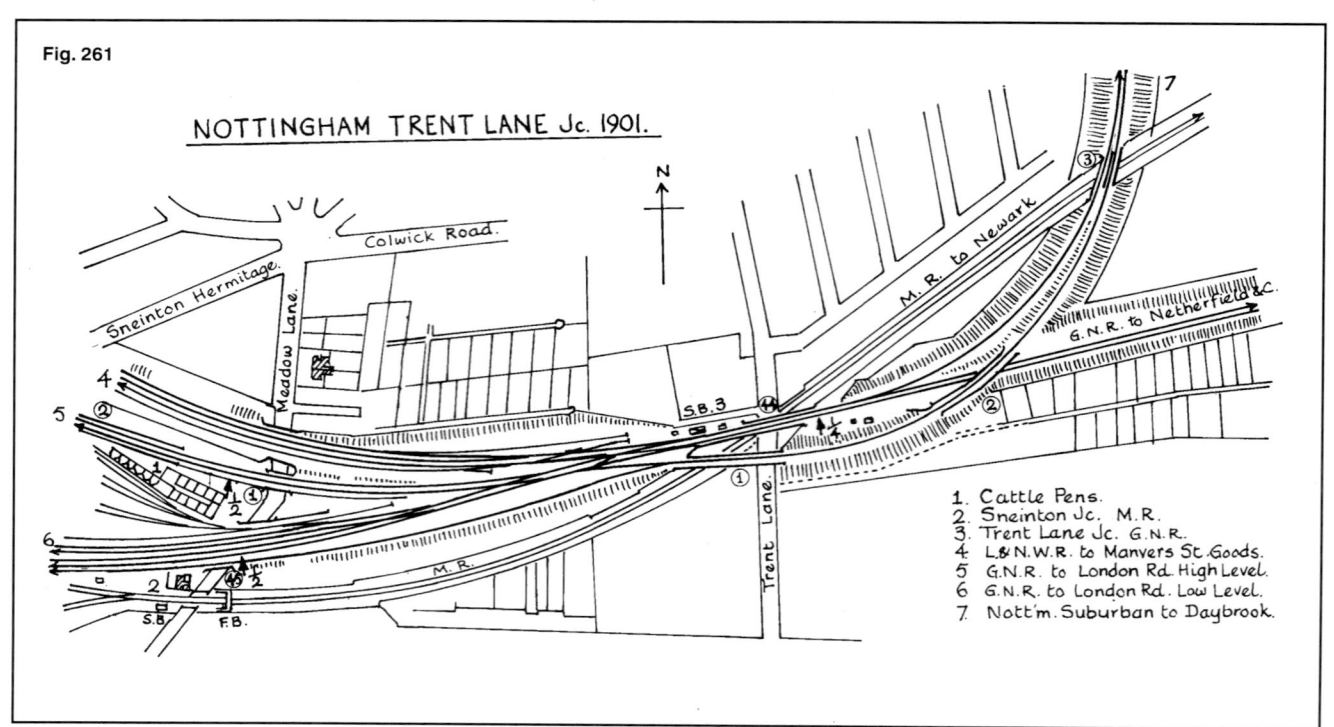

Fig. 261

NOTTINGHAM TRENT LANE Jc. 1901.

1. Cattle Pens.
2. Sneinton Jc. M.R.
3. Trent Lane Jc. G.N.R.
4. L.&N.W.R. to Manvers St. Goods.
5. G.N.R. to London Rd. High Level.
6. G.N.R. to London Rd. Low Level.
7. Nott'm. Suburban to Daybrook.

6. APPENDICES

APPENDIX 1

List of Tunnels, GNR Western Division

Name	Situated between	Length yards
Gonerby	Grantham and Allington Junction	560
Victoria Street	*Weekday Cross Junction and Nottingham Victoria	393
Mansfield Road	*Nottingham Victoria and Carrington	1189
Sherwood Rise	*Carrington and New Basford	665
Annesley	*Annesley North Junction and Kirkby South Junction	1001
Sneinton	Trent Lane Junction and Thorneywood	183
Thorneywood	Thorneywood and St Ann's Well	408
Sherwood	St Ann's Well and Sherwood	442
Ashwells	Sherwood and Daybrook Junction	70
Mapperley	Gedling and Daybrook	1132
Basford	Basford and Bagthorpe Junction (Up line)	90
Watnall	East of Kimberley station	268
Morley	West Hallam and Breadsall	238
Mickleover	Derby and Mickleover	464

*GCR

GNR Stationmaster Area Control Responsibilities
23.11.1900

Location	Signalboxes, Ground Frames, etc
COLWICK (Yardmaster)	Rectory Junction, East Junction, Locomotive junction, North Junction, Shunters' South Cabin
Netherfield	Colwick West Junction, Goods Yard, Station, Netherfield Lane
Nottingham London Road	Trent Lane Junction, Goods Yard, Low Level Station, High Level Station
Thorneywood	Station
St Ann's Well	Station
Sherwood	Station
Gedling	Station, The Kennels
Daybrook	Arno Vale, Daybrook Junction, Station, Leen Valley Junction

APPENDIX 2 BOOKED SHUNTING ENGINE DUTIES 1950

Station or Yard	Depot from which engine provided	Description or number of Pilot	Period required at station or yard	Particulars of Work
Basford & Bulwell	Colwick	No 1	8.45 am to 4.15 pm	Performs shunting in Carriage
Basford & Bulwell	Colwick	No 2	6.35 pm to 8.0 pm (off 6.05 pm ex Nottingham)	Sidings and at Station
Nottingham Vic.	Colwick	No 1	5.0 am to 2.30 am (approx)	Performs shunting and covers Up and Down passenger trains
Nottingham Vic.	Derby	No 2	6.45 am to 7.30 am	Shunts Parliament Street Dock (off 5.35 am ex Derby)
Nottingham Vic.	Grantham	No 3	7.30 am to 7.55 am	Shunts South End (off 6.35 am ex Grantham)
Nottingham Vic.	Derby	No 4	8.5 am to 8.45 am	Shunts South End (off 7.10 am ex Derby)
Nottingham Vic.	Colwick	No 5	9.0 am to 11.30 am (off 7.55 am ex Edwinstowe)	Performs shunting and makes trips to and from Nottingham LL as reqd.
Nottingham Vic.	Leicester	No 6	9.30 am to 12.30 pm	Performs shunting (off 6.35 am ex Woodford)
Nottingham Vic.	Colwick	No 7	2.0 pm to 3.30 pm	Shunts South End (off 1.33 pm ex Basford)
Nottingham Vic.	Leicester	No 8	3.30 pm to 5.0 pm **SX** 5.30 pm **SO** (off 1.20 pm ex Leicester)	Performs shunting
Nottingham Vic.	Grantham	No 9	6.0 pm to 7.30 pm (off 4.5 pm ex Grantham)	Shunts Parliament Street Dock and at South End
Nottingham Vic.	Colwick	No 10	9.0 pm to 10.30 pm (off 8.0 pm ex Edwinstowe **SX** and 8.15 ex Basford **SO**)	Performs shunting and makes trips to and from Nottingham LL as required
Nottingham Vic.	Colwick	No 11	9.0 pm to 1.0 am (off 8.15 ex Basford **SX** and 8.0 pm ex Edwinstowe **SO**)	Performs shunting
Nottingham Vic.	Colwick	No 12	11.5 pm to 1.30 am (off 10.0 pm ex Grantham)	Performs shunting
			SUNDAYS	
Nottingham Vic.	Colwick	No 1	9.15 am to 12.30 pm	Performs shunting
Bestwood Colliery	Colwick	No 1	7.14 am to 11.55 am weekdays (off No 3198 Dn)	Shunting

Station or Yard	Depot from which engine provided	Description or number of Pilot	Period required at station or yard	Particulars of Work
Bestwood Colly	Colwick	No 2	2.10 pm to 6.50 pm (approx) (off No 3258 Down)	Shunting
Colwick Sidings	Colwick	No 1	6.0 am Monday to 6.0 am Sunday	Shunting arrival end No 1 Down Goods Yard
Colwick Sidings	Colwick	No 2	6.0 am Sunday to 6.0 am Sunday	Down Goods Yard Departure end
Colwick Sidings	Colwick	No 3	6.0 am to 7.30 pm, 10.0 pm to 6.0 am each weekday	Shunting Down Empties Yard
Colwick Sidings	Colwick	No 4	6.0 am Monday to 6.0 am Sunday	Shunting arrival end Up Goods Yard
Colwick Sidings	Colwick	No 5	6.0 am Monday to 6.0 am Sunday	Shunting arrival end Up Coal Yard
Colwick Sidings	Colwick	No 6	6.0 am Monday to 6.0 am Sunday	Shunting departure end Up Yards Carlton Fields
Colwick Sidings	Colwick	No 7	6.0 pm to 2.0 am Monday to Friday	Shunting Cripple Docks
Colwick Sidings	Colwick	No 8	8.0 am to 4 pm each weekday	Transfers Yard to Yard
Colwick Sidings	Colwick	No 9	6.0 am to 9.0 pm weekdays	Work trips to Colwick Estates as necessary
Daybrook, Leen Valley Jcn Yard	Colwick	No 1	8.36 am to 1.30 pm weekdays (off 3214 Down)	Shunting
Nottingham Goods (London Road)	Colwick	No 1	4.30 am to 3.0 pm **MO** 4.0 am to 3.0 pm **MX**	Shunting
Nottingham Goods (London Road)	Colwick	No 2	12.40 pm to 12.30 am **SX** 12.40 pm to 11.0 pm **SO**	Shunting
Nottingham Goods (London Road)	Colwick	No 3	3.0 pm to 1.0 am **SX** 3.0 pm to 12 mdt **SO**	Shunting
Nottingham Goods (London Road)	Colwick	No 4	6.0 am to 12.40 pm **MO** 12.5 am to 12.40 pm **MX** 12.5 am to 6.0 am or when finished Sundays	Shunting

APPENDIX 3

Specimen Allocation of Traffic at Colwick

No 1 Yard (Down Empties)	No 4 - Old Bank (Up Goods)	No 5 - New Bank (Up coal)
1 Sugar Beet	1 Down side transfers	1 LMS
2 Digby & Lodge	2 Cripples	2 LMS
3 Shirebrook	3 Stathern	3 LMS
4 Hucknall	4 Southend	4 LMS
5 Pinxton	5 King's Cross	5 Spalding
6 Pleasley	6 Hull	6 Estates
7 Riddings	7 Newark	7 GE
8 Nottingham Midland	8 Grantham passenger	8 GE
9 Nottingham.LNER	9 Grantham Old Yard	9 GE
10 Cripples	10 Leicester	10 GE
11 Brake vans	11 Sleaford	11 Boston Docks
12 Stanley	12 Boston	12 Brakes
13 Shipley Manners	13 Various	13 Highs
14 GC Lines	14 London & Peterboro' Gds	14 Peterboro' Goods
15 Gedling	15 GC Gds	15 South District
16 Newstead	16 Doncaster mineral	16 South Lines
17 Bestwood	17 Doncaster Decoy	17 South Lines
18 Eastwood	18 York	18 London Depots
19 Summit	19 Denton	19 London Depots
20 No 3 Down Yard	20 LMS	20 GC coal
21 End door	21 LMS	21 Eastwell
22 Wait orders	22 Brakes	22 Stainby
23 Wait orders	23 Brakes	23 Loco
24 Stanton		24 Loco
25 Leen Valley		25 Nottingham
26 Annesley Colliery		26 Loco
27 Teversall Silverhill		27 Boston Docks
28 GC Lines		28 Highs
29 Spare		29 Up Goods Yard
30 Up Goods Yard		
31 Leen Valley		

Abbreviations

GC - Great Central Railway.
LMS - London, Midland and Scottish Railway.
GE - Great Eastern Railway.

APPENDIX 4

Marshalling of Traffic for Junctions and Stations in the Manchester and Western Districts

Traffic for the various Groups should be conveyed on Colwick to Deansgate, etc, trains as follows:-

6.20 pm	Colwick - Deansgate	Godley, Liverpool, Guide Bridge, Ardwick, Deansgate
3.00 pm	King's Cross - Deansgate	Guide Bridge, Ardwick, Deansgate
11.15 pm	Colwick - Mottram	Godley, Liverpool, Guide Bridge, Ardwick, Deansgate
2.25 am	Colwick - Huskisson	Godley and Liverpool
2.45 am	Colwick - Mottram	Godley, Liverpool, Guide Bridge, Ardwick, Deansgate

Sheffield

Sheffield	Blast Lane
"	Victoria
"	Bridgehouses
Rotherham	Branch
Stations	Sheffield to Penistone
	Penistone to Lockwood and Huddersfield and LMS line *via* Penistone
	Sheffield to Barnsley *via* Chapeltown
	Penistone to Barnsley inclusive

Godley

Woodley
Portwood Sidings
Stockport
Heaton Mersey
Cheadle
Northenden
Baguley
Knutsford
Northwich
Chester (Northgate)
Seacombe LMS
West Kirby
Hoylake
Bidston
Upton
Storeton
Heswall Hills
Neston & Parkgate
Burton Point
Saughall
Welsh Road
Chester (Liverpool Road)
Connah's Quay
Hawarden Bridge
Buckley Junction
Penyfford

Caergwrle Castle
Llay Main
Hope Village
Brymbo
Wrexham
Delamere
Mouldsworth
Barrow for Tarvin
Mickle Trafford
Risley Moss
Culcheth
Lowton St Marys
Golborne
Garswood Hall
Ashton-in-Makerfield
St Helens
West Leigh & Bedford
Hindley & Platt Bridge
Wigan
Knowle Lane Siding
Old Ewloe Siding
Ewloe Barn
Northorpe Hall
Mountain Colliery
LMS Line *via* Bidston
GW Line *via* Wrexham
Bramall Moor LMS
Helsby CLC & GW *via* Helsby

Romiley
Rose Hill
Bollington
Marple
Strines
New Mills
Birch Vale
Rumney's Siding
Hayfield
Peak Forest LMS
Macclesfield & LMS Railway *via* Macclesfield
Birkenhead Dock Road GC
Birkenhead Shore Road CLC
Hale
Ashley
Mobberley
Shaw Heath Siding
Plumbley
Lostock Gralam
Hartford
Cuddington
Winsford
Winnington
Parkington
Cheadle Heath LMS

Liverpool Section

- Liverpool (Brunswick)
- Liverpool (Huskisson)
- Walton
- Aintree
- Sefton
- Lydiate
- Altcar
- Mossbridge
- Woodvale
- Ainsdale Beach
- Southport
- Wavertree CLC
- Warrington
- Farnsworth
- Widnes
- Hough Green
- Halewood
- West Derby
- Gateacre
- Childwall
- Knotty Ash

Guide Bridge

- Hyde Junction
- Partington Steel & Iron Co (Glazebrook)
- Glazebrook
- Partington North Side (Shipment Fuel)
- Risley Siding
- Hyde
- Dog Lane
- Ashton Oldham Road
- Park Bridge
- Oldham Clegg Street
- Oldham Scottfield
- Ashton Park Parade
- Stalybridge
- Hyde Road
- Levenshulme
- Fallowfield
- Chorlton-cum-Hardy
- Urmston
- Flixton
- Irlam
- Sankey
- Padgate
- Cornbrook
- Fairfield
- Wilbraham Road
- Oldham Glodwick Road
- Guide Bridge GC
- LMS Stations *via* Guide Bridge ie, Cock Lane
- LMS Stations *via* Ashton Moss

Ardwick

- Openshaw
- Gorton G C Works
- Beyer Peacock's Works

- MSJ & A Line *via* Ardwick
- LMS Stations *via* Ardwick

- Crossley Bros Openshaw
- Armstrong Whitworth, Openshaw

- Ardwick
- Belle Vue
- Reddish
- Bredbury
- Ducie Street

Deansgate

- Deansgate
- Manchester Docks
- Manchester Cen

APPENDIX 5 GREAT NORTHERN RAILWAY

Weekday Passing Times at Arno Vale Box, October 1899

Reproduced by kind permission of the late Vic Forster secretary of the
East Midlands Branch of the Railway Correspondence & Travel Society

UP LINE

		From	To
am			
12.30	Goods	Burton-on-Trent	Colwick
12.45	LNW Coal	New Hucknall	Colwick MX Q
12.52		Stanton	Colwick SX
1. 6	Fast Goods	Stoke-on-Trent	King's Cross. GN works throughout
1.35	Coal	Grassmoor	Colwick MX
1.50	LNW Coal	New Hucknall	Colwick MX
1.55	Fast Goods	Manchester	King's Cross MX
2. 0	LNW Coal	Beighton	Colwick MX Q
2.10	Coal	Eastwood	Colwick MX
2.15	Goods	Derby	Colwick MX
2.23	Through Goods	Burton-on-Trent	Doncaster MX
2.30	Coal	New Hucknall	Colwick MX
2.40	Goods	Stafford	Colwick
3. 0	LNW Coal	Grassmoor	Colwick MX Q
3.10	Coal	Stanton	Colwick MX
3.17	Coal	Eastwood	Colwick MX Q
3.25	GC Goods	Annesley	Colwick MX
4. 0	NS Coal	Alsager	Colwick MX. NS works throughout
4. 5	Fast Goods	Manchester	King's Cross MX
4.10	LNW Coal	Pilsley	Colwick MX Q
4.32	Coal	Staveley	Colwick MX
4.40	Goods	Eastwood	Colwick MO
4.45	LNW Goods	beyond Egginton Junction	Nottingham
5.20	Goods	Burton-on-Trent	Nottingham MX
5.40	Coal	Eastwood	Colwick MX
5.50	Coal	Staveley	Colwick MX
6.25	Coal	New Hucknall	Colwick MX
6.35	Goods	Bestwood	Carlton Fields
6.45	Coal	Heath	Colwick MX
7.15	Ironstone Empties	Stanton Works	Denton SO
7.23	LNW Coal	Tibshelf	Colwick MX Q
7.27	Passenger	Sutton-in-Ashfield	Nottingham
7.42	Goods and Coal	Egginton Junction	Colwick MX
7.50	Coal	Chesterfield	Colwick MX
7.59	Passenger	Pinxton	Nottingham
8. 9	Passenger	Burton-on-Trent	Nottingham
8.20	Passenger	Stafford	Nottingham
8.30	Ironstone Empties	Stanton	Woolsthorpe MO
8.55	Ironstone Empties	Stanton	Woolsthorpe M & SX
9. 8	Passenger	Burton-on-Trent	Nottingham
9.35	Goods	Burton-on-Trent	Nottingham MX
10. 0	Ironstone Empties	Stanton Works	Colwick MO
10.24	Passenger	Pinxton	Nottingham
10.45	Goods and Empties	Heanor	Colwick
10.54	Passenger	Stafford	Nottingham
11. 0	Coal	Babbington Colliery	Colwick
11.10	Coal	Bestwood Colliery	Colwick SX
11.20	Goods	Newstead Colliery South	Colwick
11.45	Coal	Annesley Colliery	Colwick
11.52	Goods and Coal	Nutbrook Junction	Colwick
12.00	Coal	Hucknall No 2 Colliery	Colwick
pm			
12. 4	Passenger	Pinxton	Nottingham SO
12.15	Coal	West Hallam Colliery	Colwick MO
12.20	Goods	Burton-on-Trent	Colwick

		From	To
pm			
12.25	Coal	Newstead Colliery	Colwick Th & SX
12.33	Coal	Brinsley Sidings	Colwick SX
12.40	Coal	Linby Colliery	Colwick SX
12.55	Coal	Nutbrook Junction	Colwick
1. 0	Coal	Watnall Sidings	Colwick
1. 5	Coal	Bestwood Colliery	Colwick SX
1.20	Coal	West Hallam Colliery	Colwick M & SX
1.25	Pick-up Goods	Burton-on-Trent	Colwick MO
1.25	Goods & Coal	Burton-on-Trent	Colwick MX
1.30	Coal	Pleasley	Colwick
1.34	Passenger	Pinxton	Nottingham
1.40	Coal	Linby	Colwick SX
1.49	Passenger	Stafford	Nottingham
2. 0	Coal	Grassmoor	Colwick
2. 5	Pick-up Goods & Coal	Pinxton	Colwick
2.10	Coal	Silverhill Colliery	Colwick
2.20	Coal	Pinxton	Colwick
2.25	Coal	Annesley Colliery	Colwick
2.30	Coal & Empties	Pinxton	Colwick
2.37	Fast Cattle	Derby	Carlton Fields FO Q
2.46	Passenger	Pinxton	Nottingham
2.55	Coal	Linby Colliery	Colwick Th &SX
3. 2	Coal	Nutbrook Junction	Colwick SX
3.10	LNW Coal	New Hucknall	Colwick SO
3.15	Coal	Bestwood Colliery	Colwick
3.20	Coal	Digby & Lodge Sidings	Colwick
3.30	Coal	Eastwood	Colwick
3.37	Coal	Nutbrook Junction	Colwick
3.43	Coal	Babbington Colliery	Colwick SX
4. 0	Coal	Tibshelf Town	Colwick
4.10	Coal	Hucknall	Colwick SX
4.25	LNW Coal	Sheffield	Colwick
4.31	Passenger	Stafford	Nottingham
4.35	Coal	Pleasley	Colwick
4.40	Goods	Burton-on-Trent	Colwick
4.45	Goods & Coal	Hucknall (Newstead or Linby Q)	Colwick Wed O
5. 0	Coal	Nuthall Sidings	Colwick SX
5. 5	Coal	Linby	Colwick SX
5.10	Coal	Bestwood Colliery	Colwick
5.17	Coal	Babbington Colliery	Colwick SX
5.39	Passenger	Pinxton	Nottingham
5.50	LNW Coal	Grassmoor	Colwick SX
6. 8	Coal	Brinsley Sidings	Colwick
6.38	Passenger	Stafford	Nottingham
6.45	Goods & Coal	Burton-on-Trent	Colwick SX
6.50	Fast Goods	Burton-on-Trent	Colwick SO
6.58	Coal	Annesley Colliery	Colwick
7. 6	Passenger	Derby	Nottingham
7.25	Coal	Pinxton	Colwick
7.30	Ironstone Empties	Stanton Works	Woolsthorpe
7.37	Coal	Linby	Colwick SX Q
7.40	LNW Coal	Staveley Town	Colwick SO
7.43	Coal	Ilkeston Colliery	Colwick SX
7.50	Coal	Silverhill Colliery	Colwick
7.55	Coal	Digby & Lodge Sidings	Colwick SX
8. 2	Coal	Hucknall	Colwick SX
8. 8	Coal	Bestwood Colliery	Colwick
8.15	Coal	Pinxton Colliery	Colwick
8.24	Passenger	Pinxton	Nottingham
8.35	Coal	West Hallam Colliery	Colwick SX
8.45	Goods	Skegby	Colwick
8.50	Coal	Pilsley	Colwick Q
9. 0	LNW Coal	New Hucknall	Colwick SX
9.15	Fast Goods	Burton-on-Trent	Carlton Fields SX

		From	To
pm			
9.20	Goods	Eastwood	Colwick SX
9.30	Passenger	Stafford	Nottingham
9.35	Fast Goods	Derby	King's Cross SX
9.47	Coal	Annesley	Colwick SX
9.58	Express Milk	Egginton Junction	King's Cross
10.13	Passenger	Pinxton	Nottingham Wed & SO
10.16	Express Milk	Egginton Junction	King's Cross
10.30	Coal	Watnall Sidings	Colwick SX
10.35	LNW Coal	Staveley Town	Colwick SX
10.40	GC Goods	Annesley	Colwick
10.45	Coal	Eastwood	Colwick SX
10.50	Goods & Coal	Egginton Junction	Colwick
10.55	LNW Coal	Sheffield	Colwick
11.10	Coal	Eastwood	Colwick SX
11.15	Coal	Summit Colliery	Colwick Q
11.20	LNW Fast Goods	Sheffield	Colwick SX

DOWN LINE

		From	To
am			
12.35	Empties	Colwick Sidings	Staveley MX
12.45	Fast Goods	King's Cross	Manchester MX
1. 5	LNW Empties	Colwick	Pilsley Colliery MX Q
1.12	Empties	Colwick	Eastwood MX Q
1.25	Fast Goods	Doncaster	Burton-on-Trent MX
1.35	Goods & Coal	Colwick	Egginton Junction MX
1.56	Coal & Empties	Colwick	Derby MX
2. 2	LNW Goods & Empties	Colwick	Sheffield MX
2.35	Empties	Colwick	Chesterfield MX
2.50	Empties	Colwick	Heath MX
3.15	Empties	Colwick	New Hucknall MX
3.30	Through Goods	Colwick	Stafford MX
3.58	Ironstone	Colwick	Stanton SO
4. 5	Goods & Empties	Colwick	Burton-on-Trent MX
4.15	Goods	Colwick	Derby MO
4.15	Goods	Colwick	Burton-on-Trent MX
4.32	Fast Goods	King's Cross	Stoke-on-Trent MX GN work throughout
4.45	LNW Empties	Colwick	Tibshelf Town MX Q
4.55	Engine & Brakes	Colwick	Bestwood
5. 0	GC Goods	Colwick	Annesley MX
5.10	Empties	Colwick	Pleasley
5.23	Ironstone	Colwick	Stanton Works MO
5.20	Goods & Coal	Colwick	Heanor MX
5.27	LNW Fast Goods	Colwick	Sheffield MX
5.44	Passenger	Nottingham	Pinxton
6. 3	Passenger	Nottingham	Stafford
6.11	Goods & Coal	Colwick	Heanor MO
6.14	Ironstone	Colwick	Stanton Works M & SX
6.15	LNW Empties	Colwick	Sheffield MO
6.25	Through Goods	Colwick	Burton-on-Trent
6.34	Ironstone	Colwick	Nutbrook Junction MO
6.40	Goods & Empties	Colwick	Teversall
6.45	Empties	Colwick	Manchester MX
6.50	Goods	Colwick	Egginton Junction MO
6.55	Goods & Empties	Colwick	Pinxton
7. 5	Empties	Colwick	Babbington Colliery
7.20	Pick-up Goods	Colwick	Annesley Colliery
7.40	Empties	Colwick	Grassmoor
7.50	Pick-up Goods	Colwick	Pinxton
8. 2	Passenger	Nottingham	Daybrook
8.12	Passenger	Grantham	Stafford *via* Radcliffe and Gedling

		From	To
am			
8.25	Empties	Colwick	Bestwood Colliery SX
8.35	Goods & Empties	Colwick	Linby
8.45	Empties	Colwick	Hucknall
8.58	Passenger	Nottingham	Pinxton
9.10	Empties	Colwick	West Hallam Colliery SX
9.20	LNW Empties	Colwick	Sheffield
9.30	Empties	Colwick	Nutbrook Junction
9.45	Empties	Colwick	Brinsley Sidings SX
9.55	Empties	Colwick	Newstead Colliery Th & SX
10.10	Passenger	Nottingham	Stafford
10.18	Empties	Colwick	Pinxton
10.30	Empties	Colwick	Linby SX
10.37	Goods	Colwick	Burton-on-Trent
10.45	Empties	Colwick	Bestwood Colliery SX
10.51	Empties	Colwick	Watnall Colliery
10.59	LNW Empties	Colwick	Grassmoor SX
11. 4	Pick-up Goods	Colwick	Burton-on-Trent SO
11.10	Milk Vans	King's Cross	Tutbury
11.20	Empties	Colwick	Annesley Colliery
11.30	Empties	Colwick	Babbington Colliery SX
11.38	Empties	Colwick	Linby SX
11.45	Empties	Colwick	Nutbrook Junction
11.55	Empties	Colwick	Pleasley
pm			
12.15	Pick-up Goods	Colwick	Burton-on-Trent SX
12.30	Passenger	Nottingham	Derby
12.39	Coal	Colwick	Tibshelf Town
12.53	Passenger	Nottingham	Stafford
1. 0	Passenger	Nottingham	Pinxton
1.10	Empties	Colwick	Nutbrook Junction
1.18	Empties	Colwick	Eastwood
1.25	Empties	Colwick	Bestwood Colliery
1.33	Engine & Brake	Colwick	Linby Th & SX
1.40	Empties	Colwick	Butler's Hill SX
1.40	LNW Coal	Colwick	Staveley Town SO
1.50	Passenger	Nottingham	Heanor SO
1.55	Pick-up Goods	Colwick	Annesley Colliery
2.10	Pick-up Goods	Colwick	Pinxton
2.15	Empties	Colwick	West Hallam Colliery SX
2.25	Empties	Colwick	Brinsley Sidings
2.35	Empties	Colwick	Awsworth
2.40	Two Engines & Brakes	Colwick	Babbington Colliery SX
2.56	Ironstone	Colwick	Bestwood Ironworks
3. 5	Passenger	Nottingham	Egginton Junction
3.15	Empties	Colwick	Silverhill Colliery
3.22	Empties	Colwick	Linby Colliery SX
3.30	Empties	Colwick	Pinxton
3.43	Ironstone	Colwick	Stanton Works
3.50	LNW Empties	Colwick	Staveley Town SX
4. 1	Passenger	Nottingham	Stafford
4.10	Goods, Coal, Engine & Brake	Colwick	Derby SX
4.18	Empties	Colwick	Babbington Colliery SX
4.18	LNW Empties	Colwick	New Hucknall SO
4.25	Goods & Empties	Colwick	Egginton Junction
4.33	Empties	Colwick	Pleasley Q
4.40	Pick-up Goods	Colwick	Burton-on-Trent
4.50	Passenger	Nottingham	Pinxton
5. 8	Ironstone	Colwick	Bestwood Ironworks
5.15	Empties	Colwick	Digby & Lodge Sidings SX
5.25	Fast Cattle & Goods	Colwick	Burton-on-Trent MO
5.25	Passenger	Nottingham	Pinxton SO

pm		From	To
5.35	LNW Empties	Colwick	New Hucknall SX
5.40	Empties	Colwick	Linby SX Q
6.0	Passenger	Nottingham	Egginton Junction
6.26	Passenger	Nottingham	Stafford
6.30	Engine & Brake	Colwick	Eastwood SX
6.43	Empties	Colwick	Hucknall SX
7.1	Empties	Colwick	Nutbrook Junction SX
7.15	Engine	Colwick	Egginton Junction SO
7.20	Empties	Colwick	Annesley Colliery SX
7.30	Empties	Colwick	Summit Colliery Q
7.38	Empties	Colwick	Eastwood
7.45	Empties	Colwick	Grassmoor
8.0	Goods	Colwick	Burton-on-Trent
8.10	Empties	Colwick	Watnall Sidings SX
8.18	LNW Empties	Colwick	Beighton SX Q
8.35	Passenger	Nottingham	Pinxton Wed & SO
8.43	LNW Goods	Nottingham Goods Station	Liverpool
9.12	Goods & Coal	Nottingham Goods Station	Burton-on-Trent
9.23	Ironstone	Colwick	Stanton Works SX
9.40	LNW Empties	Colwick	New Hucknall SX Q
9.48	Passenger	Nottingham	Burton-on-Trent
10.5	Passenger	Nottingham	Pinxton
10.23	LNW Empties	Colwick	Grassmoor SX
10.30	NS Empties	Colwick	Alsager. NS Company works throughout
10.40	Empties	Colwick	Staveley Town
10.53	Ironstone	Colwick	Stanton Works
11.0	Empties	Colwick	Chesterfield SO
11.0	LNW Empties	Colwick	New Hucknall SX Q
11.15	Empties	Colwick	Watnall Sidings SX
11.20	Passenger	Nottingham	Pinxton SO
11.25	Empties	Colwick	New Hucknall SX
11.30	Empties	Colwick	Heath SO

MO - **Mondays Only**
MX - **Mondays Excepted**
Wed - **Wednesday**
Th - **Thursday**
F - **Friday**
SO - **Saturdays Only**
SX - **Saturdays Excepted**
Q - **As Required**
NS - **North Stafford Railway**

Some other RCTS Books

A TRAVELLERS GUIDE TO THE ROBIN HOOD LINE

A Travellers Guide to The Robin Hood Line presents an illustrated history of the line and its rebuilding as a traveller can now view it heading north from Nottingham to Worksop. From the full colour covers and fifteen photographs (three in colour) to the ten maps and diagrams and full art paper production, this book continues our Society's reputation for quality works. Each section of the route is dealt with in detail, using a one page map/one page narrative layout covering not only railway but also local history and topographical features. Our thanks go to the East Midlands Branch for their production efforts on this 28-page A5-sized book, especially John Hitchens and Frank Ashley, and we thank Nottinghamshire County Council for sponsoring much of its production cost to allow an extremely competitive price. Available from Hon. Assistant Publications Officer, Hazelhurst, Tiverton Road, Bampton, Devon EX16 9LJ. One reviewer, commenting on the level of detail included, made three trips on the new line before observing all the points of interest mentioned!

Just £2-95

BRITISH RAILWAYS STANDARD STEAM LOCOMOTIVES
Volume I Background to Standardisation and the Pacific Classes

Immediately British Railways was formed in January 1948, the Railway Executive instructed Robert Riddles to design a series of standard locomotive designs. The intention was to gain material savings in running and maintenance costs by adopting as standard the best practices of the four independent companies. In this major series, the Society presents for the first time the complete story of British locomotive standardisation from the days of the Robinson ROD 2-8-0s to the twelve BR Standard designs totalling 999 locomotives. This book, by Paul Chancellor and Peter Gilbert, presents the Standards design history and for each of the 66 locomotives in the popular Britannia, Duke and Clan classes its complete construction, modification, allocation and operating history.

Page size 212 x 272mm, casebound, 184 pages, 151 illustrations including 17 in colour.

BRITISH RAILWAYS STANDARD STEAM LOCOMOTIVES
Volume 3 The Tank Engine Classes

From Penzance to Wick, the Standard tank classes were designed to modernise secondary route power. Railway enthusiasts throughout the land became familiar with their high running plates which gave the 230 engines of three types their "family" appearance. Author Paul Chancellor presents their full story, from their design origins, construction, modifications, allocation, use and liveries. Whether these engines hauled you reluctantly to school - your reviewer's experience - or you only came across them in preservation, the Class 4s handsome curved tank sides will evoke many a nostalgic memory. With their construction at all six main workshops, local livery variations and national use, there is something for everyone to savour in this book, the second in the Society's BR Standard series. Diagrams of each design are included.

Page size 212 x 272mm, Casebound, 189 photographs including sixteen in colour.

GREAT NORTHERN LOCOMOTIVE HISTORY

This major four-volume work covers the complete story of the Great Northern Railway, Doncaster Works and its locomotives, from earliest days to the Grouping. Each class is covered from all six designers - Cubitt, Bury, Sturrock, Stirling, Ivatt and Gresley. 1,553 Doncaster-built engines are covered, plus those bought in. Their robust design was demonstrated by almost half of the GN stock passed to the LNER at Grouping surviving into British Railways ownership 25 years later.
The set totals 804 pages with 738 illustrations. Buy the complete set or individual volumes.

LOCOMOTIVES OF THE LNER
Part I - Preliminary Survey
Third impression, updated and revised

This series of books is the accredited expert work on LNER locomotives. The series eventually stretched to nineteen books, and this, the best-selling first volume, has been long out of print. Read how nine pregrouping railways were turned into the London & North Eastern Railway, how locomotive engineer Gresley transformed its motive power with his big engine policy that was to prove invaluable as loads grew. This book brings to life and presents comprehensive details of not only locomotive policy and construction, but also loco classification and numbering systems, liveries, naming, loco diagrams, route restrictions and the full locomotive workshops developments. The later Thompson and Peppercorn eras are also covered. Includes diagrams.
Laminated cover, 194 pages, 172 photographs, including one colour plate. LNER fold out map.

LOCOMOTIVES OF THE LNER
Part 2A - Tender Engines - Classes Al to A10
Fourth impression, updated and revised

The famous Pacific classes of the LNER are the feature of this book. Gresley's designs are prominent. Read the complete story of how he rose to the challenge of increasing loads and speeds by producing some of Europe's most elegant and respected locomotives, including of course the A4 class of which *Mallard* holds the world speed record for steam traction. The later work of Thompson and Peppercorn is also featured. Much official information is used that is in several instances at variance with previously published accounts. From just four at Grouping, by nationalisation some 139 Pacifics were running, and a total of 208 locomotives are covered, from design history, building, competitive trials and rebuilding to complete dimensions, allocation, renumbering and the use of each individual engine.
Laminated cover, 351 pages, 276 photographs, 27 diagrams and two fold out sections.

RCTS Publications List

*UK Post Free
Overseas add 25%

Title of Book	ISBN No.	*Price
The Great Northern Railway in the East Midlands	0901115843	£13-95
Guide to the Robin Hood Line	0901115835	£2-95
BR Standard Steam Locomotives:		
Vol 1 Background and the Pacifics	0901115819	£19-95
Vol 3 The Tank Engine Classes	0901115770	£18-95
Special Offer Set of Great Northern Railway		£40-95
Gt Northern Locomotive History		
1: 1847-1866	0901115614	£12-95
2: 1867-1895	0901115746	£19-95
3A: 1896-1911	090111569X	£19-95
3B: 1911-1923	0901115703	£16-95
Locomotives of the LNER:		
Part 1 Preliminary Survey	0901115118	£12-95
Part 2A Tender Engines A1-A10	0901115258	£14-95
Part 2B Tender Engines B1-B19	0901115738	£13-95
Part 9A Tank Engines L1-L19	0901115401	£10-95
Part 9B Tank Engines Q1-Z5	090111541X	£10-95
Part 10A Departmental Stock, Engine Sheds, Boiler and Tender Numbering	0901115657	£10-95
Part 10B Railcars and Electrics	0901115665	£13-95
Western Change	0901115789	£15-95
The Railways of Keynsham	0901115827	£9-95
LMS Diesels	0901115762	£19-95
LMS Locomotive Names	0901115797	£18-95
LMS Locomotive Design and Construction	0901115711	£16-95
Highland Railway Locos 1855-1895	0901115649	£12-95
Highland Railway Locos 1895-1923	090111572X	£16-95
Shildon-Newport in Retrospect	0901115673	£10-95
Lord Carlisle's Railways	0901115436	£7-95

Available from:

    **Hon. Assistant Publications Officer
    Hazelhurst,
    Tiverton Road,
    Bampton,
    Devon, EX16 9LJ.**

When ordering please quote reference PUBS10

THE GREAT NORTHERN RAILWAY IN THE EAST MIDLANDS

The Society is publishing a complete history of the Great Northern Railway in the East Midlands. Details of construction, operation and traffic will be presented covering both passenger services and the lifeblood of the system, freight, in particular mineral traffic. The Series will be extensively illustrated with photographs, track and signalling diagrams.

This book is the first in a series of four. Subsequent titles will cover Nottingham Victoria - Annesley, Leen Valley, The Shirebrook Extension, The Pinxton Branch, Ilkeston and Branches, Nottingham - Grantham and the Joint Line, and Leicester Belgrave Road.

The Railway Correspondence and Travel Society publishes a wide range of books on railway and locomotive subjects, our current Publications List appears on page xi.